# The Challenges and Prospects of *Sukuk*

# The Challenges and Prospects of *Sukuk*:

## *A Content Analysis-Based Study*

By

Essia Ries Ahmed, Md. Aminul Islam,
Ku Halim Ku Ariffin and Azlan Amran

**Cambridge Scholars** Publishing

The Challenges and Prospects of *Sukuk*: A Content Analysis-Based Study

By Essia Ries Ahmed, Md. Aminul Islam, Ku Halim Ku Ariffin
and Azlan Amran

This book first published 2022

Cambridge Scholars Publishing

Lady Stephenson Library, Newcastle upon Tyne, NE6 2PA, UK

British Library Cataloguing in Publication Data
A catalogue record for this book is available from the British Library



ISBN (10): 1-5275-8072-5
ISBN (13): 978-1-5275-8072-5

# TABLE OF CONTENTS

# PREFACE

Over the past decades, *Sukuk* (Islamic bonds) have emerged as one of the most important tools for Islamic investment and financing. They have become the most successful financial product in the Islamic financing industry. The International Islamic Financial Market (IIFM) believes the global *Sukuk* market will be able to sustain its expansionary phase into 2015, with total issuance likely to top US$150 billion, despite the uncertainty in the global economy. Total *Sukuk* issues crossed the US$130 billion mark in 2014. The world *Sukuk* issuance crossed the landmark US$100 billion mark in 2012, when a total of US$137.45 billion was raised in the corporate year. However, the controversy over *Sukuk* became heated when Taqi Usmani critically commented on unscrupulous *Sukuk* issuance. Taqi Usmani is reported to have said that 85% of the *Sukuk* issued worldwide are un-Islamic. The pricing of *Sukuk* is one of the main contributory factors to this controversy. Currently, conventional finance benchmarks, such as KLIBOR, LIBOR etc. are used to determine the cost of funds, and the return to financial investments, which creates controversy. The LIBOR benchmark has been employed as a reference guide for long-term investment pricing among Islamic financial institutions. It is generally accepted and recognized in the Islamic banking industry, without making any serious or innovative moves to become free from a usury-based benchmark. The arguments made are based on complete replication of the conventional (usury-based) financial indicators, and the unjustified view of some scholars is that it is a complete surrender to the long-lasting control of western practice to the financial markets, since modern Islamic finance is still in its infancy.

The rise in the Muslim population around the globe begs for *Shariah* (Islamic law)-compliant financial instruments, as the conventional products in the market go against the religious orientation of Muslim clients. *Sukuk* (Islamic bonds) are among the most promising and popular Islamic financing instruments which are promoted as being *Shariah*-compliant. However, *Sukuk*'s compliance to *Shariah* became questionable when a breach of *Shariah* principles in *Sukuk*'s issuance was reported. Thus, this study is aimed at examining the factors that affect *Sukuk*'s legitimacy and the moderating role of the *Shariah* Supervisory Board (SSB) in relation to *Sukuk* legitimacy determinants (pricing, type of structure, *Shariah* risk,

*Shariah* auditing, and *Shariah* documentation). Based on indebtedness and institutional theories, a conceptual model is developed and tested using the data from 82 *Sukuk* products listed in the Bursa Malaysia's exempt regime. This study adopted a mixed research method to build a framework based on qualitative findings, verified by literature, and tested quantitatively. The study began by first analysing data obtained from interviews (primary source) and *Shariah* reports (secondary source) between the years 2005 to 2015. Using descriptive statistics, the existence, and the extent of existence, of legitimacy in Islamic *Sukuk* in Islamic financial institutions in Malaysia was ascertained. The research found that the pricing, rating, *Shariah* compliance risks, *Shariah* auditing, and *Shariah* documentation, significantly influence *Sukuk* legitimacy. An analysis of the quantitative data was then made using the Partial Least Squares (PLS). The research found that pricing, type of structure, and *Shariah* auditing, have a significant effect on *Sukuk* legitimacy. In contrast, *Shariah* risk has a negative effect on *Sukuk* legitimacy, while *Shariah* documentation has no significant effect on *Sukuk* legitimacy. As for the moderating role of the SSB, the study proves that the combination of the determinants and SSB leads to greater monitoring, and therefore resulting in higher disclosure levels, which is in compliance with *Shariah* tenets and rules. The results from the interviews confirmed and validated the results obtained from the quantitative analysis done in the current study. These findings could be used as subjects of references in determining the existence of legitimacy in *Shariah* pronouncements. This study contributes to the literature by presenting a systematic framework that demonstrates the underlying indebtedness theory, and introduces a disclosure index as a measurement to represent *Sukuk* legitimacy. In addition, the moderating role of SSB as a governance mechanism that can influence *Sukuk* compliance to *Shariah* is strengthened positively. These findings also contribute to the practitioners by promoting the importance of disclosing elements of *Shariah* compliance among the *Sukuk* legitimacy determinants, as well as affirming the pivotal role that SSB plays in enhancing the legitimacy of *Sukuk*.

Although the Islamic finance industry has been developing rapidly in many respects, and the growing demand for Islamic *Sukuk* is noticeable, both domestically and internationally, there are a number of challenges that the Islamic *Sukuk* products are facing. Some scholars have argued for the need to reconsider the existing method of structuring and marketing Islamic *Sukuk*, which impedes the desired goals. The target audience for *Sukuk* is mostly a conventional bonds audience; while the return of *Sukuk* is more like the return of conventional bonds, in terms of their relation to (LIBOR), in terms of risks, or in terms of subscriptions and marketing through brokers.

This contributes towards limiting the liquidity of *Sukuk* due to the restricted quantity of *Sukuk* that are offered for trade in the secondary market. In general, we can focus on the following three most important contemporary challenges that the Islamic *Sukuk* has been facing: the challenges of the *Sukuk* market; the challenges of developments of *Sukuk*; and challenges based on the mechanisms of *Sukuk*. There are some controversial issues and challenges that need prompt *solutions* in order to sustain the development of the *Sukuk* market. This requires close cooperation among *Shariah* scholars and financial experts on one hand, and more interaction among *Shariah* Committees on the other. In order for the *Sukuk* market to be acceptable to the international financial institutions, the *Sukuk* products must overcome their limitations against the conventional market. However, *Sukuk* compliance with Islamic *Sharia* remains the first and foremost criterion. A well-defined, and well-developed *Sukuk* system can help in the growth of a real economy and socio-economic development. Towards the end of this book, we have attempted to propose an alternative Islamic Pricing Benchmark Model (IPBM) that will help to determine *Sukuk* cost of capital. This proposed benchmark will assist in pricing *Sukuk* that is usury-free and *Shariah* compliant.

This book is written on our content-analysis-based research of Malaysian *Sukuk*. It is primarily meant for researchers, academics, practitioners, and policy makers, who are interested in understanding and finding solutions in order to sustain the development of the *Sukuk* market. This book will be highly useful for lecturers teaching *Sukuk*, researchers, PhD scholars, and practitioners concerned about the challenges and prospects of *Sukuk*. This book is organized into 10 chapters. Chapter One describes a general understanding of *Sukuk* for readers. Chapter Two describes the history and development of *Sukuk*. Chapter Three presents types of *Sukuk* and their modes of operation. Chapter Four reviews relevant literatures and explains theoretical foundations in conducting research on *Sukuk*. Chapter Five presents our research backgrounds, while Chapter Six describes research methodology, and Chapters Seven and Eight present our research findings and their implications. The challenges and prospects of *Sukuk* and our recommendations are presented in Chapter Nine.

# ACKNOWLEDGEMENTS

*Alhamdulillah,* to our creator and sustainer, we surrender and offer our praises for all the blessings. Many people have helped along the path that brought us to the writing of this book. We would like to begin with joint 'thank you's'. We both offer our heartfelt appreciation to Yang Berbahagia Brig. Jen. Datuk Professor Dr. Kamarudin Hussin, the Vice Chancellor of UniMAP for motivating us to embark on this CSR book project. We also want to thank Associate Professor Dr. Hazry Desa, the Dean of the School of Business Innovation and Technopreneurship, UniMAP, for his words of encouragement. We would also like to extend our appreciation to UniMAP's Publication unit, especially its Director, Professor Dr. Asiah bt. Sarji and its Publication Officer, Zulhillizan Bin Othman for giving us all the support and assistance in the process of publishing this book. Our appreciation also goes to Jay Lee Sze Fern for her excellent editing job on this book. We also want to thank Associate Professor Dr. Idris Md. Noor from the School of Business Innovation and Teachnopreneurship, UNIMAP for his valuable feedback and reflections. Many thanks to Ajinder Kaur, Timbalan Pendaftar (Academic Affairs and International Department, USM), Dr. Tarsame Singh, (a Teacher Trainer at the Institut Pendidikan Guru Kampus Tuanku Bainun) and Dr. Jasbir Singh from Singapore for their words of encouragement and support. Last but not least, we would like to thank Sentral College Penang, and its CEO Dr. Chiang Geok Liang, for her support and encouragement in working on this book project. To our parents, our spouses, and our children, we remain ever so grateful for their love, and to whom we dedicate this accomplishment.

# ABOUT THE AUTHORS

**Dr. ESSIA RIES AHMED, PhD**

**Essia Ries Ahmed** is currently working as an Asst. Professor of Accountancy at University of Nizwa. He is instructor (trainer) in a training program prepared by the International Center for Training and Development (ICTD) in Kuala Lumpur.

He is an Auditor and a member of the Iraq Institute of Accountants. Dr Essia Ries received his Bachelor's degree majoring in commercial science from the Baghdad College of Economic Science University, and his Master's degree in Accounting from Universiti Sains Malaysia (USM). He received his PhD from University Malaysia Perlis (UniMap). Dr Essia's primary research interests concern financial reporting, and accounting and Islamic finance. He has published articles in the *Journal of Accounting and Business* and the *Journal of Islamic Accounting and Business Research*, as well as contributing to proceedings and presenting papers at both national and international conferences. Dr Essia Ries Ahmed is a reviewer and a member of the editorial boards of several journals.

## ASSOC. PROF. MD. AMINUL ISLAM, PhD

**Md. Aminul Islam** is currently working as a Professor in the School of Business Innovation and Technopreneurship at Universiti Malaysia Perlis. He received his Bachelor's degree from the International Islamic University Malaysia, and his MBA and Doctor of Philosophy degrees from Universiti Sains Malaysia. He also completed an advanced diploma in teaching in higher education from Nottingham Trent University, in the UK.

An award-winning academic and researcher, Professor Islam received the Raffles Education Founder's Award for being the most deserving academic staff member of Olympia College Malaysia in 2006, the Excellent Academic Support Award 2009, the Best Lecturer Award in 2010, and the Best Supervisor Award in 2018 and 2019, for producing the greatest number of PhD graduates, as well as the Research Excellence Award in 2020 from Universiti Malaysia Perlis. He also won the Best PhD Thesis Award for the most outstanding PhD dissertation at Universiti Sains Malaysia in 2011.

He is a member of the Asian Academy of Management, the Malaysian Institute of Management, and an associate member of the Malaysian Finance Association. He is a visiting Professor of Northern University Bangladesh, Daffodil International University, East Delta University, Thammasat University Thailand, and an Academic Advisor of Sentral College Penang. He has authored and co-authored three books, two book chapters, and about 200 research papers. His writings have so far attracted about 400,000 readers through the Research-gate, and about 3500 citations in Google Scholar. His recent research has spanned issues related to Entrepreneurship, IPO under-pricing, Earning Management, Block chain, Blue Economy, Islamic banking, and *Sukuk*.

## ASSOC. PROF. KU HALIM KU ARIFFIN

**Ku Halim Ku Ariffin** is an Associate Professor in the School of Business Innovation and Technopreneurship at Universiti Malaysia Perlis, Malaysia. He received his Bachelor's degree and MPA from the University of Science Malaysia. Ku Halim Ku Ariffin served as Dean, Deputy Dean and University Registrar. He has been involved in university management development and consulting for many entrepreneurship training schemes. Ku Halim Ku Ariffin has authored or co-authored eight books, including *Islamic Entrepreneurship* (University Malaysia Perlis, 2010), *Islamic Entrepreneurship Value* (University Malaysia Perlis, 2011), *Business and Innovation* (University Malaysia Perlis, 2012), *Successful Entrepreneurship* (University Malaysia Perlis, 2010), *Perspective and Alternative on Islamic Entrepreneurship* (University Malaysia Perlis, 2012), *Development Transformation* (University Malaysia Perlis, 2011), *Islamic and Asia Civilization* (Pearson, 2012), and *Ethnic Relation* (Oxford, 2006). He has also authored or co-authored dozens of scholarly articles, papers, and chapters. His undergraduate and graduate teaching is primarily focused on management, leadership, strategic management, human resource management, business innovation, engineering entrepreneurship, and marketing.

**PROFESSOR DR AZLAN AMRAN**

**Professor Dr Azlan Amran** is the Dean of the Graduate School of Business, Universiti Sains Malaysia (USM). Prior to joining USM, he worked as an accountant for several years. He has published a significant number of articles in the area of Corporate Sustainability Reporting and Corporate Social Responsibility in both local and international journals. He has been involved in several training and consultancy projects in Accounting-related issues and Corporate Social Reporting. He is also a member of the editorial board for several international journals. At the national level, he has been involved as a Technical Committee member for ISO 26000.

# CHAPTER 1

# INTRODUCTION

Muslim populations are expected to increase rapidly, growing from about 1.6 billion in 2010 to nearly 2.8 billion in 2050 (Lipka & Hackett 2015). This rise in the Muslim population is the key motivating driver for the growth in the Islamic finance industry whose reach has also begun to extend beyond the Muslim majority emerging markets (Mitchell, Rafi, Severe, & Kappen 2014). The main factor for the acceptance of Islamic finance globally is the compliance of the Islamic banking services with the religious orientations of their clients, illustrated by the Islamic law, the *Shariah* (Metawa & Al-Mossawi 1998, Naser, Jamal, Al-Khatib 1999, Bley Kuehn 2004, Alnasser & Muhammed 2012). The *Shariah* involves a series of prohibitions as well as guidance regarding the practices to be undertaken in a Muslim's day-to-day life. The prohibitions, in relation to the financial aspect, include paying or receiving interest (*riba*) speculating or gambling (*gharar* or *maysir*) and being involved in prohibited (*haram*) industries, such as those related to alcohol, pork, pornography, weapons, or conventional banking (Gheeraert 2014). It is crucial, therefore, that the Islamic finance product meets the basic requirement of being in compliance with the *Shariah* (Dawood 2008) in order to be deemed acceptable by Muslims.

*Shariah* stems from the nexus of Islamic rules derived from two foundational sources. The primary source is the *Qu'ran*, God's (Allah's) revelation to the Messenger Prophet Muhammad (peace be upon him [PBUH]). The other is the habitual practices of Prophet Muhammad's (PBUH) actions and precepts, collectively called the *Sunnah*. While the primary source of *Shariah* is the *Qu'ran*, for cases that are not addressed explicitly in either the *Qu'ran* or the *Hadith*, especially concerning the recent (modern) Islamic issues, other sources are used, such as *Ijma* (general agreement), *Qiyas* (analogical deduction), and *Ijtihad* (interpretation of one or a few scholars) (Aksoy 2005). The availability of these sources exhibits the flexibility of Muslims in finding solutions to their problems everywhere, and under any circumstances. Hence, when conventional banks are established under the principles of capitalism, and transect business by charging interest, which is unacceptable (forbidden) by *Shariah*, Muslims resorted to finding alternatives under Islamic principles (Hanif 2010), by applying the various aforementioned Islamic jurisprudence. One such Islamic innovation under the capital market is *Shariah*-compliant financial instruments known as *Sukuk* (Islamic bonds or Islamic Investment Certificates) (Tahmoures 2013). *Sukuk* are asset-based securities, while conventional bonds are debt-based securities. Unlike conventional bonds, the holders of these certificates are the true owners of the underlying asset, and therefore, can share in the actual success, or otherwise, of the venture.

The Islamic capital market (ICM) consists of the debt market and the equity market. *Sukuk* are the most active Islamic debt market financial instruments to date. *Sukuk* (the plural of *Sakk* meaning a deed or check) can be defined as trust documents or investment certificates representing a contract of transference of rights and revenues or obligations earned in alignment with the Islamic *Shariah* law (Abdullah 2011). The Accounting and Auditing Organization for Islamic Financial Institutions (AAOIFI) has defined *Sukuk* as "certificates of equal value representing undivided shares (in the ownership of) tangible assets, usufruct, and services or (in the ownership of) the assets of particular projects or special investment activities" (AAOIFI 2008). *Sukuk* are asset-backed, stable income and tradable trust certificates. The primary condition for the issuance of *Sukuk* is the existence of assets on the balance sheet of the government, the monetary authority, the corporate body, the banking and financial institution, or any entity that wants to mobilize its financial resources (Tariq & Dar 2007).

Malaysia is the pioneer in *Sukuk* issuance, capturing the global *Sukuk* market, and has played an important role in the development of *Sukuk* (Kamaluddin, Manan, Khadijah, Sufian, & Htay 2012). According to Malaysian Rating Cooperation Berhad (MARC 2010), the appeal of *Sukuk* as a funding source has grown tremendously with an increasingly large investor base, which is attributed to their appeal as a *Shariah*-compliant alternative to conventional fixed-income instruments (Haron 2012). It is anticipated that *Shariah*-compliant financial institutions' assets, worldwide, will expand in the next few years, from the current $2 trillion to approximately $3 trillion, despite the moderate level of growth of the Islamic finance industry forecasted in 2016 (Standard & Poor's Ratings Services). The Islamic financial institutions' (IFI) market share is expected to be 12 percent in Malaysia, in comparison to 17 percent in the six Gulf Cooperation Council (GCC) countries of Kuwait, Saudi Arabia, Qatar, the

United Arab Emirates, and Oman, where the market share is growing at a faster rate than elsewhere in the world.

Figure 1.1 allows several observations to be made. The global *Sukuk* market in 2010 reached US$52.97 million, which was an increase of 50 percent in comparison to 2009, when the total global market only reached US$37.09 million, according to Islamic Finance Information Services (IFIS) sources. However, in 2014, the *Sukuk* issuance declined to $120.85 million from $138.17 million in 2013. Despite that, as forecasted, Malaysia continued to dominate the *Sukuk* issuance market in 2015, and remains as the global *Sukuk* market leader. Figure 1.2 below provides the geographic distribution of *Sukuk* issuance by country in 2014, with Malaysia easily outstripping the other countries.

In 2011, Malaysia's primary *Sukuk* market was seen to be one of the most active markets, with an 86.1 percent increase over a two-year period, growing from an issuance of $32.7 billion in 2010, to an issuance of $60.9 billion in 2011. Furthermore, Malaysia continues to retain its position as the number one country in the world for *Sukuk* issuance, maintaining a 71.6 percent market share. Malaysia's government has supported this level of growth through a significant level of *Sukuk* issuance, in addition to a robust corporate sector which is flourishing as a consequence of Malaysia's healthy economic growth, coupled with an active Islamic capital market (KFH 2014). By the end of 2013, Malaysia's secondary *Sukuk* market claimed a record increase of 9.6 percent year-on-year, with $173.4 billion. The Bank Negara Malaysia, being the central bank of Malaysia, is recognized as the leader in *Sukuk* issuance, and its operations are being leveraged by other central banks globally. In 2014, the Central Banks' total issuance of *Sukuk* reached $50.2 billion globally, which represented 43.1 percent of all securities issuance. Of this sum, Malaysia accounted for 92.1 percent at the 2014 year-end, followed by Qatar's Central Bank, at 3.7 percent.

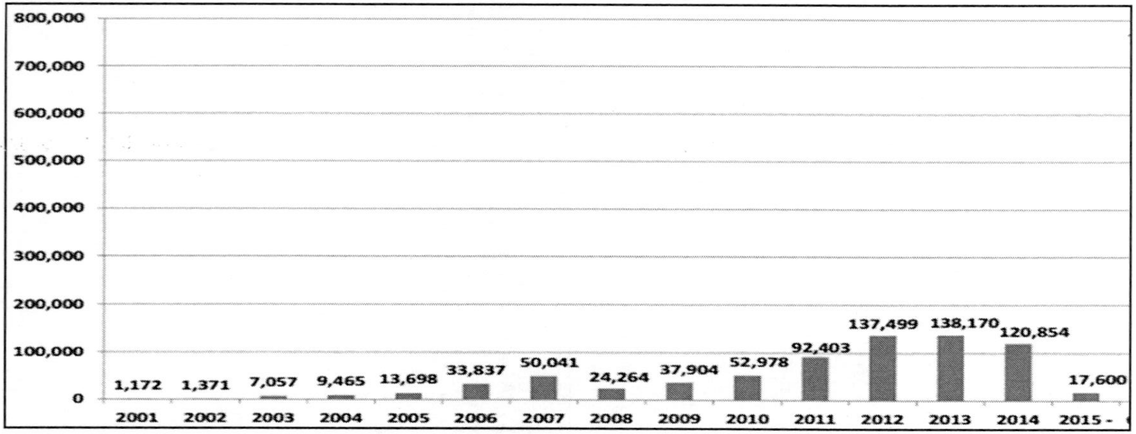


Figure 1: Total Global *Sukuk* Issuance 2006 – 2015
Source: International Islamic Financial Market (IIFM) *Sukuk* Database

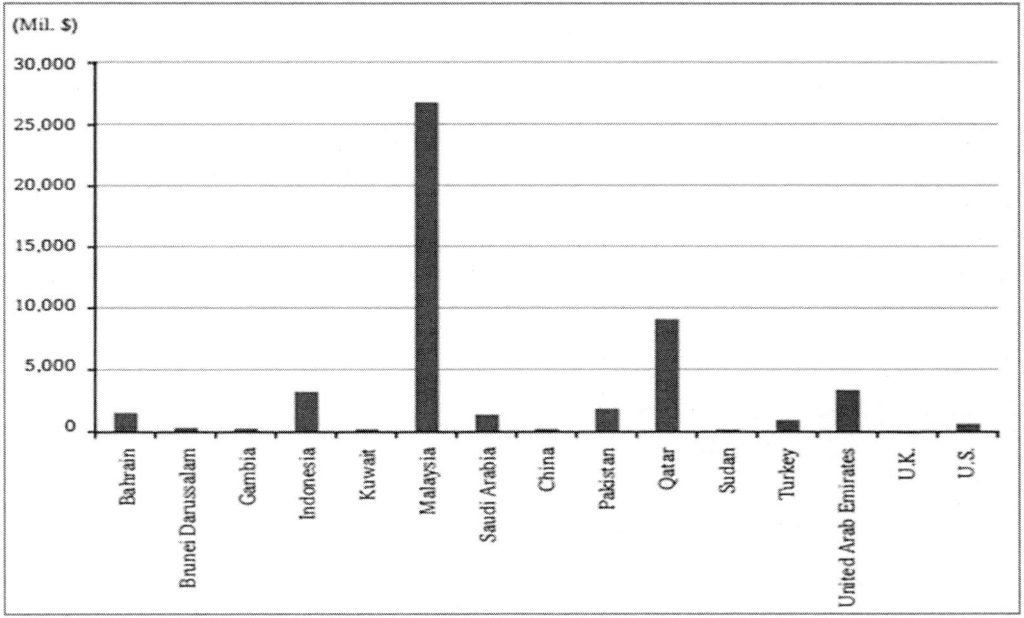


Figure 2: Geographic Distribution of *Sukuk* in 2014
Source: Standard & Poor's

A number of strategic initiatives are in place for Malaysia to emerge as the ICM international hub. The intent is to introduce more services and products, for funds to be mobilized in an effective way, and a comprehensive tax, accounting, and regulatory framework founded on *Shariah* principles to be established. *Sukuk*, in comparison to conventional bonds, are different in terms of their very structure, their classifications of 'asset-based' and 'asset-backed', and the risk/return mechanisms (Usmani 2002, Kantakji & O'haj, 2010). *Sukuk* issuance involves global investors, issuers and intermediaries, and their transactions require certain standards to be met in relation to governance, transparency, and compliance (Laldin 2013). Accordingly, there are efforts in Malaysia to ensure that *Sukuk* issuance is benchmarked with international standards and complies with *Shariah* best practices (Ginena 2014). The standardization and coordination of the *Shariah* ruling is essential to minimize any divergence amongst *Shariah* scholars regarding *Shariah* interpretations (SC 2003, 2007).

## *Sukuk* Legitimacy

*Sukuk* have several legitimacy (lawfulness or authenticity) determinants that are of interest to investors, financial institutions, and regulators, such as pricing, rating, *Shariah* auditing, *Shariah* risk, and *Shariah* documentation (Lahsasna, Ibrahim, & Othman 2014, Grassa 2015b). Although there are other factors that may influence the legitimacy of *Sukuk*, these determinants are general in nature and are found in *Sukuk* reports that are available for review by IFIs, investors and regulators (Haron & Ibrahim 2012, Hasan & Sabirzyanov 2015). However, the Chairman of AAOIFI, Taqi Usmani, in 2007, criticized the fact that most of the *Sukuk* products in the market were not fully compliant with *Shariah,* and thus required an urgent review (Usmani 2008). In reaction to that, the Muslim Council of Britain (2008), in co-operation with the Utrujj Foundation and the Islamic Finance Council, released the *Islamic Finance Transparency Standard*, a consultative document with a threefold purpose: to improve the level of consumers' understanding of retail products that are Islamic; to reduce consumers' skepticism about non-compliance of *Shariah* products; and to enhance the protection of consumers (Ginena 2014). A document entitled *Guiding Principles on Shariah Governance Systems for Institutions offering Islamic Financial Services* was released by the IFSB in December 2009. Bank Negara Malaysia (BNM) followed shortly thereafter in 2010, by issuing its own document on the subject, called the *Shariah* Governance Framework.

Acknowledging the requirements for stringent measures to validate *Sukuk* legitimacy, numerous guidelines and rulings were put in place. In July 2011 the Malaysian Securities Commission amended its Islamic Securities Guidelines to provide a comprehensive direction on the subject, covering topics such as the applicable *Shariah* rulings, the approval process, disclosure requirements, and ratings for *Sukuk* issuance. In addition, Malaysia has also listed *Sukuk* on Bursa Malaysia under an exempt regime for *Sukuk* that are issued, offered, or subscribed, in accordance with section 229(1) and section 230(1) of the Capital Markets and Services Act 2007 (CMSA). The exempt regime is specifically meant for issuers who intend to list their *Sukuk* or debt securities on Bursa Securities for listing status and for profiling purposes only, but not to be quoted or traded. This listing enables investors to participate in bonds trading in a transparent manner (Securities Commission Malaysia 2009). Furthermore, the Securities Commission (SC), under the Private Debt Securities (PDS) Guidelines (paragraph 32), requires the Islamic Private Debt Securities' (IPDS) issuers to appoint an independent *Shariah* advisor, approved by the SC, to advise on all aspects of the IPDS, including documentation, investment, and structuring (SC 2003). These advisors-cum-*Shariah* scholars play a crucial role in maintaining and ensuring public confidence in the ICM by guaranteeing that the *Sukuk* issued by the market participants are fully compliant with *Shariah* principles, both from the accounting perspective with regards to the *Sukuk* issuance process, as well as in a complete and transparent disclosure on its determinants' legitimacy limitations.

## The *Sukuk* Market in Malaysia

Recently, more efforts have been directed towards the development of the *Sukuk* market, which has now increased to such a state that it encompasses in excess of fifty percent of the bond market in Malaysia (Abdel-Khaleq & Richardson 2006). This situation has been made possible through the participation of international corporations and multilateral agencies that have raised substantial amounts of funds and invested in the *Sukuk* issuances outside Malaysia (Jobst, Kunzel & Mills 2008). In lieu of this foreign participation, proportionally continuous innovation has been witnessed, and an increasing number of issuances in foreign currency have occurred. Zeti Akhtar (2010) vowed that Malaysia will offer international participation in the Islamic financial system, opening up an international gateway, leading to the strengthening of the link between the two important dynamic growth regions of Asia and the Middle East.

Malaysia's *Sukuk* market was initialized by Shell MDS Sdn. Bhd. with a modest issue in the order of RM125 million in 1990. Since that time, continuous and encouraging development has been seen. The recent issue of RM15.4 billion ($4.7 billion) by Binariang GSM Sdn. Bhd. is the largest *Sukuk* issuance, demonstrating a positive ongoing development. Incidentally, with an average annual growth of 22 percent issued for the period 2001 to 2007, the *Sukuk* market in Malaysia is among the fastest-growing funds in the world for the corresponding period. Since the inception of the first sovereign global *Sukuk* in the world in 2002, more successes followed with the introduction of innovative *Sukuk* structures, such as the convertible *Sukuk musharakah* issued by Khazanah Nasional Berhad, the Malaysian government's investment holding institution. This pioneering measure brought together the features of the first full convertibility that is usually only used for conventional equity-linked transactions (BNM 2007). Meanwhile, in an attempt to further improve *Sukuk* funds, Malaysia extended its cooperation with other regulatory authorities to guarantee financial stability in the Islamic financial system.

This cooperation involved Malaysia actively collaborating with the Islamic Financial Services Board (IFSB), the Islamic Financial Stability Forum (IFSF), the Islamic Development Bank (IDB), and the International Islamic Liquidity Management Corporation (IILMC). In addition, secondary trading in the Malaysian *Sukuk* market has increased the depth and liquidity of the market with the participation of more companies, including foreign-owned companies which continue to use this market for funding purposes (Bin Ibrahim & Wong 2006). Naturally, a large number of corporate issuances serve to finance long-term funding needs. In practice, this has helped to create an energetic secondary market due to the diversity and size of *Sukuk* transactions, which possess an increasing value proposition that is appealing to investors out to vary their asset portfolios (Tariq 2004).

Apart from this, the Malaysian *Sukuk* market has also developed sufficiently to handle the varied risk-return profiles and requirements of both issuers and investors, innovatively and in a sophisticated way (Wedderburn-Day 2010). In order to encourage the participation of both local and foreign investors in the market, the propagation of new types of instruments with extended maturity profiles have been put into operation by the *Sukuk* issuers (Zin, Sakat, Ahmad, Bhari, Ishak & Jamain 2011). In 2005, the Malaysian government threw in more support by liberalizing the market to allow for the issuance of debt securities by foreign corporations and multilateral agencies in Ringgit-denominated papers (Hamid 2000). Subsequently, the issuance of debt securities was extended to foreign currency-denominated issuances in 2007. As a result, many foreign corporations, multinational corporations, and multilateral agencies, began to raise funds and invest in issuances and originations out of Malaysia (Zin, Hashim, Khalid, Opir, and Sulaiman 2011). This indirectly strengthened the Malaysian market, and simultaneously forged stronger bonds with other international financial markets. On the whole, this illustrated the government's efforts to transform the Malaysian economy into a more diversified and private sector-driven economy, through the development of the *Sukuk* market in Malaysia (Zaid 2011a).

This diversification reflected the government's effort to transform a market dependent on its debt securities into long-term financing requirements for the private sector. This move has certainly boosted the market capitalization of the private sector in Malaysia. The debt securities and *Sukuk* market helped to meet the financing requirements from one-third, ten years ago, to almost three-fifths currently. More significant and liquid debt securities as well as *Sukuk* markets have directly helped to stabilize the financial system. Therefore, Malaysia has the world's largest *Sukuk* market with the total of *Sukuk* issues standing at 58.1 percent, or US$308 billion of the total global outstanding amount at the end of 2015. Last year, the total global *Sukuk* outstanding was a little over $300 billion with Malaysia accounting for more than half of the total at $173 billion. Saudi Arabia came in second, making up 16.7 percent of the total global *Sukuk* outstanding.

Interestingly, Malaysia possesses the most developed *Sukuk* market in terms of total *Sukuk* issuance, and also the introduction of innovative *Sukuk* structures which are competitive enough to attract more investors (Ab Majid, Shahimi & Bangaan 2010). Furthermore, Malaysia aims to promote the Malaysian debt security market and increase the capital market investment options offered. As a result, debt securities and *Sukuk* have been listed on Bursa Malaysia under the exempt regime, by both listed and non-listed issuers, for *Sukuk* that are issued, offered, or subscribed, in accordance with section 229(1) and section 230(1) of the Capital Markets and Services Act 2007 (CMSA). This regime enables institutions and investors to enhance the transparency of *Sukuk* issued, as well as offering profiling opportunities for the instrument issuers. It allows any currency denominations by either listed or non-listed local or international entities, but is subjected to the rules of Bursa Malaysia Listing Requirements which are comparable with other Exchanges which provide similar listing facilities. In short, the *Sukuk* market has developed into the most successful Islamic financial product in the financial industry, and among the global finance sectors, it is one of the fastest-growing sectors (Zin et al. 2011).

# CHAPTER 2

# THE HISTORY AND DEVELOPMENT OF *SUKUK*

The current chapter reviews and describes the history and development of *Sukuk*. It begins with an explanation about the definition of *Sukuk*, their history, and the basic foundations of *Sukuk* in *Shariah* (Islamic law), and outlines the sources from *Shariah*, as well as the concepts of *Ijtihad*. It also gives an explanation of the basic principles of the Islamic financial system, and the concept of debt and equity in Islam. Finally, the chapter continues with an outline of the development of the *Sukuk* market and the *Sukuk* structure.

## The Definition of *Sukuk*

There have been many definitions for *Sukuk* derived from previous studies, and from recognized organizations, globally, and locally within a Malaysian context. According to Al-Jumuah (2000), *Sukuk* are property certifications. *Sukuk* are also sometimes referred as Islamic bonds or *Sukuk sanadat* (negotiable papers) and ownership (Al-Bastawaisi 2006). In comparing *Sukuk* to bonds, *Sukuk* have more generalized meaning than bonds (Engku Ali 2005). Furthermore, *Sukuk* refer to securities characterized as compliant with Islamic *Shariah* rules and with the principles of investment which prohibit and prevent dealings with interest charges (LMC 2008). In addition, as mentioned by Al-Buolayan, (2006) and LMC (2008), *Sukuk* are represented by their stability; being asset-backed, they are compatible with *Shariah* rules, and can be considered as trust certificates. The Accounting and Auditing Organization for Islamic Financial Institutions (AAOFI, 2012) defines *Sukuk* as "Certificates of equal representing undivided shares in ownership of tangible assets, usufructs and services or (in the ownership of) the assets of particular projects or special investment activity". There are several kinds of *Sukuk*. Nevertheless the common ones, as mentioned by AAOFI, are: *Musharakah Sukuk*; the *Ijarah Sukuk*; *Murabahah Sukuk*; *Mudarabah Sukuk*; *Istisna Sukuk*; *Salam Sukuk*; and the Hybrids.

The Islamic Financial Services Board (IFSB) defines *Sukuk* thus, "*Sukuk* (plural of *sakk*), frequently referred to as 'Islamic bonds', are certificates, with each *sakk* representing a proportional undivided ownership right in tangible assets, or a pool of predominantly tangible assets, or a business venture. These assets may be in a specific project or investment activity in accordance with *Shariah* rules and principles" (IFSB 2009b).

On the other hand, the Malaysian Debt Securities and *Sukuk* Market (2009) provides another definition to explain *Sukuk* as follows: "Certificates of equal value that represent an undivided interest (proportional to the investor's interest) in the ownership of an underlying asset (both tangible and intangible), usufruct, services or investments in particular projects or special investment activities". Also, the Securities Commission (SC) Malaysia (2012) has defined *Sukuk* as "[…] any securities issued pursuant to any *Shariah* principles and concepts approved by the *Shariah* Advisory Council (SAC) of the SC, as set out in Appendix 1 […] (and subsequently) Appendix 1 (B): A document or certificate which represents the value of an asset" (SC 2004 and SC 2009).

Al-Buolayan (2006) stated that the *Sukuk* Security Model is derived from traditional securitization procedures that are based on a special purpose vehicle (SPV) which lies in gaining assets and issuing financial compensation on these assets. Such assets represent appropriate aspects with beneficial ownership to the *Sukuk* investors.

The *Sukuk* issuance process lies in the following steps (LMC 2008):

1. A feasibility study must be prepared in detail;
2. A general framework is to be prepared in addition to setting up an organizational structure;
3. The work should be in line with the structure and principles of *Shariah;*
4. Issuance must be conducted by a leading manager;
5. Arrangement of agreed Islamic legal documentation;
6. Arrangement of special purpose vehicles (SPV) to represent *Sukuk* holders;
7. Circulation of the *Sukuk* into the financial markets.

## Difference between *Sukuk* and Debt Bonds

A *Sukuk* certificate duplicates some of the functions of the tradable bonds and conventional securities to inject liquidity into the reserves of government and corporations, to mobilize market resources and to provide a steady source of income for investors or *Sukuk* holders (LMC 2008). However, there are a number of distinctions between bond debts and *Sukuk*. Amongst these, the most significant is that in the creation of *Sukuk*, they are founded on an array of contracts to underpin the financial commitment between the investors and issuers. A lease (*Ijarah*) and others such as *Musharakah* (partnership) are such examples, whereas debt bonds are issued on the basis of loan contracts to secure the debt (AL-Bashir 2008).

Furthermore, the profit from *Sukuk* for the investors is derived from the margin of the intrinsic revenue in the lease or partnership contracts, whilst the return for holders of conventional debt bonds is derived from the interest, which is the additional sum of monies charged on the principal loan amount. For *Sukuk*, there is also a requirement to be backed by tangible asset, but such is not the case for conventional debt bonds where the investors can be sold simple receivables (Afshar 2013).

The pricing mechanism between *Sukuk* and conventional bonds varies as well. *Sukuk* pricing is based on the market, and, therefore, is dependent upon market supply and demand. Hence, the asset's underlying value may depreciate or appreciate, but in the case of conventional debt bonds, returns are solely dependent upon the issuer's creditworthiness (Al-Maghlouth 2009). Another difference is that *Sukuk* are security-based and the holders of *Sukuk* have ultimate ownership against the assets. However, in relation to a conventional debt bond, the investors' interest is not the owner of the underlying asset (AL-Bashir 2008).

The structure of *Sukuk* provides a mechanism which is self-controlled and operates as a safety valve, so that in the event of the issue being oversubscribed, the issuer of the *Sukuk* is already conscious of its limitation, and has retained a certain amount, so that the total subscription is not able to surpass the leased asset's value. Conversely, in the event of over-subscription of a debt bond, the action from the issuer to preserve the maximum possible amount may not prove to be responsible, and may, indeed, put the investor's interest at risk. Should a problem occur in relation to the asset-backed *Sukuk*, the investors will still be able to reclaim a significant part of their investment as they own an undivided share in the *Sukuk* ownership (AL-Bashir, 2008). Finally, in evaluating the issuance of *Sukuk*, the investment involves the production of tangible assets or the funding of trade, so that there is direct linkage of the *Sukuk* to real sector activities. In other words they are linked to the economy, and therefore, do not, in the short-term, create speculative movement of funds leading to possible financial crises (LMC 2008, Usmani 2009).

There is a fundamental requirement for the structure of *Sukuk* to follow the structure set by Islamic finance to be *Shariah* compliant (Chik 2012). This fundamental requirement involves the observance of a number of factors: avoiding interest (or *Riba*) that is derived from *bay' al-Inah*, which means to sell and buy back immediately; *Bay' al-Dayn*, at a discounted rate whereby preference is given to those investors who participate in terms of a dividend or liquidation; the avoidance of any type of gambling (or *Maysir*); the avoidance of uncertainty (or *gharar*); as well as the avoidance of transactions prohibited by Islam, such as conventional financial service products including tobacco, alcohol, and pork, and entertainment viewed as immoral (LMC 2008). Further to the discussion above, Table 2.1, below, provides a summary of the main differences between a debt bond and *Sukuk* (AL-Bashir 2008, Usmani 2009, Zaid 2011b).

**Table:1 The Main Differences between Debt Bonds and *Sukuk***

| Debt Bonds | Islamic *Sukuk* |
|---|---|
| A debt bond is characterized by a pure debt for the issuer. | *Sukuk* are characterized by the ownership of stakes in existing and or well-defined assets. |
| Bonds basically create a relationship between borrower and lender, in the form of a contract for which the sole purpose is to earn interest. | The *Sukuk* contract is founded on the lease or a defined undertaking of business between the *Sukuk* issuers and the *Sukuk* holders. |
| In relation to bonds, the condition of an underlying asset does not apply, and it is possible for bonds to be issued for purposes which are not legitimate. | In relation to the underlying *Sukuk* asset, a project or business must be of the type such that their use is possible and permissible. |
| The sale of a bond fundamentally equates to the sale of a debt. | The sales of *Sukuk* are signified by the sale of a share of assets, project or business activity. |

Source: Compiled from Jamilah, and Abdul Rahman 2012, AL-bashir 2008, Zaid 2011b, and Usmani 2009.

However, there are some similarities between a debt bond and *Sukuk*, and the commonalities include: their ratability, in that *Sukuk* can also be readily rated, with marketability, because *Sukuk* are real assets in financial markets which are monetized, liquid, readily traded, and transferable; differing *Sukuk* structures feature an improved ability for credit enhancements; and adaptability, allowing an array of *Sukuk* structures across fiscal and legal domains, as well as options for variable and fixed income options.

## Basic Foundations of *Sukuk* in Islamic Law

The rationale for *Sukuk* and their issuance lies in Islamic *Shariah* and its principles (Saeed & Salah 2012). *Shariah* literally refers to an Islamic religious law body (Abdal-Haqq 2006). However, Islamic law is not a jurisdictional black-letter law based on technical legal rules which are not subject to a reasonable dispute. Instead, Islamic law is based on a set of religious-based concepts and moral principles, as well as Islamic-based rules developed over time (*Qu'ran* and *Sunnah*). As an example, *fiqh* is the understanding of *Shariah's* regulations and practical rules. The term *fiqh muamalat* equates to financial and banking activities that are a part of the economic activities through one area of *fiqh* (Mat & Ismail 2008).

## *Shariah* Sources

According to the classical theory of Islamic jurisprudence, there are two primary sources, and a range of secondary sources of *Shariah* (Saeed & Salah 2012). The primary sources are the Holy Scripture of Islam; the *Qu'ran*, which was revealed to the Prophet Muhammad. Although there are doubts as to whether the legal injunctions in some verses in *Qu'ran* are obligatory or permissive, eighteen verses of the *Qu'ran* refer to strictly legal matters (Pearl 1979). The second most important source is the *Sunnah* (the normative behaviour of the Prophet) which is considered to be documented in the various reports describing the words, actions, or habits, of the Islamic prophet known as the *Hadith* (Janin & Kahlmeyer 2007). The secondary sources of *Shariah* include scholarly consensus (*Ijma*), analogous deduction (*Qiyas*) and independent analytical reasoning (*Ijtihad*) (Visser 2013, Jobst 2010).

*Ijtihad* is literally defined as a striving, or an effort to do something. It was the terminology applied to a jurist's deduction of a point of law in the sources (Waines 2003, Abdelaal 2012). *Ijtihad* is almost considered as a secondary source of Islamic *fiqh* in *Shariah*. Nonetheless, *Ijtihad* is not specifically a source of law, but one of the functions of the jurist (*faqih or mujtahid*) who makes known the interpretation of the original foundational texts and rules of *Shariah* sources (*Qu'ran* and *Sunnah*) (Harasani 2013, Saeed & Salah 2012). While *al-Faqih* has the complete authority to propose interpretations of rules and texts, it is only when the interpretations are supported by a subsequent scholarly consensus (*Ijmaa*) that they obtain the necessary authority in *Shariah* (Farooq 2006). *Sukuk* are not referred to in the *Qu'ran* and *Sunnah* which are the primary sources in Islamic law. It is as a result of *Ijtihad* that ideas have been developed with regard to *Sukuk*, including the way in which they could be structured and their use (Saeed & Salah 2014). Therefore, it can be argued that the concept of *Ijtihad*, and its importance, must be taken into consideration when examining *Sukuk*. Accordingly, the following subsections provide more information in relation to *Ijtihad*.

## *Ijtihad* Method for *Sukuk*

In examining *Ijtihad* during the classical period, there is an association between the development and explanation of *Ijtihad* with the growth of a society's intellectual, economic, legal, political, cultural, and moral aspects (Safari, Ariff & Mohamad 2014). Therefore, *Ijtihad* can be defined as a process and mechanism of the *Usul al-fiqh* (principles of Islamic jurisprudence) method. It is a fact that the rules and laws of *Qu'ran* and *Sunnah* are represented through *Ijtihad*.

According to Weiss (1998), a law was passed, based on the *Mujtahid,* which was considered to be suitable for the actual life of human beings. Therefore, it is important to view *Ijtihad* as generosity. In particular the *Mujtahid,* who is a Muslim recognised as an original authority on Islamic law, can explain the Islamic rules and principles to other people, and society in general. According to Saeed & Salah (2014), although the *Qu'ran* provides the rules and guidance for human beings, its source is still limited, which means that detailed responses and solutions are inadequately provided through the law. That causes difficulties for the Muslim community. Therefore, the significant role of *Ijtihad* is highly appreciated and has become an effective tool of growth of *Shariah* rules. Today, *Sukuk* are, in fact, developed in that context (Ariff, Iqbal & Mohamad 2012). According to Omar, Abduh and Sukmana (2013), the requirement of the fund through financial markets leads to an Islamic financial instrument, which replaces conventional bonds. Based on *Ijtihad* practice, researchers proposed that *Sukuk,* as *Shariah*-compliant securities, replace conventional bonds (Hassan & Mahlknecht 2011). Saeed

& Salah (2014) also stated that *Ijtihad* is considered as the most flexible institution, compared to the experience of earlier generations of Muslims. Indeed, the notation or documentation of *Shariah* sciences such as the *hadith*, history, and exegesis, theology, and jurisprudence principles, was, and continues to be, greatly appreciated.

In particular, Imam Shafi'i (a prominent Muslim jurist) has succeeded in formulating and disseminating *Usul al-fiqh,* and the further development of the *Usul* by later scholars, which led to a gradual reduction in the flexibility available to scholars of all aspects (Safari et al. 2014). A formal, systematic, and rule-governed, approach emerged due to a lack of formalism in the 1st century of the *Hijrah* calendar (Ariff et al. 2012). Before the 10th century, the *Usul al-fiqh* methodology had been established (Weiss 2002). By the 4th century AH (Anno Hegirae, i.e. in the year of *Hijrah),* and by the 6th century, the legal scholarship of Islam had caught the attention of a number of famous researchers (Al-Juwayni [d. 478] AH and al-Ghazali [d. 505 AH]). Then, the main aspects of *Usul* were given due attention (Izz b. Abd al-Salam [d.660 AH] and Imam Al-Shatibi [d.790 AH]).

In examining *Ijtihad* in the modern period, the practice of *Ijtihad* is more legalistic, formalistic, and literalistic, in nature (Ariff et al. 2012, Safari et al. 2014). In the 19th and 20th centuries, due to the complexity of Western concepts, including historical criticism, rationalism, human rights, and nationalism, a number of qualified Muslims, with a range of different degrees in Islamic areas, attempted to determine the appropriate approaches of *Ijtihad* in *Shariah*-related studies (Saeed and Salah 2014).

In recent years, in the Islamic world, there has been a new perception, and critical attitude (Ariff et al. 2012). Moreover, Saeed and Salah (2012) confirmed that Muslim scholars have differing ideas. Local circumstances have a strong effect, with demographics, levels of development, internal and external threats, educational opportunities, and contact with different cultures, all being impacting factors. The perceptions of the social, political, economic and legal problems also vary among scholars when examining differing circumstances (Safari et al. 2014).

In the modern period, scholars have identified three dominant forms of *Ijtihad*. The first one is the text-based *Ijtihad* that uses the traditional methods of *Usul al-fiqh* to derive new laws (Ahmed 2011b). This *Ijtihad* method was found in ancient times, and the practice of this method still remains in traditional Islamic legal scholarship (Saeed 2006). It provides a foundation as well as a consensus (*Ijma*), and an analogy *(Qiyas*) based on the principles and rules of jurisprudence (Moaddel 2005). According to scientists, it is necessary to take into consideration each new legal problem in a deeply well-thought-out manner. In particular, scholars have attempted to find solutions to existing or forthcoming problems, and then provide scientific evidence of *Shariah* prior to applying and implementing the rules of *Usul al-fiqh* (Yahaya, Samsudin & Lalulddin 2013). However, it has been suggested that the new problem, text, previous rules, and decision-making, should all be linked together (Saeed et al. 2014). The text, for instance, could be a verse of the *Qu'ran*, a *Hadith*, a saying of a *Sahabah* (one of the companions of the Prophet Muhammad (PBUH), or the view of an *Imam.* This method emphasizes reading texts literally, applying the *Usul* rules strictly, and paying much attention to compatibility and traditionalism.

*"Eclectic Ijtihad is the second type of Ijtihad, in which scholars do not confine themselves to their respective schools"* (Ahmed 2011a). In eclectic *Ijtihad*, the scholar faces a problem or issue, and must decide whether or not it is acceptable from an Islamic perspective. In fact, the *Shariah* compliance of the issue persuades the scholars; therefore, they can justify their views by selecting texts, including verses, *Hadith*, sayings of the Companions, and views of *Imams*, supporting their preconceived opinions (Ariff et al. 2012).

However, the limitation of this approach is not systematic. That means it does not follow the rules (Saeed 2006). The *Usul al-fiqh* approach is not taken into account, and thus the possible textual or historical evidence is ignored (Saeed & Salah 2014). Although there is a focus on intellectual honesty, this method remains problematic. Indeed, the boundaries, signposts, or approaches, remain ambiguous, and therefore it is difficult to give an interpretation in a conceptualized way (Ahmed 2011b). In the fields of Islamic finance, banking, and economics, examples of eclectic *Ijtihad* can be found (Safari et al. 2014).

The third approach of *Ijtihad* is context-based *Ijtihad*. Context-based *Ijtihad* is known as the third approach of *Ijtihad.* Nevertheless, this approach did not exist in a developed form in early Islamic history. It is a fact that, today, context-based *Ijtihad* is known as a relatively new phenomenon (Saeed 2006). Therefore, gaining an insight into this problem is of crucial importance, and should be taken into consideration in both the modern and historical contexts. Accordingly, there is a need to determine problems from an Islamic viewpoint in which a detailed problem should be firstly, carefully considered. Its features should be identified, and the purpose of the problem, the current function, and the role of today's society, should be determined as well (Ariff et al. 2012). Similar problems were also found in the time of the Prophet Muhammad. The scholars have, therefore, attempted to examine the previous historical problems. In this case, the concept of *maslaha* (public interest, or common good) was used to guide the scholars.

In examining a problem, a scholar places more of a focus on the aims of *Shariah* associated with the modern and historical problem, than on the outward form of the problem itself (Saeed 2006). A decision will then be made as to the attitude Muslims ought to take to examine the problem in the current environment face-to-face. With respect to context-based *Ijtihad*, the scholar does not have an interest in specific *Ijma* created in the classical era, or in certain *Usul*-based tools like *Qiyas*, but mainly conducts what is referred to as so-called 'context analysis', both for the modern situation, and that of the classical era (Safari et al. 2014).

## History and Roots of *Sukuk*

According to De Vroede (1981), the word 'check' in the US, is associated with the British spelling of the word 'cheque', and the modern Western word 'cheque' appears to have been derived from the Arabic word *Sakk* (Heck 2006). *Sukuk* can be defined as documents which represent contracts of transference of rights and obligations, or revenues earned in accordance with the Islamic law, or *Shariah*. Empirical evidence has shown that *Sukuk* (Islamic bonds), the plural form of *Sakk*, were products broadly used during medieval Islam for transferring financial duties and obligations derived from trade and other business activities (Ahmed et al. 2014). The essence of *Sukuk* in the modern Islamic perspective depends on the concept of securitizing 'asset monetization', which is achieved based on the process of issuing *Sukuk taskeek*. Its great potential lies in transforming asset future cash flow within present cash flows. *Sukuk* may be issued on existing as well as specific assets, which could become available at a future date (Taher & Al-Hajjar 2013).

The next sub-sections provide a particular focus on the origins of the word *Sukuk*, their use in the Middle Ages, and the recent history of *Sukuk* in Islamic capital markets.

## The Origins of *Sukuk*

As previously indicated, the Arabic word *Sukuk* is the plural of the word *sakk*, meaning 'certificate' or 'order of payment' (Khan 2004, Cakir & Raei 2007). Documentary evidence confirms the use of the word *sakk* in early

Islamic caliphates (Adam & Thomas 2004a). The Muslim societies of the pre-modern period used *Sukuk* as papers representing financial obligations originating from trade and other commercial activities (Jaffer 2004, Khan 2004, Adam, & Thomas 2004b). In the earlier theoretical legal works, written instruments of credit were present. Such written instruments are encountered frequently in *genizah* documents (Udovitch 1981). *Genizah* documents are documents that were stored in the Middle Eastern mosques and synagogues, because the word 'God' was written either in Arabic or Hebrew, and, therefore, the merchants were reluctant to destroy such documents. The Cairo *genizah* documents contain fragments that indicate the existence of *sakk* in the 12th century CE, and these money orders are remarkably similar in form to modern-day checks (Khan 1993). They state the sum to be paid, the order, the date, and the name of the issuer (Khan 1993, Goodwin 2003). During the Middle Ages, a *sakk* was a written vow to pay for goods when they were delivered, and it was used to avoid money having to be transported across dangerous terrain (Vallely 2006). As a result, these *Sukuk* were transported across several countries and spread throughout the world. The Jewish merchants from the Muslim world transmitted the concept, and the term '*sakk*' to Europe (Braudel 1995). An interesting outcome of the trade and transport of these *Sukuk* is that they functioned as a source of inspiration for modern-day checks.

## *Sukuk* in Present Times

Today, *Sukuk* are known as tools of the Islamic capital markets. In modern-day Islamic finance, *Sukuk* refers to Islamic securities with rather distinctive features. One of the very first definitions of modern day *Sukuk* was given in February 1988 during the fourth session of the Council of the Islamic *Fiqh* Academy in Jeddah. Resolution No.30 (5/4) of the Council of the Islamic *Fiqh* Academy dealt with the matter. This resolution made was in respect of investment certificates, and more specifically on *muqarada* bonds (also known as *mudaraba Sukuk*), which are a specific form of *Sukuk*. The Council defined these *Sukuk* as:

> "[…] investment instruments which allocate the (*muqarada*) capital (*mudaraba*) by floating certificates, as an evidence of capital ownership, on the basis of shares of equal value, registered in the name of the owner, as joint owners of shares in the venture capital or whatever shape it may take, in proportion to […] each one's share therein" (IDB 2000).

This is arguably the first description of *Sukuk* in present times. Shortly after this description, in 1990, the first *Sukuk* were issued by Shell MDS in Malaysia (Dusuki 2009b). After this issuance, there were no other active issuances by other *Sukuk* issuers until the beginning of the 21st century. From 2000 onwards, a number of institutions started issuing *Sukuk*, and the *Sukuk* market took off from there (Haneef 2009). The immense growth of the market required certainty in regard to *Shariah*-related matters and standardization. Hence, the Accounting and Auditing Organization for Islamic Financial Institutions (AAOIFI) issued its *Shariah* Standard No.17 on 'Investment *Sukuk*' in May 2003, which became effective from January 1 2004. This *Shariah* Standard provides a definition of *Sukuk* in s.2 of the *Shariah* Standard. The AAOIFI defines investment *Sukuk* as:

> "[…] certificates of equal value representing undivided shares in ownership of tangible assets, usufruct, and services or (in the ownership of) the assets of particular projects or special investment activity […]" (AAOIFI 2012).

The AAOIFI *Shariah* Standard on *Sukuk* describes that there are fourteen different *Sukuk* structures founded on the basis of Islamic financial contracts, such as the first decade of the 21st century, when the market witnessed several *Sukuk* issuances in different forms and structures. In 2007, the *Sukuk* market reached its peak in terms of issuance volume (Mokhtar 2009). The AAOIFI *Shariah* Standard No.17 on *Sukuk* also provides specific rules to safeguard the *Shariah* compliance of each *Sukuk* structure.

## Basic Principles of an Islamic Financial System

The basic framework for a financial system in Islam is a set of laws and rules, collectively referred to as *Shariah*, governing social, political, economic, and cultural, aspects of Islamic societies (Elasrag 2011). Islamic law (*Shariah*) originated from the principles and rules dictated by the Holy *Qu'ran* and its practices, as well as explanations rendered, known as the *Sunnah* by Prophet Mohammad (Iqbal 1997). Furthermore, scholars elaborated upon the rules of Islamic jurisprudence within the framework of the *Qu'ran* and *Sunnah*. The basic principles of the Islamic financial system can be summarized in the following way:

*i.* **The prohibition of *riba*:** *Riba* is a term that literally means 'an excess' and interpreted as "any unjustifiable increase of capital whether in loans or sales". It is the central tenet of the system. More precisely, any positive, fixed, predetermined rate tied to the maturity and the amount of principal, in other words, guaranteed, regardless of the performance of the investment, is considered *riba*, which is prohibited in Islam (Bertillo, Julius, Salando, Nieva & Ortega 2013). The general consensus among Islamic scholars is that *riba* covers not only usury, but also the charging of interest as it is widely practiced. This prohibition is based on arguments of social justice, equality, and property rights. Islam encourages the earning of profits, but forbids the charging of interest, because profits, determined ex-post, symbolize successful entrepreneurship and the creation of additional wealth, whereas interest, determined ex-ante, is a cost that is accrued irrespective of the outcome of business operations, and may not create wealth if there are business losses (Iqbal & Mirakhor 2011). Social justice demands that borrowers and lenders share rewards as well as losses in an equitable fashion, and that the process of wealth accumulation and distribution in the economy be fair and representative of true productivity (Ahmed 2011).

ii. **Risk sharing:** As interest is prohibited, suppliers of funds become investors instead of creditors (Bellalah and Ellouz 2004). Furthermore, the provider of financial capital and the entrepreneur share business risks in return for shares of the profits (Mounira & Anas 2008).

iii. **Money as actual capital:** Money is treated as potential capital, that is, it becomes actual capital only when it is combined with other resources to undertake a productive activity. Islam recognizes the time value of money, but only when it acts as capital, not when it is potential capital (Choudhury 2005).

iv. **Prohibition of speculative behavior:** The Islamic financial system discourages hoarding, and prohibits transactions featuring extreme uncertainties, gambling and risks (Iqbal 1997).

v. **Sanctity of contracts:** Islam upholds contractual obligations and the disclosure of information as a sacred duty (Musa & Obadi 2009). This feature is intended to reduce the risk of asymmetric information and moral hazard (Srivastava & Surana 2006).

vi. ***Shariah*-approved activities:** Only those business activities that do not violate the rules of *Shariah* are qualified for investment (Iqbal & Mirakhor 2011). For example, any investment in businesses dealing with alcohol, gambling, and casinos, is strictly prohibited.

## The Concept of Debt and Equity in Islam

*Shariah* governs all aspects of an individual's life, from matters of state such as governance and foreign relations, to issues of daily living and financial transactions (Iqbal & Mirakhor 2011). It is the set of rules and principles that Muslims believe in, and they represent God's guidance for the individuals to lead their lives (Sachedina 2005). *Shariah* is derived from two primary sources, the Holy *Qu'ran* and *Sunnah* (Rehman 2007).

*Shariah* lays several general and specific principles which govern how financial transactions should be conducted (El-Hawary & Grais 2003). In relation to debt and equity, the following rules are applied:

1. Prohibiting any interest being applied when money is lent and paid back with interest, irrespective of whether it is fixed or floating.
2. Prohibiting uncertainty (*gharar*) is covered off, as any agreements containing a material degree of uncertainty are not recognized as valid under the Islamic *Shariah* law.
3. Prohibiting of speculation (*maisir*), in that transactions relying on mere chance are not permitted under *Shariah* law.
4. Prohibiting investments (*haram*) that are not acceptable from the *Shariah* perspective, in that *Shariah* stipulates that the nature of the underlying investment must also be acceptable from the *Shariah* viewpoint. It cannot be used to promote unlawful investments, for instance, investment in the alcohol trade, armaments, and gambling, is prohibited.
5. Risk taking (*mukhatarah*), in that *Shariah* prohibits the guarantee of a fixed return on an investment; the parties must assume some risk in a transaction.

The key principles that have been set out above, shape the way in which *Shariah*-compliant transactions are structured. Although in principle, *Shariah* requires an Islamic investor to assume a propriety interest in the asset or project being financed, *Shariah*-compliant investments can be structured to yield returns that resemble both equity and debt type returns (Ibrahim, Eng & Parsa 2009). Equity structures mainly use partnership models. Debt structures use devices such as leases, forward sales, and deferred payment obligations, on assets or real estate which guarantee the economic effect of returns on lending (Simmons & Simmons LLP 2010). On both sides of financial intermediation, banks can use either equity or debt instruments. In the early literature concerning Islamic economics and finance, Islamic banks were envisioned to use equity or quasi-equity instruments on both asset and liability sides (El-Gamal 2005). In this regard, they would have become the polar opposite of commercial banking practice, wherein debt instruments dominate both the asset and liability sides (El-Gamal 2007).

Evidence concerning the current practices by Islamic banks worldwide suggests that the majority of financing operations are not based on equity; instead they take the form of debt-like instruments (Aggarwal & Yousef 2000, Wajdi & Abdullah 2006, Mehmet 2007). This is because, according to Mehmet (2007), Islamic banks and financial institutions have opted for profitable Islamic financing such as *murabahah* instead of *musharakah* (*musharakah* is equity-finance oriented and *murabahah* is debt-financing). This phenomenon is described by Farooq (2006) as the *murabaha* syndrome, as the Islamic Banking and Financial Institutions overly use debt-based financing as their products. This has been proved, when Mehmet (2007), by quoting *Hasan's* recent data while studying the Malaysian case, stated that, "the percentage share of *musharakah* declined from 1.4 percent in 2000 to 0.5 percent in 2003". Evidently, it seems that the major modes of Islamic financing are in the form of *Bai` Bithaman Ajil* (BBA) (a contract that refers to the sale and purchase) and *Ijarah Thumma al-bay* (a type of lease contract in which the legal title of the leased asset will be passed to the hirer at the end, or at the completion of, the rental period) with 47.4 percent and 27.9 percent respectively in 2003.

Islamic Financial Institutions have currently built the bulk of their assets in the form of debt-based instruments, through *murabaha, ijarah*, and various *Sukuk* structures (Dusuki 2010a). The finance (loan) officers at those Islamic Banks would, as they do currently, utilize the same criteria used by their conventional bank counterparts (prospective debtors' earnings before interest, taxes, and depreciation, credit risk scores, etc.) (Roy 1991). In the meantime, the liabilities side of the bank will consist mainly of shares (after excluding various owed debts, e.g. for leased bank buildings, etc.), whereby shareholders and investment account holders will be put on a par (El-Gamal 2005). While this does not eliminate information asymmetry problems, it does eliminate the substantial short-term conflict of interest that currently exists between Islamic bank shareholders and investment account holders, which is addressed by the AAOIFI standard quotes in the previous sections. In other words, this would reduce the corporate governance and regulatory issues for Islamic banks to their well-studied counterparts for mutual thrift institutions such as mutual savings banks, credit unions, and so forth (Nomani 2013).

# CHAPTER 3

# THE STRUCTURE AND TYPES OF *SUKUK*

*Sukuk* is an Arabic word for financial certificates which can be viewed as the Islamic equivalent of bonds (Alam 2011). However, in Islam, interest-bearing fixed-income bonds are not permissible (Ayub 2005). Accordingly, *Sukuk* are securities that are *Shariah*-compliant and follow the investment principles of *Shariah*, in that the paying or charging of interest is prohibited. Those financial assets that are *Shariah*-compliant are grouped as to whether they are non-tradable or tradable in the secondary markets (Rizvi 2014). From the perspective of modern Islam, in essence, *Sukuk* are founded on the concept of monetization of an asset; in other words, securitization which is obtained through the process of *Sukuk* issuance (*taskeek*) (Ahmed et al. 2013). The *Sukuk's* huge potential rests in their being able to transform the future cash flow of an asset into the present cash flow (Jaffer 2004). As such, *Sukuk* may be issued on an existing asset in addition to specific assets which may become available at a later date in the future (Hasan 2007).

From their basic structures, *Sukuk* have evolved by way of innovative moves in order to gain popularity in the financial markets (Al-Amine 2008). However, not all *Sukuk* innovation has been seen as positive, as demonstrated by a failure of some *Sukuk,* after being tested by the Islamic financial industry to pass the grade of *Shariah*-compliance as financing instruments which are an alternative to conventional bonds (Nazar 2015). *Sukuk,* in line with conventional debt securities, are issued for a fixed period of time, rather than in perpetuity, as is the case with equity. According to the principles of *Shariah*, the *Sukuk* must be backed by a real asset, for instance a building, land, or equipment. Accordingly, when *Sukuk* are bought and sold, the vendor and purchaser are indirectly dealing with real assets, not merely trading paper (Mseddi & Naifar 2013). The *Sukuk* can be structured in a number of ways, and the types of structures are dependent on the types of Islamic financing modes and trades utilized in *Sukuk* structuring (Mseddi & Naifar 2013). Fourteen prototypical *Sukuk* (with differing characteristics of risk and return) have been developed by the AAOIFI in line with its standards for *Sukuk* investment, whereby some

*Sukuk* are non-tradable in the secondary market whilst others have tradability, depending upon the characteristics and type of the *Sukuk* issued (Nathif & Abdulkader 2004). *Sukuk* can also be structured alongside other techniques, as stated by Wilson (2008), El-Quqa, Hasan, Rout and Joubaili (2008) and Shaikh and Saeed (2010). *Sukuk* can constitute a partial ownership of a debt (*Sukuk Murabaha*), an asset (*Sukuk Ijara),* a business (*Sukuk Musharakah*), a manufacturing project (*Sukuk Istisna*), an investment (*Sukuk Istithmar*), financing (*Sukuk Mudarabah*), future delivery (*Salam Sukuk*), irrigation (*Sukuk Musaqah*), sharecropping (*Sukuk Muzara'ha*), agriculture (*Sukuk Mugharasah*) or a combination of these forms (hybrid *Sukuk*).

However, the *Sukuk* structures are not without their critics. According to Moody's report (Howladar 2009), many of the applied *Sukuk* structures have literally been reduced to forms that duplicate conventional unsecured bonds. Many *Sukuk* which are asset-based may possess the form of asset-backed *Sukuk,* however not the substance (Khan 2013). In accordance with several researchers (Usmani 2007, Alam, Hassan & Haque 2013, Zulkhibri 2015), some of the existing practices of *Sukuk* issuance mirror the conventional bonds' structure in terms of not having ownership, and a guarantee of the principal to be repaid and a right to a fixed rate of return. Some researchers believe that the majority of *Sukuk* structures are not in accordance with the principles of *Shariah.* Miller, Challoner, and Atta (2007), and Wilson (2008), similarly claimed that *Sukuk* are not financial innovative instruments, as in general, they are structured along the lines of securitization rules in Western countries. As predicted by several scholars there is a view that there is a convergence between conventional finance and Islamic finance, and specifically in the case of *Sukuk,* this viewpoint is gaining momentum (Mirakhor 2006). Howladar (2009) claimed that the majority of *Sukuk* structures to date have not been asset-backed, rather they have been asset-based, which is the equivalent of conventional unsecured bonds. Some scholars have highlighted the issue in the market of *Sukuk* structures guaranteeing the return of the *Sukuk*-holders' capital and the provision of purchase guarantees for credit enhancement by related businesses. From a *Shariah*-related perspective, Wilson (2004) contends that the present structures of the *Sukuk* have been developed by investment bankers and lawyers, and, as they are not *Shariah*-based, and given that the traditional Islamic jurisprudence '*fiqh*' contracts are appreciably different, the present structures' legitimacy is in question. Currently, some analysts are attempting to create Islamic financial tools which are homologous with conventional financial tools by pursing the same path of logic, and at the same time being *Shariah*-compliant (Mseddi & Naifar 2013). For instance, in undertaking an arrangement of *Sukuk* as an Islamic financial instrument, the instrument is seen to be *Shariah*-compliant when approval has been granted by the relevant institution's *Shariah* Supervisory Board (SSB). However, in some instances the SSB may not have been party to the discussion in the structuring of some of the financial instruments (Kamso 2013).

In following equity-based or debt-based principles, the *Sukuk* structures can be formulated (Saeed & Salah 2014). In accordance with *Shariah* principles, those instruments which are debt-based, such as *murabaha* (cost-plus sale) and *ijarah* (lease or rental agreement) pay to investors a prearranged rate of return, and receive less praise in comparison to those investments which are equity-based (Godlewski, Turk & Weill 2014). Nevertheless, these structures are permitted as they do not comprise a component of interest. On the other hand, investments that are equity-based follow the principles of profit-and-loss sharing of *musharaka* and *mudaraba*, and these equate to partnership contracts in which the entrepreneur and financier are able to share in the profits on the basis of pre-agreed ratios whereby any loss corresponds to their physical or financial contribution to the partnership (Farooq 2007). Although *Sukuk* are a favoured type of financing, those *Sukuk* created on the basis of partnership contracts received criticism in 2007, by a well-known *Shariah* scholar, for not being structured *de facto* along the lines as prescribed by *Shariah* principles (Faiz 2011). Given it is dubious as to whether the structures are *Shariah*-compliant, these instruments may well succumb to an unfavourable selection mechanism, as outlined by Godlewski et al. (2014). Indeed, these types of *Sukuk* may cause a damaging stock market reaction compared with debt-based instruments. Nevertheless, in the modern Islamic financial market for most *Sukuk,* the practice of *Shariah*-compliance has not been adhered to. Accordingly, the structures of *Sukuk* ought to be modified to enable *Shariah*-compliance. To do this would necessitate the joint efforts of the states, regulators, market players and providers, investors, *Shariah* scholars, and legal experts (Yean 2009 & Nanaeva 2010).

In the structuring process, there are a number of steps which vary according to the category. The structuring process can be encapsulated in five steps, as outlined in sub-section 2.8.1.2. There are many different types of *Sukuk*. However, they are dependent on the types of Islamic modes of trade and financing utilized in the structuring (Nisar 2007, Krichene 2012). The standards for the Accounting and Auditing Organization of Islamic Financial Institutions (AAOIFI) have allowed for fourteen different types of *Sukuk*. Of these, the most significant and commonly used ones are:

*Mudarabah, Ijarah, Istisna, Murabaha, Musharakah, Salam,* and even some versions which are hybrid.

## *Ijarah Sukuk*

*Ijarah Sukuk* represent ownership in equal shares in a rented real estate, or the usufruct of the real estate (Zakaria, Md Isa & Abidin 2012). These *Sukuk* give their owners the right to own the real estate, receive the rent, and dispose of their *Sukuk* in a manner which does not affect the right of the lessee; in other words, they are tradable (Nisar 2007). The holders of such *Sukuk* bear all costs of maintenance and are obliged to repair any damage to the real estate (AAOIFI 2008).

*Ijarah Sukuk* are securities which represent ownership of well-defined existing and known assets tied up by way of a lease contract, the rental of which is the return payable to *Sukuk* holders (Wilson 2008). Payment of *Ijarah* rentals can be unrelated to the period of taking usufruct by the lessee. It can be made before the beginning of the lease period, during the period or after the period, as the parties may mutually decide (Ayub 2005). This flexibility can be used to evolve different forms of contract and *Sukuk* which may serve different purposes for issuers and holders (Shaukat 2010).

## Features of *Ijarah Sukuk*

It is necessary for *Ijarah* contracts for the assets being leased and the amount of rent to be clearly known to the parties at the time of the contract, and, if both of these are known, *Ijarah* can be contracted on an asset or a building that is yet to be constructed, as long as it is fully described in the contract. This is made on the proviso that the lesser should normally be able to acquire, construct, or buy the asset being leased by the time set for its delivery to the lessee. The lesser can sell the leased asset provided it does not hinder the lessee to take full benefit of the asset. Furthermore, the new owner would be entitled to receive the rentals (Kahf 1997).

Rental in *Ijarah* must be stipulated in clear terms for the first term of the lease, and, for future renewable terms, it could be constant, increasing or decreasing by benchmarking or relating it to any well-known variable (Ayub 2005). As per *Shariah* rules, expenses related to the corpus or basic characteristics of the assets are the responsibility of the owner, while maintenance expenses related to its operation are to be borne by the lessee (Nisar 2007). With respect to the procedure for issuance of *Ijarah Sukuk*, an

SPV is created to purchase the asset that issues *Sukuk* to the investor, enabling it to make payment for purchasing the asset (AL-Maghlouth 2009). The asset is then leased to a third party for its use. The lessee makes periodic rental payments to the SPV, which, in turn, distributes the same to the *Sukuk* holders.

*Ijarah Sukuk* are completely negotiable and can be traded in the secondary markets. *Ijarah Sukuk* offer a high degree of flexibility from the point of view of their issuance management and marketability (Rohmatunnisa 2008). The central government, municipalities, *Awqaf* or any other asset users, private or public, can issue these *Sukuk.* Additionally, they can be issued by financial intermediaries or directly by users of the leased assets (Kahf 1997). Figure 2.1, below, outlines the *Sukuk Ijarah* transaction structure.

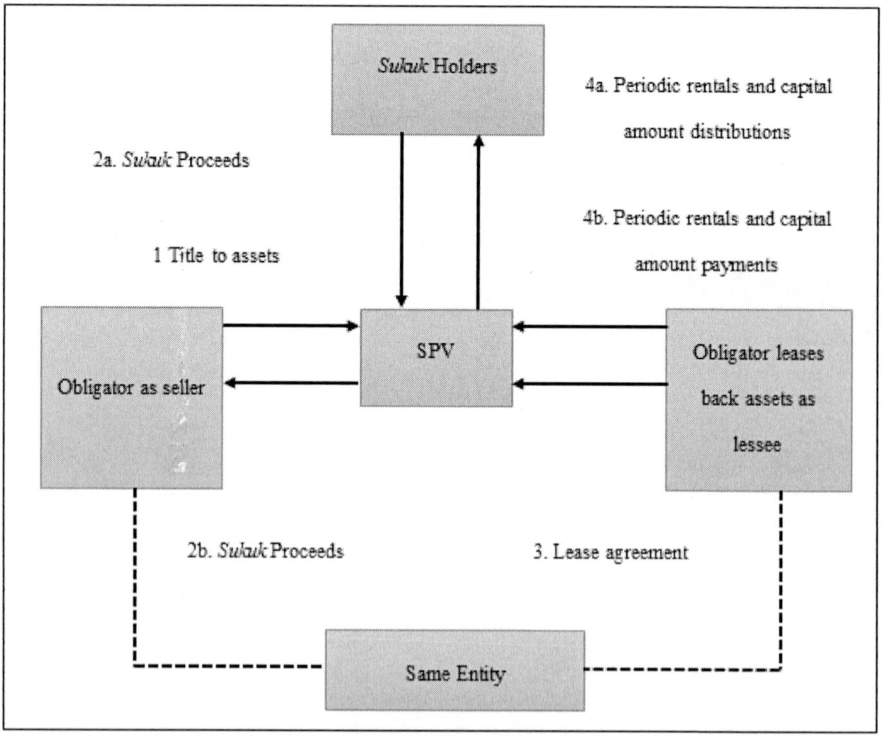


Figure 1: *Sukuk Ijarah* Transaction Structure
Source: Rohmatunnisa 2008

## Steps involved in the Structuring

The structuring process can be encapsulated in following five steps outlined below:

1. A company's identifiable well-defined assets are placed by the originator or seller into a special purpose vehicle (SPV) at a pre-determined price (Nisar 2007) and the proceeds of the *Sukuk* issuance will then be obtained. This is specifically undertaken as an asset transfer to identify and set aside the assets from the associated risks with the originator's or obligator's potential insolvency or bankruptcy, and placing them in an SPV means that there is a lessened likelihood of being involved in insolvency or bankruptcy proceedings (McMillen 2008).
2. It is the entity of the SPV that in fact issues the *Sukuk*, and it raises the finances by issuing *Sukuk* certificates in an amount which is equal to the purchase price (Vishwanath & Azmi 2009). The SPV hands on the comparative ownership rental payments from the originator or obligator to the investors.
3. Investors purchase the *Sukuk* issuance and provide the payment of the principal amount to the SPV. A lease agreement is signed between the SPV and the obligator or originator for a fixed period of time, and the obligator or originator leases back the assets as a lessee (Nisar 2007).
4. The originator or obligator therefore has responsibility to make recurring payments by way of rent for the use of the assets and the rental monies are passed on to the investors by the SPV.
5. At the maturity of the *Sukuk*, or in the event a dissolution occurs, the SPV sells the assets back to the originator or obligator, and the sale proceeds will be utilized to repay the investors or *Sukuk* holders. That value should be equal to any amounts still owed under the terms of the *Ijarah Sukuk* (Ferry 2010).

## *Musharakah Sukuk*

In examining the types of *Sukuk* structures, *Musharakah Sukuk* relate to the sharing of profit and loss (Arshad & Ismail, 2010). Moreover, they represent a partnership where profits are shared as predetermined ratios agreed by partners while the losses are shared in proportion to the capital or investment of each partner (Mirakhor & Zaidi 2007). In addition, all partners contribute funds and have the right, but not the obligation, to exercise executive powers in that project. This is similar to a conventional partnership structure and the holding of voting stock in a limited company. It is widely considered as the purest form of Islamic financing (LMC 2008).

*Musharaka Sukuk* are used for mobilizing the funds for establishing a new project, or developing an existing one, or for financing a business activity on the basis of partnership contracts (Vishwanath & Azmi 2009). The certificate holders become the owners of the project or the assets of the activity, in accordance with their respective share's holdings. These *Musharaka* certificates can be treated as negotiable instruments, and can be bought and sold in the secondary market (Shaukat 2010).

In accordance with AAOIFI Standard 17, 3/6, "these are certificates of equal value issued with the aim of using the mobilized funds for establishing a new project, developing an existing project, or financing a business activity on the basis of any partnership contracts, so that the certificate holders become the owners of the project or assets of the activity, as per their respective shares, with the *Musharaka* certificates being managed on the basis of participation or *Mudaraba* or an investment agency". Figure 2.2 outlines the way in which the *Sukuk Musharakah* transactions operate.

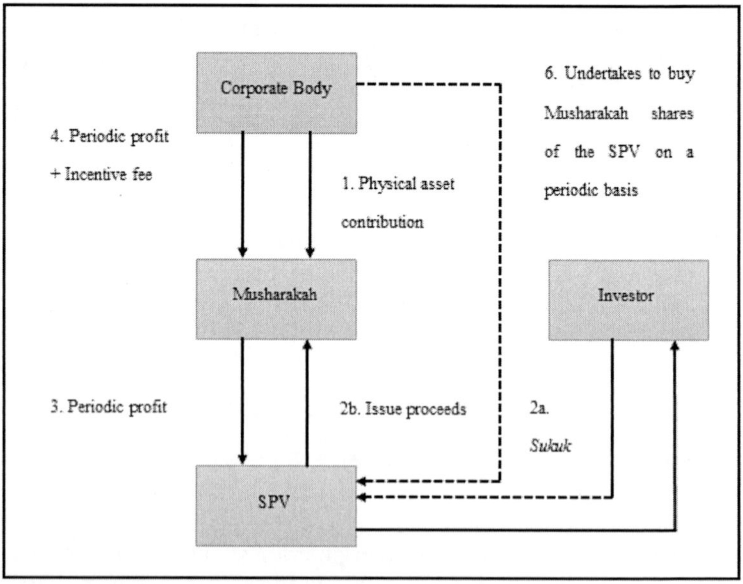


Figure 2: *Sukuk Al-Musharakah* Transaction Structures
Source: Compiled from Al-Amine, 2008 and Wilson, 2008

From examining Figure 2.2 above, the following points can be observed:

1. The corporate body (as *Musharik*) contributes land or other physical assets to the *Musharakah* (Kamil, Abdullah, Shahimi & Ismail 2010).
2. (a & b) The Special Purpose Vehicle (SPV) (as *Musharik*) contributes cash (i.e., the issue proceeds received from the investors to the *Musharakah*) (Kamaluddin, Manan, Khadijah, Sufian & Htay 2012).
3. The *Musharakah* appoints the corporate body as an agent to develop the land (or other physical assets) with the cash injected into the *Musharakah* and sell/lease the developed assets on behalf of the *Musharakah* (Vishwanath & Azmi 2009).
4. In return, the agent (i.e. the corporate body) will get a fixed agency fee plus a variable incentive fee payable (Kamil et al. 2010).
5. The profits are distributed to the *Sukuk* holders (Usmani 2008).
6. The corporation irrevocably undertakes to buy, at a pre-agreed price, the *Musharakah* shares of the SPV on, say, a semi-annual basis. At the end of the fixed period, the special purpose vehicle will no longer have any shares in the *Musharakah* (Hassan & Shahid 2010).

## *Mudharabah Sukuk*

*Mudharabah* means an agreement between two parties, according to which one of the two parties provides the capital (capital provider) for the other (the *Mudharib*) to work with, on the condition that the profit is to be shared between them according to a pre-agreed ratio (Ahmed et al. 2013). For *Mudharabah* certificates, the issuer of these certificates is the *Mudharib*, the subscribers are the capital providers, and the realized funds are the *Mudarabah* capital (Kamil et al. 2010). The certificate holders own the assets of *Mudarabah* and the agreed-upon share of the profits; losses, if any, are borne by capital providers only. *Mudarabah Sukuk* give their owner the right to receive his capital at the time the *Sukuk* are surrendered, and an annual proportion of the realized profits as agreed (Nisar 2007). They play a vital role in the process of development of financing because they are related to the profitability of the projects (Shaukat 2010).

Furthermore, any company that intends to issue *Mudarabah Sukuk* will issue them to the investors in order to finance its project. Then, it will start working on the project and the profit that is generated from the business will be divided between the partners according to the predetermined percentage (Ahmed et al. 2013). Revenues generated from the project are considered

*Sukuk* payments for the investors. At maturity, if the project generates enough revenue to pay off *Sukuk,* the *Sukuk* holders will receive their face value and their interest at the time (Ali 2011). However, if the project does not generate enough revenue, the *Sukuk* holders will either receive their principal and interest later, or nothing at all (AL-Maghlouth, 2009).

## Salient Features of the *Mudharabah Sukuk*

The *Mudharabah Sukuk* have a number of salient features. Firstly, the *Mudharabah Sukuk* represent common ownership which entitles their holders to hold shares in the specific projects against which the *Mudharabah Sukuk* have been issued (Ayub 2005). Secondly, the *Mudharabah Sukuk* contract is based on the official notice of the issue of the prospectus, which must provide all information required by *Shariah* for the *Qirad* contract, such as the nature of the capital, the ratio for profit distribution, and other conditions related to the issue, which must be compatible with Islamic *Shariah* (Kamil et al. 2010). Thirdly, the owners of *Mudharabah Sukuk* have the right to transfer the ownership through selling *Mudharabah Sukuk* in the stock market at their discretion (Zin et al. 2011). The sale of *Mudharabah Sukuk* must follow three rules, as follows:

(i) In the event the *Mudharabah* capital prior to the operations of the project commencing is still in the form of money, the trading of *Mudharabah Sukuk* can be likened to the exchange of money for money. In this case, the rules of *bay al-sarf* will be applied.
(ii) If the *Mudharabah* capital is in the form of a debt, then it must satisfy the principles of debt trading in Islam.
(iii) If capital is in the form of a combination of cash, receivables, goods, real assets and benefits, trade must be based on the market price evolved by mutual consent.

The fourth feature is when managers/SPVs receive the funds collected from the subscribers to the *Mudharabah Sukuk* and are able invest their own funds (Nisar 2007). Thus, they will get profits for their capital contribution in addition to their share in the profit as a *Mudharib* (Ismail 2009). Fifthly, neither prospectus nor *Mudharabah Sukuk* should contain a guarantee from the issuer or the manager for the fund for the capital or a fixed profit, or a profit based on any percentage of the capital (Zin et al. 2011). Accordingly, the prospectus or the *Mudharabah Sukuk* issued pursuant to it, may not stipulate payment of a specific amount to the *Mudharabah Sukuk* holder. Furthermore, the profit is to be divided, as determined by applying the rules of *Shariah*; that is, an amount access of the capital, and not the revenue or the yield. Finally, the profit and loss account of the project must be published and disseminated to *Mudharabah Sukuk* holders. Sixthly, it is permissible to create reserves for contingencies such as loss of capital by deducting from the profit (Ayub 2005). Seventhly, the prospectus can also contain a promise made by a third party, totally unrelated to the parties to the contract, in terms of legal entity or financial status, to donate a specific sum, without any counter benefit, to meet losses in the given project, provided such commitment is independent of the *Mudharabah* contract (Lahsasna & Lin 2012). On the expiry of the specified time period of the subscription, the *Sukuk* holders are given the right to transfer the ownership by sale or trade in the securities market at their discretion (Kamil et al. 2010). Figure 2.3 outlines the structure of a *Sukuk Mudharabah* transaction.

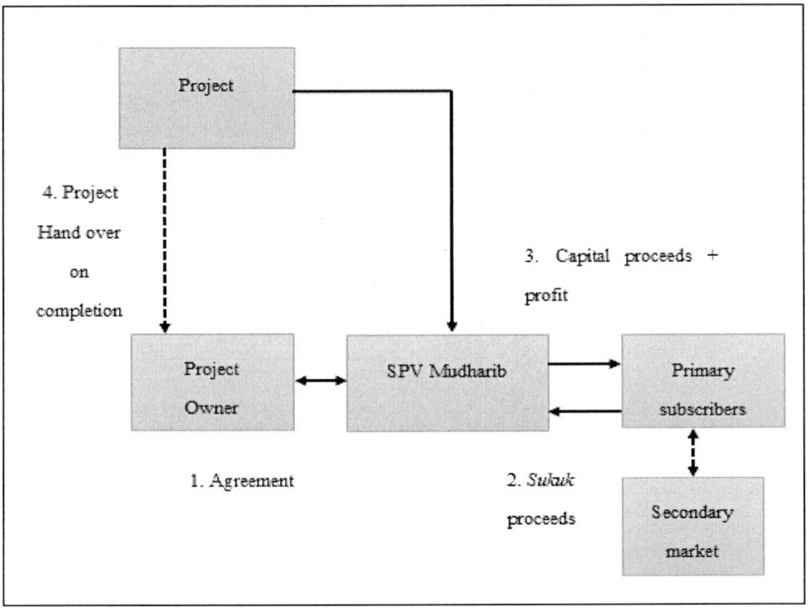


Figure 3: *Sukuk Mudharabah* Transaction Structure
Source: Ismail (2009)

In examining Figure 2.3 above, the following observations can be made:

1. The *Mudharib* enters into an agreement with the project owner for construction/commissioning of the project (Shafi & Redzuan 2010).
2. The Special Purpose Vehicle (SPV) issues *Sukuk* to raise funds.

3. The *Mudharib* collects regular profit payments and final capital proceeds from project activity for onward distribution to investors.
4. Upon completion, the *Mudharib* hands over the finished project to the owner.

## *Murabahah Sukuk*

*Murabahah* is, basically, the sale of goods at a price comprising the purchase price plus a margin of profit agreed upon by both parties concerned (Al-Amine & Al-Bashir 2001). *Sukuk* al-*Murabahah* are certificates of equal value issued for the purpose of financing the purchase of goods through *Murabahah*, so that the certificate holders become owners of the *Murabahah* commodity (Ab Majid et al. 2010). The issuer of the certificate is the seller of the *Murabahah* commodity, the subscribers are the buyers of that commodity, and the realized funds are the purchasing cost of the commodity (Shaukat 2010).

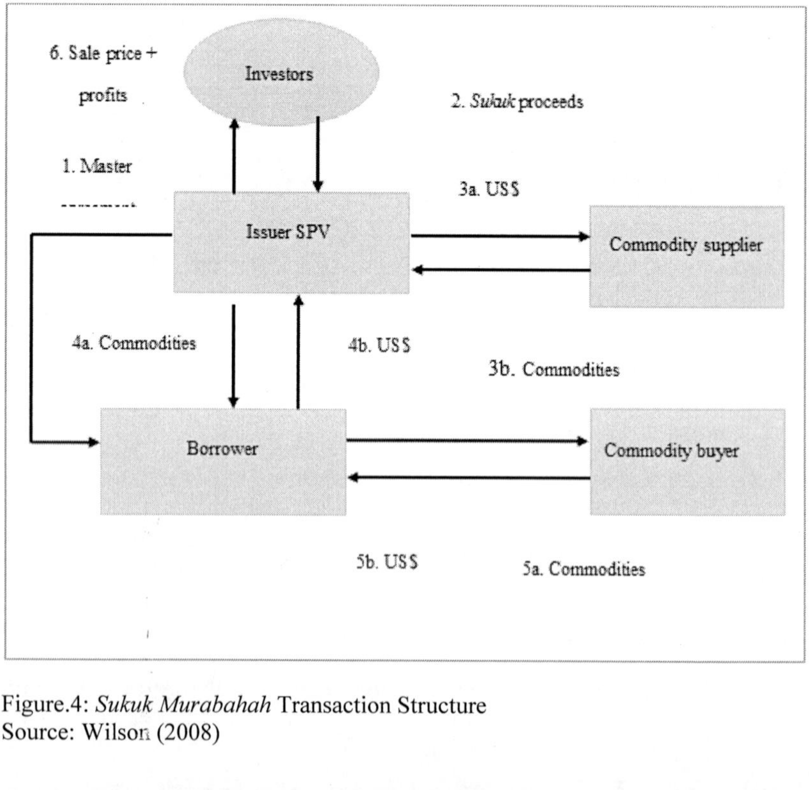


Figure.4: *Sukuk Murabahah* Transaction Structure
Source: Wilson (2008)

The possibility of having legally acceptable *Murabahah*-based *Sukuk* is only feasible in the primary market (AIMS 2011). Neither the negotiability of these *Sukuk,* nor their trading in the secondary market, are permitted in accordance with the principles of *Shariah*, as the certificates represent a debt owing from the subsequent buyer of the commodity to the certificate-holders, and such trading amounts to trading in debt on a deferred basis, which will result in *riba* (Ahmed et al. 2013). Despite being debt instruments, the *Murabahah Sukuk* could be negotiable if they are the smaller part of a package or a portfolio, the larger part of which is constituted of negotiable instruments, such as *Mudharabah*, *Musharakah* or *Ijarah Sukuk* (Shaukat 2010). *Murabahah Sukuk* are popular in the Malaysian market due to a more liberal interpretation of *Fiqh* by Malaysian jurists permitting the sale of debt (*bay'-al-dayn*) at a negotiated price (Ab Majid et al. 2010). Figure 2.6 below, demonstrates the structure of a *Sukuk Murabahah* transaction.

## Steps involved in the *Sukuk Murabahah* Transaction Structure

From Figure 2.4 above, the following six observations can be made:

1. A master agreement is signed between the Special Purpose Vehicle (SPV) and the borrower.
2. (a & b) The SPV issues the *Sukuk* to the investors and receives the *Sukuk* proceeds.
3. (a & b) The SPV buys the commodity on an 'on the spot' basis from the commodity supplier.
4. (a & b) The SPV sells the commodity to the borrower at the 'on the spot' price plus a profit margin, payable in instalments over an agreed period of time.
5. (a & b) The borrower sells the commodity to the commodity buyer on the 'on the spot' basis.
6. The investors receive the final sale price and profits.

## *Salam Sukuk*

In relation to *Salam* contracts, two parties agree on the sale and purchase of an underlying asset on a future date, but at a price determined and fully paid for today (Bacha 1999). Therefore, the seller agrees to deliver the asset in the agreed quantity and quality to the buyer at a future date. This is similar to the conventional forward contract, but the principle is different, by which the buyer in *Salam* pays the entire amount in full, at the time the contract is initiated (LMC 2008).

*Salam*-based securities may be created and sold by a special purpose vehicle (SPV) under which the funds mobilized from investors are paid in advance to the company, by SPV, in return for a promise to deliver a commodity on a future date (Vishwanath & Azmi 2009). The SPV can also appoint an agent to market the promised quantity at the time of delivery, perhaps at a higher price (Ahmed et al. 2013). The difference between the purchase price and the sale price is the profit to the SPV, and hence to the holders of the *Sukuk* (Nisar 2007). All standard *Shariah* requirements that apply to *Salam* also apply to *Salam Sukuk*, such as full payment by the buyer at the time of affecting the sale, the standardized nature of the underlying asset, clear enumeration of quantity, quality, date and place of delivery of the asset, and the like (Shaukat 2010).

One of the *Shariah*-related conditions, with respect to *Salam,* as well as the creation of *Salam Sukuk*, is the requirement that the purchased goods are not re-sold before actual possession at maturity (Nisar 2007). Such transactions would amount to the selling of the debt. This constraint renders the *Salam* instrument illiquid, in other words not easily converted into cash, and hence, somewhat less attractive to investors (Vishwanath & Azmi 2009). Thus, an investor will buy a *Salam* certificate if he expects prices of the underlying commodity to be higher on the date of maturity. Figure 2.5 below outlines the structure of the *Sukuk Salam* transaction.

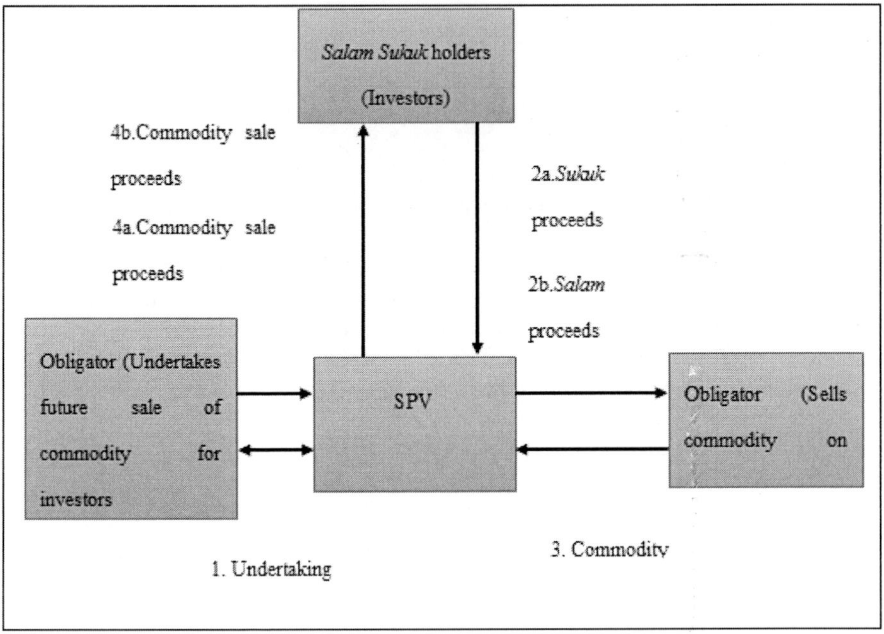


Figure.5: *Sukuk Salam* Transaction Structure
Source: Al Istithmar 2006 "An Introduction to the Underlying Principles and Structure"

## Steps Involved in the *Sukuk Salam* Transaction

From Figure 2.5 the following four observations can be made:

1. The special purpose vehicle (SPV) signs an undertaking with an obligatory to source both commodities and buyers. The obligator contracts to buy the commodity on behalf of the end-*Sukuk* holders, and then sell it for the profit of the *Sukuk* holders.
2. (a) *Salam* certificates are issued to investors, and the SPV receives the *Sukuk* proceeds.
   (b) The *Salam* proceeds are passed on to the obligator who sells the commodity on a forward basis.
3. The SPV receives the commodities from the obligator.
4. (a) The obligator, on behalf of *Sukuk* holders, sells the commodities for a profit.
   (b) *Sukuk* holders receive the commodity sale proceeds.

## *Sukuk Istisna*

*Istisna* is a contractual agreement for manufacturing goods and commodities, allowing cash payment in advance, and future delivery, or a future payment and future delivery (Ahmad & Hassan 2006). A manufacturer or builder agrees to produce well-described goods, or to build a well-described building, at a given price on a given date in the future. The price can be paid in instalments, step by step, as agreed between the parties (Benjelayel 2011). *Istisna* can be used for facilitating the financing of the manufacture or construction of houses, plants, or projects - including the building of bridges, roads, and highways. *Istisna Sukuk* are certificates that carry equal value, and are issued with the aim of mobilizing the funds required for producing products that are owned by the certificate holders (Vishwanath & Azmi 2009).

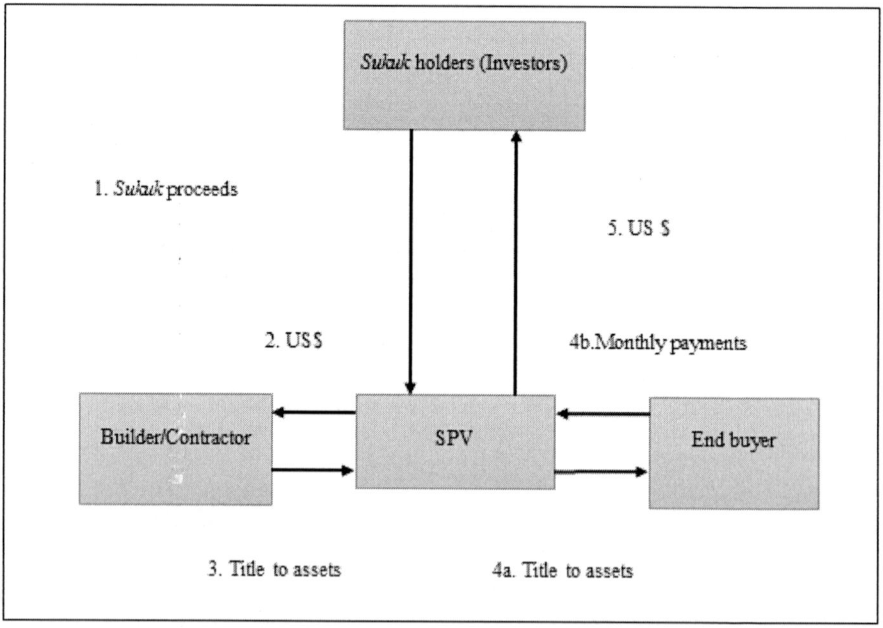


Figure 6: *Sukuk Istisna* Transaction Structure
Source: MIFC 2013 "The Malaysia International Islamic Financial Centre (MIFC)"

The issuer of these certificates is the manufacturer (supplier/seller), and the subscribers are the buyers of the intended product, while the funds realized from subscription are the cost of the product (Ahmed et al. 2013). The certificate holders own the product, and are entitled to the sale price of the certificates, or the sale price of the product sold on the basis of a parallel *Istisna*, if any. *Istisna Sukuk* are quite useful for financing large infrastructure projects (Shaikh and Saeed 2010). The suitability of *Istisna* for financial intermediation is based on the permissibility for the contractor in *Istisna* to enter into a parallel *Istisna* contract with a subcontractor (Haron & Hock 2007). Thus, a financial institution may undertake the construction of a facility for a deferred price, and sub-contract the actual construction to a specialized firm. *Shariah* prohibits the sale of these debt certificates to a third party at any price other than their face value (Zarqa 1997). Clearly, such certificates cannot be traded in the secondary market. Figure 2.8 below outlines the structure of the *Sukuk Istisna* transaction.

## Steps Involved in the Structure of the *Sukuk Istisna* Transaction

From Figure 2.6 the following observations can be made:

1. The Special Purpose Vehicle (SPV) issues *Sukuk* certificates to raise funds for the project.
2. *Sukuk* issue proceeds are used to pay the contractor/builder to build and deliver the future project.
3. The title to assets is transferred to the special purpose vehicle.
4. (a & b) The property/project is leased or sold to the end buyer. The end buyer pays monthly instalments to the special purpose vehicle.
5. The returns are distributed among the *Sukuk* holders.

## Hybrid *Sukuk*

Considering the fact that *Sukuk* issuance and trading are important means of investment, and taking into account the various demands of investors, a more diversified *Sukuk*, which is a hybrid, or mixed asset *Sukuk*, has emerged in the market (Nisar 2007). In a hybrid *Sukuk*, the underlying pool of assets can comprise an *Istisna*, or *Murabahah* receivables, as well as *Ijarah* (Saeed & Salah 2012). Having a portfolio of assets comprising of different classes allows for a greater mobilization of funds. However, as *Murabahah* and *Istisna* contracts cannot be traded on secondary markets as securitized instruments, at least 51 percent of the pool in a hybrid *Sukuk* must comprise of *Sukuk* tradables in the market, such as *Ijarah Sukuk* (Salami & Alkhadhari 2010). Due to the fact the *Murabahah* and *Istisna* receivables are part of the pool, the returns on these certificates can only be at pre-determined fixed return rates (Nazar 2011). The hybrid *Sukuk* have yet to make headway in the market. However, the structure does represent the potential of new structures and benefits for the investors (Tariq 2004). Figure 2.9 below, outlines the structure of a hybrid *Sukuk* transaction.

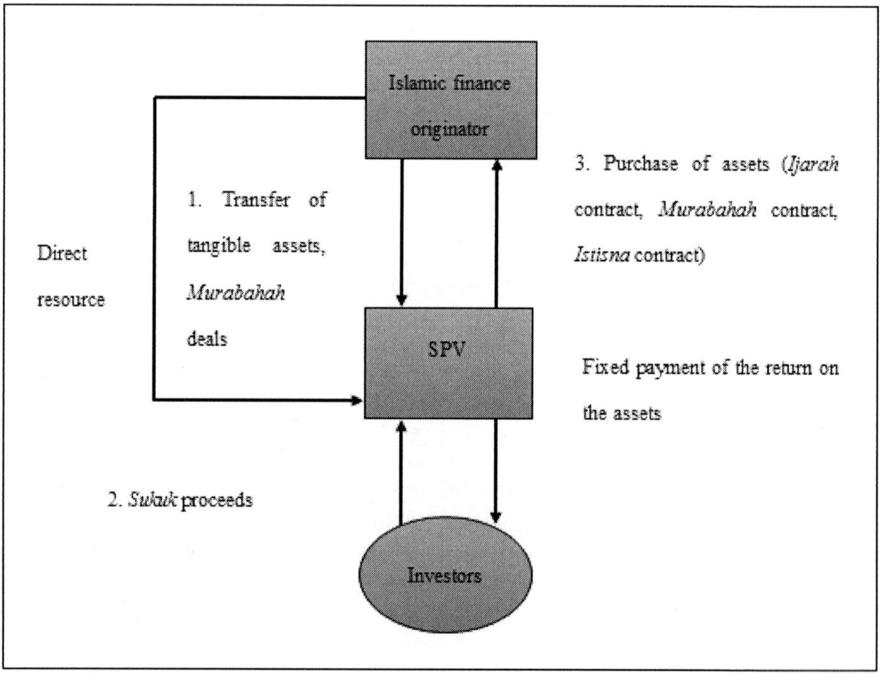


Figure.7: Hybrid *Sukuk* Transaction Structure
Source: AL-Maghlouth (2009)

## Steps Involved in the Hybrid *Sukuk* Transaction Structure

From Figure 2.7 above the following observations can be made:

1. The Islamic finance originator transfers tangible assets, as well as *Murabahah* deals, through the Special Purpose Vehicle (SPV).
2. The SPV issues certificates of participation to the *Sukuk* holders and receives funds. The funds are used by the Islamic finance originator.
3. The Islamic finance originator purchases these assets from the SPV over an agreed period of time.
4. Investors receive a fixed payment of return on the assets.

Globally, *Sukuk* have become a robust part of the Islamic finance industry, through their involvement in the international market and via the significant cross-border flow of funds which are reaching well beyond the domestic markets. Along with hard work, growth, and a balanced development agenda, all countries have the potential to expand the role of Islamic finance, which is increasing its contribution to global growth and financial stability.

# CHAPTER 4

# LITERATURE REVIEW

In the previous chapter, the conceptualization of *Sukuk* was discussed. For example, the definition of *Sukuk*, differences between *Sukuk* and debt bonds, and the basic foundations of *Sukuk* in *Shariah,* were highlighted. The purpose of Chapter Three is to review the literature in order to determine an applicable theoretical basis, and to identify specific objectives related to this study. Thus, a review of the existing literature has been undertaken, and this involved examining the concepts, perspectives and findings from past research which revolve around the legitimacy of *Sukuk* and the disclosure of *Shariah* compliance, pricing, type of *Sukuk* structure, *Shariah* auditing, *Shariah* risks, *Shariah* documentation, and other relevant themes, to support the current research endeavor. In addition, the chapter discusses and sheds light on the *Shariah* Supervisory Board (SSB) as a moderator. Finally, the rationale for choosing the theory of indebtedness (*Al-Mithaq*) and the institutional theory, will be presented.

## Legitimacy of *Sukuk*

*Shariah* can be explained as a guide to a Muslim's life in all its aspects (Kasim 2012). *Shariah* consists of a nexus of Islamic rules, parameters and principles. Muslims follow both the Holy *Qu'ran* that consists of the words of Allah, *Subhanahu Wa Ta'ala* (SWT) as well as the habitual practices of the Prophet Muhammad (Peace Be Upon Him [PBUH]), in the form of the *Hadith*. The most important source of *Shariah* is the Holy *Qu'ran*. For cases that are not addressed explicitly in both the *Holy Quran* and the *Hadith*, *Shariah* uses another source, which lies in *Ijma*, *Qiyas*, and *Ijtihad*. All such things refer to the solution for matters that need a judgment under Islamic law, in that Islam is a religion characterized by flexibility in explaining issues that need to be cleared, sometimes by giving more than one explanation in terms of the fact that such explanations have no negative impact, or distortion of the Islamic identity.

Globally, the business world has witnessed waves of crises, bankruptcies, and collapses, in large companies, in several developed and developing countries. Such harmful crises have led to the collapse of a large number of global companies, even those with good reputations in the business world (Chen, Lindeke, & Wyrick 2010, Ongena, Smith, & Michalsen 2003, Radelet & Sachs, 1998). Carmassi and Herring (2013) mentioned that these crises revealed that there is a lack of, and thus a need for, coherent business systems in global and large financial institutions. Therefore, the current study aims to deal with processes of financial instruments from the *Shariah* perspective, especially with respect to the *Sukuk* structure and its legitimacy. The current study focuses on such important issues because previous studies have revealed an importance of the rule of Islamic *Shariah* principles to these companies during global crises. A number of relevant studies were found in the existing literature in that regard. For example, Hasan and Dridi (2011) concurred with this view. They examined the impact of crisis on performance by examining the impact on asset growth, profitability, and credit, of both Islamic banks and conventional banks, for a group of countries. For their study, they elected to solely examine the banks which were characterized as having a significant and important market share, and they examined the period from 2008 to 2009. Their findings revealed that certain elements related to Islamic banks' business structures mitigate and protect these banks from having a negative impact on their profitability. Moreover, Islamic banks performed better than conventional banks with regard to credit and asset growth during the period 2008 to 2009. In addition, Islamic banks contributed positively to the stability of the financial and economic aspects of the group of countries they examined.

*Sukuk* has a feature as a financial instrument that should be undertaken in accordance with *Shariah* rules. Therefore, as Hamid, Craig, and Clarke (1993) have argued, it is important that *Sukuk* implementation is compliant with *Shariah* principles in order to be a preferred alternative choice in the current business environment. The role of *Shariah* is so important in the business world because of its concern for justice, honesty, and goodwill, and in the prevention of any prohibitions on uncertainties and fraud. The recommendations of *Shariah* to Muslims for conducting their business transactions are based on the side of ethical behavior, alongside giving attention to social responsibility (Kasim 2012). Although pursuing and gaining profit is not forbidden, it must not be gained at the expense of the underpinning virtues of *Sukuk*, which involves social guarantees, mutual risk sharing, cooperation, mutual protection, and solidarity. Such virtues are constructed with a wider aim than making profit (Ahmed et al. 2014).

As far as *Sukuk* legitimacy is concerned from the perspective of *Shariah*, Wilson (2004) claimed that the current structures are not *Shariah*-based, in that these structures have been developed by investment bankers and lawyers, and as such, there is a significant difference in the contracts in the sense of traditional Islamic jurisprudence - *fiqh*. Furthermore, he contended that *Sukuk,* in general, are structured in accordance with Western rules of securitization and, therefore, are not deemed as financial innovation. An analysis of the role of the various aspects of the market participants, including firms that issue *Sukuk*, was made by Azmat, Skully, and Brown (2014a). This included regulators, *Shariah* advisors, and *Shariah* investors. Their study found that, to attract further issue of *Sukuk*, certain factors can be modified. The findings also indicated that, due to competition with the issuers, *fatwa* shopping, and also amongst *Shariah* advisors, this competition has resulted in Islamic financial instruments which are non-compliant, or less than fully-compliant.

One such study examined the aspects concerning issues or controversies with respect to *Sukuk*, in particular the *Shariah* Board of AAOIFI's observations and the issue of resolutions (Yean 2009). This study claimed that the problems confronting the *Sukuk* industry include: the issue of whether the contracts are enforceable; the existing legal framework's legal constraints in certain jurisdictions; the lack of a secondary *Sukuk* market that is well-regulated and well-structured; and cross-border problems. Therefore, the structure of *Sukuk* ought to be modified, and in doing so, the joint efforts of the states, market players and providers, regulators, investors, legal experts, and *Shariah* scholars would be required.

A critical review of the empirical and theoretical literature examining the *Shariah*-compliance of bonds from three perspectives has been made (Zulkhibri 2015). The *Shariah*-compliance of the bonds' operational structures and issues in relation to *Sukuk* and their underlying nature and theory, and the role of *Sukuk* in economic development were all under examination. Zulkhibri indicated that the concept of *Sukuk* amongst *Shariah* scholars was uncertain, and that a lack of accreditation and standardization of a global standard for courses of Islamic finance constituted a problem which ought to be resolved.

Due to the increasing numbers in the Muslim community, and the growing awareness and importance placed on due diligence to comply with the law of *Shariah,* it is a crucial factor that the activities of businesses ought to have compliance with Islamic law, as claimed by Dawood (2008), so that the increasing requirement for Islamic *Sukuk* can comply with the rules of

*Shariah*. For those Muslims wishing to invest, an important issue to be addressed is that business transactions comply with the requirements of *Shariah*, as it places a focus on the purity of the expenditure and income earned, whilst in not being compliant, a negative connotation is associated with a firm's revenue. Furthermore, any revenue earned from the disclosure of *Shariah* compliance which is not legitimate, is solely to be considered for donations or charitable purposes (Lahsasna 2014). *Shariah* compliance refers to the purity factor of business operations, and, as such, enables Muslim investors to fulfill their religious duty by choosing *Sukuk* products as their favorite choice (Radzi & Muhamed 2012). The legitimizing of *Sukuk* and its provision represents a rare valuation that can satisfy the requirements of Muslim investors and their desire for dealing with *halal* (meaning lawful or permitted) *Sukuk* products (Ahmed et al. 2013). In this regard, the Islamic *Sukuk* are not direct substitutes for conventional bonds, since they could be used to gain a competitive advantage. Haniffa and Hudaib (2007) determined that the following information, and its details, represent an ethical identity of Islamic financial institutions (IFIs) in the area of reviews by the *Shariah* Board. Furthermore, Maali et al. (2006) indicated that IFIs are required to disclose information in detail concerning unlawful or forbidden operations. Disclosure is expected when compliance has not been achieved, and the disclosure ought to provide the reason for the IFIs' non-compliance and delve into the ways of undertaking such operations, the expenditure or revenue amounts, and the ways in which such revenue was disposed. In accordance with Kasim (2012), to prevent occurrences of non-compliance of *Shariah* in the future, an explanation of how to rectify the situation ought to be included in the disclosure. Ahmed, Islam & Ariffin (2015) determined that the factors of pricing, rating, *Shariah* auditing, *Shariah* compliance risk, and *Shariah* documentation are essential elements that have an important impact on *Sukuk* legitimacy. This study found that the selected factors influencing *Sukuk* legitimacy could be used as subjects of references in determining the existence of legitimacy in *Shariah* pronouncements.

## Disclosure of *Shariah* Compliance

According to Sulaiman (2001), religion is generally considered a crucial part of some cultures. Particularly for Muslims, Islam affects the way in which Muslims conduct their lives, including their involvement in business activities. Hence, Islam's impact on accounting and economics is noticeable. Islam has more influence in accounting at the level of disclosure, rather than the measurement of financial reporting, as the basic accounting measurement techniques are fundamentally similar to the conventional system (Baydoun & Willett 1997). Consequently, from an Islamic perspective, the emphasis will be on proper disclosure rather than measurement techniques. The Islamic perspective of disclosure is based on two general requirements of Islamic accounting; the concept of social accountability, and the full disclosure concept (Baydoun & Willett 1997, 2000, Haniffa & Hudaib 2007).

The concept of the unity of God is an important concept in Islam. The belief that there is only one ultimate creator leads to the notion that the ultimate creator has absolute ownership, and human beings are merely trustees in this world. As trustees, man is responsible for God's other creations, and will be accountable for his actions in the hereafter (Baydoun & Willett 1997, Maali et al. 2006). Therefore, in Islam, man's accountability includes accountability to the community and the environment. Thus, in Islamic accounting, organizations such as banks are accountable to society, and hence they ought to disclose information which can help discharge this accountability (Baydoun & Willett 1997).

The social accountability concept in Islam has resulted in the concept of full disclosure, whereby the community has the right to know about the effects of the organizations' activities and operations in their society (Baydoun & Willett 1997, Maali et al. 2006). Therefore, the concept of conservatism of information disclosure has no place in Islamic accounting in accordance with the findings of Alam (1998). Baydoun and Willett (1997, 2000) argued that full disclosure does not mean to disclose information to the last detail, but to disclose everything that is of importance to users. Similarly, Haniffa and Hudaib (2007) argued that the full disclosure of relevant and reliable information should assist external users in making both economic and religious decisions, in addition to assisting management in fulfilling their accountability to God and to society. Based on the social accountability and full disclosure concepts, users of annual reports from *Shariah* approved companies may expect voluntary disclosure of relevant information, particularly Islamic-related information, as discussed below. This information forms a basis for developing the Islamic items in the disclosure index.

Ibrahim, Wirman, Alrazi, Nor, and Pramono (2004) argued that the disclosure of *Shariah* compliance is one of the fundamental Islamic accounting objectives. Thus, this information should be disclosed voluntarily, even though it may not be required mandatorily. The information about *Shariah* compliance is similar to that in the *Shariah* Supervisory Board (SSB) report, in the case of IFIs. However, since some *Shariah*-approved companies do not have SSBs, the information on *Shariah* compliance is based on the Board of Director's declaration. *Shariah*-approved companies are presumed not to be involved in non-permissible activities or operations. However, should *Shariah*-approved companies be involved in prohibited activities, minimally (as allowed by the *Shariah* Advisory Council), it is the company's responsibility, based on social accountability and full disclosure, to disclose information about these non-permissible elements. This can help users to understand how amounts generated from such activities are disposed, and to monitor a company's efforts to reduce involvement in such activities in the future. In addition, previous studies such as Haniffa and Hudaib (2007) and Maali et al. (2006) claimed that IFIs and their insights are very useful for improving disclosure in the *Shariah* Board's report of the Islamic financial tools. They mentioned that improving disclosure concerning *Shariah*-compliance is inevitable, not only to distinguish amongst the Islamic financial products themselves, but also from that of the traditional financial institutions (Ahmed et al. 2013).

## Determinants

According to a number of researchers (Wilson 2004, Tariq & Dar 2007, Lahsasna & Idris 2008, Wilson 2008, Rahman 2008, Howladar 2009, Yean 2009, Usmani 2009, Kasim et al. 2009, Khnifer 2010b, Herwany & Febrian 2010, DeLorenzo 2010, Shafii et al. 2010, Kaseb 2010, Nanaeva 2010, Ali 2011, Zakaria et al. 2012, Kantakji & Ohaj 2010, Casper 2012, Hidayat 2013, Van Wijnbergen & Zaheer 2013, Ahmed et al. 2013, El Shazly & Tripathy 2013, Abdulmalik 2013, Abdullah et al. 2014, Mizushima & Mizushima 2014, Azmat, et al. 2014b, Ginena 2014, Rauf & Ibrahim 2014, Lahsasna 2014, Zulkhibri 2015, Aloui et al. 2015), there are a host of essential elements influencing the legitimacy of *Sukuk*, such as pricing, type of structure, *Shariah* auditing, *Shariah* risks and *Shariah* documentation. Arguably, they are the significant determinants with which investors, IFIs, and regulators, will look at in determining *Sukuk* legitimacy according to the *Shariah* rules. Furthermore, the selected determinants are very general in nature, and readily available in the *Sukuk Shariah* reports which are disclosed by the SSB.

## *Sukuk* Pricing

Pricing is one of the most important factors that impacts upon the legitimacy of the *Sukuk* (Al-Amine 2008, Wilson 2008, Zulkhibri 2015). Pricing is also a point of contention in relation to the issuance of Islamic *Sukuk* (Usmani

2002). *Shariah* scholars and Muslim economists have not come up with an alternative to the interest rate as a readily available indicator of profitability (Al-Bashir 2008). Hence, the use of the London Interbank Offered Rate (LIBOR) as a pricing benchmark has become part of the practice of IFIs. The factors for computing the pricing benchmark ought to be free from interest rates, non-real economic activities, and non-*halal* activities, such as indices of financial derivatives instruments (Omar et al. 2010). However, in noting that while it is permissible to use LIBOR as a pricing benchmark, it is not correct to rely on it for a determination of returns (Kantakji 2012).

A conventional benchmark like LIBOR has been used in IFIs as a reference guide, leading to long-term investment pricing (Mirakhor & Zaidi 2007). It is generally accepted and recognized in the Islamic financial sector, without making any serious or deviant moves, to be free from usury-based benchmarks that do not reflect real investment behavior (Selim 2008). The arguments made are based on a complete replication of conventional usury-based financial indicators, and the views of some scholars who align their views with the long lasting outlook of adhering to the control of Western practices to the financial markets, especially with the modern Islamic financial industry being in its infancy (Usmani 2002, Kantakji 2012).

Conventional interest-based financial institutions use interest rates for debts, and charge the borrowers for the cost of the borrowed money as well as other risk factors reflected in the formula (Omar et al. 2010). This represents a behavior that has exhausted the economic cycle due to the imbalance among the parties in the investment process. As a result, the return is guaranteed to one side, and the risk is transferred to the other, upon which the result will be of zero impact on the economy, with the likelihood that a loss will apply to the owners of the fund as well (Obaidullah 2005). Both the conventional banks and the Islamic banks generally transfer the liability to the borrower, and freeze their assets from further productive investment (Zahan, Ron, & Kenett 2012). Moreover, both systems proactively share the use of the same index (LIBOR) as it is the most practical and commonly-used index, according to the widely spread belief. Conventional financial institutions justify themselves in applying a usury-based indicator, such as LIBOR, due to the adherent nature of usury-based structures in their system. Such an act is not justified for IFIs and cannot be excused based on the views of its proponents (Lane 2006). Herwany & Febrian (2010) cautioned that, due to the absence of an appropriate *Sukuk* pricing model, the industry currently uses the same pricing benchmark (i.e. LIBOR) for the issuance of both conventional and *Sukuk* products.

In the existing literature, there are a number of pertinent studies that have examined LIBOR. For instance, Wilson (2008) claimed that, for *Sukuk* pricing, the use of LIBOR as the benchmark is not appropriate, in accordance with the Islamic scholars' opinion, and it was recommended that corporate *Sukuk* ought to be benchmarked against the financial institutions' performance indicators. Wilson further added that share prices are not suitable as indicators, as the share prices sit differently to *Sukuk* securities in relation to yielding a regular income which is fixed, and debt and equity investment is unclear. Accordingly, a proposal which is suitable, is to apply profit indicators or dividends that can be utilized to underpin a new type of *Sukuk* based on the structure of a partnership (Wilson 2008). In addition, a monetary indicator such as Nominal GDP could be utilized for the pricing of a Sovereign *Sukuk*.

A study by Hayat and Kraeussl on the risk and return characteristics of Islamic Equity Funds (IEFs) between the years 2000 – 2009, found that IEFs are underperformers compared to Islamic, as well as conventional, equity benchmarks (Hayat & Kraeussl 2011). This study, which was done by analyzing pricing data from Bloomberg for 51 IEFs in Malaysia, using the Kuala Lumpur Composite Index (KLCI) as the conventional benchmark, and the Kuala Lumpur *Shariah* Index (KLSI) as the Islamic benchmark, suggests that financial improvements for Muslim investors could be improved by investing in index tracking funds, rather than individual IEFs.

An immediate cessation by the IFIs of the practice of *riba* is upheld by Usmani (2009). The argument put forward is advanced by the view that using interest rates as a benchmark is undesirable for *halal* products. Furthermore, the philosophy of an economy based on Islamic principles has not been promoted, and, therefore, does not have an effect on the system of distribution. An examination of the interactive linkages between *Sukuk* and the *Shariah* stocks in Gulf Cooperation Countries (GCC) was undertaken by Aloui et al. (2015). Their study found *Sukuk* and the *Shariah* stocks and GCC markets are not mutually exclusive, in that there are linkages between the two; however they are also regime-dependent. In other words, volatility in the *Shariah* stock market reacts in an asymmetrical way to events in the *Sukuk* markets. Crucially, this study provided support for the claim that a change in the GCC *Sukuk* price index can significantly impact upon the likelihood of transmission across the regimes.

## Mechanism of Pricing

As *Sukuk* issuance is a relatively new concept in comparison to conventional bonds, it is only natural for it to face some challenges (Muhammed & Radzi 2011). Furthermore, pricing is a main concern for *Sukuk*, as the concept is new to the market and there has yet to be any development of any suitable mechanisms to determine its price. According to Zaidi (2007), the challenges in setting the price for *Sukuk* include:

(i) There is an absence of an Islamic benchmark rate due to a lack of agreement among the issuers. Hence, it has to depend upon the conventional market benchmark rates, such as LIBOR, or the Euro Interbank Offered Rate (EURIBOR) to determine the pricing of Islamic instruments (Khan 2007).
(ii) The situation of a relatively small number of participants has led to low levels of liquidity, lack of market depth, and a lack of critical mass of issuances.
(iii) There is an absence of a standard price validation mechanism to assist in distributing up-to-date news and upcoming related issues.
(iv) There is a lack of a focused risk-based pricing mechanism related to Islamic finance.
(v) There is a lack of risk mitigation to manage and hedge the risk of fluctuations in the market value of instruments, on account of movements in the benchmark rate.
(vi) Only certain listed assets can be accepted as guarantees.

In addition, *Shariah* law contains restrictions on trading indebtedness in lieu of the increasing *Sukuk* issuances. Therefore, *Sukuk* contracts are separated into two major categories in terms of their tradability in a secondary market, with different pricing mechanisms, as follows:

(i) Tradable *Sukuk* at a market price: e.g. *Sukuk Ijarah*, *Mudarabah* and *Musharak;* and
(ii) Transferable *Sukuk* at face value: e.g. *Sukuk Murabahah* and *Istisna*.

The rating of credit is a main factor in determining the price of traditional bonds, and its importance has been highlighted as it has become a significant factor in the pricing of *Sukuk* as well (Rahman, Omar & Kassim 2013). As mentioned previously, LIBOR is the most commonly utilized benchmark to determine the pricing of a *Sukuk* rental-based return or profit, and the use of LIBOR as a benchmark is not desirable under *Shariah* law, due to the fact that it is interest-based (Wilson 2006). The process of *Sukuk* pricing utilizes the same mechanism of pricing as bonds, by using the difference between the bid and the asking price, which is generally referred to as the bid-ask spread, and it is also dependent upon the trading volume (Ahmed et al. 2013). Ahmed et al. (2014) indicated that the mechanisms of rating and pricing *Sukuk* are significant, and are essential elements impacting on the issuance of *Sukuk*. In accordance with this viewpoint, the current study supports the notion that the selected factors influencing *Sukuk* ought to have prompt solutions presented in order for the development of the structure of *Sukuk*, and for the *Sukuk* market to be sustained. In order to do so, a close cooperation amongst financial experts and *Shariah* scholars is essential.

In the context of the country of Malaysia, a study outlined the importance of pricing in relation to the legitimacy of *Sukuk*, as legitimacy of *Sukuk* is an essential factor (Ahmed et al. 2015). This study indicated that a positive relationship exists between *Sukuk* legitimacy and pricing, as pricing influences the IFIs' application of legitimacy and structuring of *Sukuk*. There is deemed to be more compliance with the principles of *Shariah* when the pricing increases the level of legitimacy of *Sukuk*, by way of an induction of an audit *Sukuk*-structure ensuring the *Sukuk* are compliant with the principles of *Shariah*.

Lane (2006) contended that a fixed rate of payout of annual interest to investors, for instance as in the case of conventional bonds, ought not be applied for *Sukuk* bonds. As an alternative, *Sukuk* returns could be sourced from sales or profits of assets such as property, leases, and joint business ventures, or from equipment. In principle, these profits, sales, or leases, could be structured in such a way to provide a suitable alternative to a fixed rate of annual interest, as these profits, sales, or leases, are not considered to be prohibited payments of 'interest'. In accordance with Nanaeva (2010), a method of distancing the pricing of *Sukuk*, away from the benchmarks of conventional debt financing such as LIBOR, to those underpinned by the platform of the principles of *Shariah*, is a significant challenge for the Islamic capital market (ICM). Given that it is such an inordinate challenge, in accordance with Godlewski, Turk Ariss and Weill (2011), there is difficulty in creating a platform for pricing on a daily basis of *Sukuk* for the facilitation of *Sukuk* trading, and to gauge an active secondary market.

## Pricing from the Islamic Perspective

The initial typical Islamic jurisprudence (*fiqh*) records indicate that pricing in Islam has been extensively deliberated and explained in the following records: *Adab al-hisbah* (al-Malqi, Abdullah al-Saqti Muhammad ibn Ahmad, 11th century); *Nihayat al-ratibah fi tolab al-hisba*h (Abd al-Rahman ibn Nasir, 589); *al-Hisbah fi Islam* (Sheikh al-Islam Ibn Taimiyyah); *Ma'alim al-qurbah fi ahkam al-hisbah*,(al-Qurashi, Muhamad ibn Ahmad al-Shafi'i, 729H); the book of *al-Turuq al-hukmiyyah fi al-siyasah al-syariyyah* (Ibn Qayyim al-Jawzi); and *Ahkam al-suk* (Yahya ibn Umar al-Kanani, 213-289h), which was the initial manuscript placing a specific emphasis on the matter of pricing; followed by the book *al-Taysir fi ahkam al-tas'ir* (Ahmad ibn Said al-Majlidi, 1094H).

Among the existing works in Arabic concerning the mechanism of pricing, and its acceptability from the *Shariah* viewpoint, along with the involvement of government in pricing are: *Ahkam al Tas'ir fi al-Fiqhi al* – Islamic, written by Muhammad Abu al Huda al Ya'kubi al Husni (2000); *Al-Ru'ya al-Islamiyyah li tas'ir al-sila' wa al-khadamat* written by Dr. Muhammad bin Ahmad bin Salih al-Salih (2001); *Jara'im al-tas'ir al-jabari* written by Mahmud Muhammad Abdul al-Zaini (2004) and *Dirasat fi takalif al-intaj wa tas'ir fi Islam* written by Dr. Auf Mahmud al-Kufrawi (1985), wherein the attention was on the revenue, cost, and the computation of price and profit rates on the basis of the *Shariah* perspective.

There are a number of modern works written in the English language examining the benchmark of pricing based on the *Shariah* perspective, and these include: *The Book of Indexation of Financial Assets an Islamic Evaluation* (Zaman 1993); *An Introduction to Islamic Finance* (Usmani 2007), and *Pricing of Murabahah* and *Ijarah Product in Malaysia* (Fitri 2007); *Cost of Capital and Investment in a Non-Interest Economy* (Mirakhor 1996); *An Islamic Pricing Benchmark* (Omar et al. 2010). The other contemporary relevant research, entitled *Performance Benchmark for Islamic Financial Transactions as a substitute to LIBOR (MQAM),* was written by Kantakji & O'haj (2010).

However, studies examining Islamic pricing along with the Islamic cost of capital are still comparatively uncommon. Selim (2008) established the approach of Islamic finance to the capital asset pricing model (CAPM), on the basis of the principle of the elimination of *riba* (usury), and the principle of universal compliments, as well as the principle of justice in *Al-Hisbah.* He examined the theoretical application to the method of Islamic financing on the basis of direct *musharakah* to the orthodox capital asset pricing model. Through his study, it has been found that financing based on *musharakah* has less beta-risk in financing than that measured with the marketplace. By definition, the marketplace has a beta of 1.0, and each stock is rated in accordance with how much they deviate from the market. A high-beta stock is supposed to be a higher risk, and therefore financing based on *musharakah* presents a lower level of risk for the investors.

Shubber and Alzafiri (2008) focused on computing the cost of capital for Islamic banks, and this computation differs from the case of traditional banks. Their study revealed that, for the Islamic banks, it is very easy to understand that accounts of deposits were not an obligation, as these accounts can be given the definition of sharing of profit-and-loss for the instruments. Furthermore, the correlation coefficient was found to be a high-positive, seeming to be a fit between the market value and the volume of deposits of the Islamic banks. Also an Islamic bank's market value was clearly independent of its cost of capital. This means that the risks related to deposit-taking requirements are to be seen a little differently for the cases of IFIs. Similarly, the returns delivered to stakeholders result in those being higher than that of the depositors.

Mohd Yusof et al. (2011) suggested the implementation of the equilibrium property rental values as a substitute to the traditional rates of interest. Also, he adopted an extrapolative method for the modeling of the rental values of the retail property to scale against the traditional rates of interest such as LIBOR, EURIBOR, and the Kuala Lumpur Interbank Offered Rate (KLIBOR). Omran, Sharara, and Struyk (2007), in their study on alternatives to the fixed rate mortgage instruments for Egypt, considered that mortgage instruments had adjustable mortgage rates, as alternative mortgage instruments for inflationary environments and affordability enhancing mortgages, and income generators that could be introduced in Egypt, where people are not as financially sophisticated in comparison to other countries.

Fitri (2007) attempted to evaluate the working function of pricing adopted by the Islamic banks to define the pricing of the two most prominent agreements, i.e., *Ijarah* and *Murabahah* products, which were suggested by the IFIs in Malaysia. He also revealed that in the environment of dual banking systems in Malaysia, the IFIs must propose a reasonable rate for every commodity if they intend to compete with the traditional banks. The traditional banking system implements a basic rate of lending as a standard to set the price value for its commodities. According to some modern-day scholars, to some extent, the base lending rate can be allowable as the standard for the fixing of the pricing. The necessity of a new pricing standard for the commodities of the IFIs is also revealed in this study.

In a study examining the cost of capital and investment, Mirakhor (1996) found that it is a non-interest economy, and in his study, he suggested that, without the assistance of the predetermined rate of interest, the measurement of the cost of capital can be performed. The standard benchmark can be set based on Tobin's Q model (Mirakhor 1996). According to Mirakhor's opinion, if a predetermined fixed rate of interest is not present, the solo source of financial capital will be equity financing. In the event that the basis of the financial system of any economy is its equity, then the measurement of the cost of capital can be made through the equity market.

A standard can be fixed by producing a mutual share that finances asset-backed instruments, such as *Ijarah*, *Musharakah*, etc. (Usmani 2002). Units of the assets can be bought and vended, according to the net value of assets, on a periodic basis, when the mainstream assets become tangible. These kinds of units can be passable, and can be implemented for financial purposes. The financial organizations that hold spare capital can procure such units, and at the time of the necessity of liquidity, these can also be sold. This kind of procedure forms the inter-bank market, and the worth of units could work as an index to measure income. The Accounting and Auditing Organization for Islamic Financial Institutions (AAOIFI) standard 27/5/3 states that it is acceptable to borrow and lend based on interest, i.e. the LIBOR or the KLIBOR as a standard to determine the pricing of Islamic financial commodities and facilities. According to the observation of Usmani (2007), most of the IFIs define the rate of profit on the basis of the recent rate of interest, mostly based on the LIBOR as the standard. The criteria to determine the mark-up of the *Murabahah* contract should be equivalent, or some percentage above, LIBOR, if the LIBOR is four percent. This type of practice for transactions is frequently criticised for the rate of its profits being based on the rate of interest, and ought to be forbidden as interest. Interestingly, according to Taqi Usmani, the use of interest rates as a measure for evaluating profits of a *Murabahah* contract does not mean that the transaction itself is *haram* (forbidden), since the deal itself does not contain *riba* (interest). The interest rate, in this instance, is only an indicator. The scholar also detailed an analogy to support the position taken by him. He mentioned the case of two traders. The first trader sells lawful products, as per the laws of Islam, such as soft drinks. However, the second trader sells liquor, which is *haram*, as per the Islamic law. Since there is competition, the first trader may wish to make as much money or profit as the second trader makes from his liquor business. Therefore, the first trader can charge his clients the amount necessary to make a similar profit to that of the second trader. From this perspective, the profit made by the first trader is *halal*, although he used the profit earned from a *haram* trade by the second trader only as a benchmark. The researcher also discussed the issues of calculation of cost in *Murabahah* contracts. According to the researcher, the *Murabahah* contract contemplates the concept of cost-plus, where it can be affected only when the seller can ascertain the exact cost incurred in acquiring the commodity when the trader wishes to sell. Thus, in this light, if the exact cost cannot be ascertained, *Murabahah* transactions are not possible (Usmani 2002).

Bank Negara Malaysia (BNM) started a new framework in 2001, whereby they reshaped the standardization of the return rate, which is the method of calculating distributable profits and the deviation of the rates of return to the depositor's derivation. The framework was intended for:

(i) The creation of a standard for calculating the rates of return;
(ii) The implementation of the equal level and terms of reference for deriving the rates of return in IFIs;
(iii) Setting a standard for evaluating the level of efficiency of the IFIs.

The framework consists of two main elements: the calculation table; and the distribution table. The calculation table describes the expense and income items which are supposed to be reported, and obtains the net distributable income by standard calculations. The distribution table informs the distribution of the net distributable income which is obtained from the calculation table and includes savings, general investments, and demands, related to their structure, maturities, and pre-agreed profit-sharing ratios among the institution and the depositors.

Ul Haque & Mirakhor (1998) described some conceptual matters including the introduction of a nationally-presented article as an appliance of government finance, and outlined the method of calculating a corresponding rate of return. They also investigated different theories including examining simple ratios to more complicated market models. They suggested separating out the private sector from the rate of return for the potential future profits, which is an important component of stock market pricing. Indeed this very component can be a take of the private sector by the passage of time, and seasonal variations along with the derivation of the rate of return on government papers. It is very important to eliminate an estimate of risk premiums that may relate to private defaults.

Ebrahim, & Khan (2002) proposed a model which is a flawless convertible facility for sponsoring infrastructure in Muslim countries. The mortgage is set out as a combination of an Islamic credit facility, by conceding the debt collateralization of the assets of the institution, and an addition of real warrants to decrease the agency cost of debt. With the help of a numerical simulation, they solved the natural evolution for the rate of return, tenure, and partial ownership supported to the financier upon conversion of the facility, without resorting to any interest-based indicator. In conclusion, they have carried out a sensitivity analysis of the study of the effect of exogenous variables, and resolved it into the present mainstream finance literature.

In 2010, the International *Shariah* Research Academy for Islamic Finance (ISRA) developed an Islamic pricing model for the Islamic banking industry specifically for Malaysia. This model utilized the Capital Asset Pricing Model (CAPM) to estimate the pricing model, so as to establish a direct link between the market risk of projects or businesses and their required rate of returns. It found that the Islamic pricing model was more stable than the KLIBOR alternative. However, there were a number of issues that the model raised about whether the effort was productive, in terms of giving the Islamic financial industry a useful alternative to interest rate benchmarks, such as LIBOR and KLIBOR. However, the critical aspect of this method is that they used 'real' economy factors to determine their benchmark, when it is not clear that the cost of financing in the Islamic financial industry, as it operates today, ought to be based on these factors and not on an interest rate. This means that the structures of the Islamic banks' financing are much more debt-like, and resemble the products offered by conventional banks in their risk and return.

An Islamic pricing model to estimate the return rate of any project proposed by considering the anticipated future cash flows relative to the invested capital was proposed by Kantakji and O'haj (2010). For any model, it is important to take into account the current economic conditions. Accordingly, based on the needs of the customer, a feasibility study for the proposed project can indicate the expected cash flows as well as other indicators. In taking the approach based on the prediction of cash flows, such as the difference between cash outflows and inflows, it is in alignment with several prior studies evaluating investment.

## Type of Structure (Asset-Backed and Asset-Based)

Customarily, an Islamic asset-backed transaction's underlying asset ought not to contain any elements that depart from the principles of *Shariah* (Ismail, Ali, Serguieva & Gregoriou 2008). However, by simply pooling the non-interest bearing assets alone, this scenario does not give rise to an Islamic securitization scheme automatically. In reality, each component of the program of Islamic securitization needs to be compliant with *Shariah* (Engku Ali 2005). As an example, aside from the removal of the interest factor, an underlying asset would also be required to fully meet any other conditions set. "*This might well include the following: the existence of an asset or an assurance concerning its deliver-ability; that the asset is of benefit to the Muslim Ummah; that an asset is deemed as halal (lawful) in accordance with the principles of Shariah; the performance or availability of an asset at a nominated date in the future; that an asset can be provided free from encumbrances; that the seller has ownership of the asset; and that the principal subject matter can be adequately recognized, characterized, or specified, in the absence of any underlying ambiguity*" (Ahmed, Ahmed, Hashim, & Islam, 2019).

In general, *Sukuk* can be classified into two different categories: equity-based; and asset-based instruments (IFSB guidelines No. 2, 2005). Previously, *Sukuk* offered a rate of return which was predictable and fair; for example in the event of *Ijarah*, *Salam,* and *Istisna*. On the contrary, through this, the rate of return is gained from the sharing of the profit and loss of a joint business venture, which makes the return unpredictable if the return is based on contracts such as *Mudharabah* or *Musharakah*. The practical implementation of *Sukuk* is, therefore, different from the ideal theoretical concept of *Sukuk*. In this regard, it is difficult to distinguish between genuine and non-genuine *Sukuk*, especially for the execution of sale and risk factors. With these acknowledgments, three types of *Sukuk* are specifically identified, as follows:

(i) Asset-Based *Sukuk* (ABS).
(ii) Non Asset-Based *Sukuk*:
  a) Pay through structures; and
  b) Pass through structures.

This classification is in accordance with the joint approach of *Real Estate Investment* (2009), and *Capital Adequacy Requirement for Sukuk* (IFSB Guideline 7) *and Securitizations*. With respect to these specific guidelines, asset-based *Sukuk* (ABS) can be defined as "structures that meet the requirement for being an asset-backed structure as assessed by a recognized external credit assessment institution (such as rating bodies)". According to this guideline, it can be stated that the asset-based *Sukuk* constitute two factors. The first factor is that in the event of any damage or deficiency in relation to the asset of the *Sukuk*, the user (the holder of the *Sukuk*) will suffer the loss. The second one is the main risk factor of the asset-based *Sukuk* which is the principal asset of the *Sukuk*. Consequently, the user or holder of the *Sukuk* originates the return and the risk out of the cash flows of the principal asset of the *Sukuk*. According to Hussin and Sariff (2010), there is another dimension of the ABS which the execution of the true sale is. In this dimension, there is an involvement of the transfer of the real asset from the creators to the users with the impact of liberating the assets from the balance sheet of the issuer to the investors. For that reason, the insurance of the ABS should be supported by the original asset, which symbolizes the ownership of the *Sukuk*, and also includes the risks involved with it. On the contrary, according to Aziz, Pahlavi, and Gintzburger (2009), there is no involvement of the true sale transactions in the ABS, only the handover of the financial rights to the asset and the revenue originated from the obligations of the financial rights involved with the debt. The main reason for the absence of the true sales transaction is that, in the event of a default, the users of the *Sukuk* hold resources to the initiator (the originator) rather than the principal asset. This, then, permits a pay-through and pass-through basis, which is well-defined by the guidelines of IFSB-7 (2009a), wherein the prior one establishes assets to the initiator through procurement agreements, whereas the latter one establishes assets to the issuer through assurance. As a result, the asset-based *Sukuk's* rate of return and risk is determined by the obligor, rather than from the principal asset of the *Sukuk*. Accordingly, in cases of default, the financiers have other options to the obligators or the issuers and the protected creditors would be unable to direct the pathway of the asset. Therefore, the parameter that calculates the risk is only dependent upon the ability of the obligator or issuer to repay the capital. Accordingly, it comes as no surprise that financiers are mostly focused on corporate/sovereign credit aspects, and are rarely concerned about the original essential performance of the asset when obtaining Sovereign *Sukuk* (Nazar 2015). According to this argument, *Sukuk* holders are faced with the certainty that in the event of bankruptcy of the obligator, the *Sukuk* holders will get their capital back.

**Table:1 Differences between Asset-Backed and Asset-Based *Sukuk***

| **Categories** | **Asset-Backed** | **Asset-Based** |
|---|---|---|
| **Source of Payment** | The source of payment comes from the revenue generated by the underlying asset. | The source of payment comes from the originator/obligator's cash flows. |
| **Presentation/Disclosure of the Asset** | The asset is separated from the originator's book. | The asset stays on the balance sheet of originator/obligator. |
| **Type of *Sukuk* Holders** | Legal ownership with right to dispose of the asset. | Beneficial ownership with no right to dispose of the asset. |
| **Recourse** | *Sukuk* holders only have recourse to the asset, thus the asset plays a genuine role in defaults. | Purchase undertaking at par from the obligator is the ultimate recourse. The recourse is only to the obligator and not the asset. |

Source: Hidayat (2013)

Moody's[1] created a special rating method for *Sukuk*. This rating method takes into account a *Sukuk*'s dependency on assets in terms of the income generated from the underlying assets. The income can also be asset-based depending on the originator for payment through a repurchase undertaking, despite the fact that all transactions are likely to include a set of underlying asset risks which are shared by the issuer and the investors. Alsaeed and Sulaiman (2012) held a similar view to Moody's by stressing the consequence of the principal assets used to ascertain the *Sukuk* principal repayment and the applicable law.

[1] Moody's is an essential component of the global capital markets, providing credit ratings, research, tools, and analysis that contribute to transparent and integrated financial markets. Moody's Corporation (NYSE: MCO) is the parent company of Moody's Investors' Service, which provides credit ratings and research covering debt instruments and securities, and Moody's Analytics, which offers leading-edge software, advisory services and research for credit and economic analysis and financial risk management.

## Studies Related to the Structure of *Sukuk*

The studies included in this evaluation are based on the period of time between 1990 and 2015, and these studies also discussed several general issues with regard to the concept and structure of *Sukuk*. Some of the issues highlighted are as follows: Preliminary studies (early research) focused on the interpretation and explanation of the basic concept of Islamic securitization and the relationship with the concept of *Sukuk*, and the process and the parties involved, as well as the points of view and opinions of the scholars in this regard (Idris 2008). Furthermore, the studies focused on the innovation and engineering of new ways, instruments (tools), and products. Meanwhile, some studies focused on how to introduce new products, or how to make conventional products comply with *Shariah* law, i.e. how to make conventional bonds comply with the principles of *Shariah* (Al-Salem 2009). There are other studies during the same period which focused on the factors that may assist in the process of developing new financial products. These factors include the support of government policy, which gives players more rights and freedom in choosing the business products and services:

(i) Studies in the middle focused more on the legal and *Shariah*-related issues (Wilson 2008). Although issues related to Islamic law have been discussed in the early period of Islamic *Sukuk* issues, more studies have become specialized after the tremendous development in the market of *Sukuk*, and these studies have provided the background knowledge for many financial products coming into existence and different contracts being developed and used. In this stage, studies have mostly addressed issues in depth; these include issues such as the process involved in the *Sukuk* issuance, issues related to the nature of relationship between the parties involved, the applicability of such *Shariah*-based contracts in some of the *Sukuk* issuance, and issues concerning the identity and positions of the parties involved (Nisar 2007). Recent studies focused on the standardization, harmonization, and globalization of *Sukuk* (Idris 2008). The new trend of recent studies places more emphasis on the way in which standardized *Sukuk* can be created by providing the views of *Shariah* on the issues of standardization. Some *Shariah* issues are related to *Sukuk* products, such as the process of issuance, nature of the underlined assets, and other controversial issues in this regard. Studies in this stage also stressed the importance of the role played by the central banks, and the *Shariah* regulatory institutions, as well as the Auditing and Advisory Boards of the IFIs (Siddiqi 2006).

In the existing literature, a number of pertinent studies were identified. For instance, Howladar (2009) contended that, for asset-based *Sukuk*, the framework is able to fulfill the pattern of an agreement, however, there is too much complexity involved, and this, in turn, translates to an Islamic equivalent of a traditional bond that is unsafe. As a result, in accordance with Haneef (2009), the *Sukuk* holders can solely place the assets with the lessee, and these are deemed as unsafe creditors, or graded on an equal footing with other creditors considered as unsafe.

An examination of three types of issuance of *Sukuk*, undertaken by Khnifer (2010b), analyzed: the *Tamweel* asset-backed Residential Mortgage Backed Securitization (RMBS); the *Tamweel Sukuk* Limited (TSL) structure which was asset-based; and the asset-backed East Cameron Gas (ECG) issuance, which was subject to a default. The findings indicated that asset-backed *Sukuk* expose the holders to higher levels of risk, and these types of *Sukuk* might lead to a default from the obligator. An examination from the *Shariah* perspective of the structures of the asset-backed and asset-based *Sukuk* was undertaken by Hidayat (2013). It found that there is more compliance with the principles of *Shariah* with an asset-backed *Sukuk* structure, both in substance and form, in comparison to the structure of asset-based *Sukuk*. Similarly, Shabana (2013) analyzed the operations of both asset-based and asset-backed *Sukuk*. The findings demonstrate the differences between asset-based and asset-backed *Sukuk*; and in particular they examined the issue of *Sukuks'* true ownership. A study analyzed the differences between the conventional bonds issued by Cagamas (the National Mortgage Corporation of Malaysia) and the *Shariah* residential mortgage-backed securities through the examination of rating grades, an equal issuance year, and the period of maturity (Ahmed, Ahmed, Hashim, & Islam, 2019). Their study indicated that those securities which were *Shariah* mortgage-backed, outperformed the conventional securities that were mortgage-backed. Therefore, a much higher rate of return on investment was provided to the investors of the *Shariah* residential mortgage-backed securities.

In the event of *Sukuk* defaults, the consequence in each scenario of default of asset-backed and asset-based *Sukuk* was analyzed by Abdulmalik (2013) by examining the differences from a market and from a *Shariah* perspective. The study found that *Sukuk* that are asset-backed are more in alignment with the principles of *Shariah*, and thus allow increased levels of protection to the holders of *Sukuk* in the event of default. Azmat et al. (2014b) analyzed the factors impacting on the choice of *Sukuk* structure of an issuer in comparison to financial instruments that are conventional. The study revealed that significant differences exist between a conventional bond and an Islamic issuer's choice of determinants, and this can be attributed to the specific characteristics of *Sukuk*.

## *Shariah* Auditing

The Accounting and Auditing Organization for Islamic Financial Institutions (AAOIFI) GSIFI No. 2 states that the principal role of a *Shariah* review is to ensure that all financial operations by an IFI are compliant with the principles of *Shariah*, and that the regulations are enacted properly, and effectively reflect the *fatwas*, rulings, and guidelines, articulated by the *Shariah* committee members (Haji Besar, Sukor, Abdul Muthalib & Gunawa 2009). To this effect, the AAOIFI recommends many procedures which must be adhered to by the *Shariah* reviewers of IFIs. These consist of the proper planning of review procedures, execution of the review procedures, preparation, and review of a working paper, as well as procedures in documenting conclusions, and the generation of a report as a final step. At the first stage, i.e. the planning and development of the *Shariah* review, the concerned reviewer ought to develop a comprehensive outline in accordance with the findings of Aida (2012). This plan ought to deal with pertinent information related to the operations of the IFIs, including such items as its products, size, locations, branches and subsidiaries. These are required to be stated explicitly in the plan, and thus developed in order to make certain that the *Shariah* reviews can be completed successfully and systematically. Also, along with the above list, all relevant *fatwas*, rulings, and guidelines should be detailed in the plan so developed. Thus, for the *Shariah* reviewer to give an accurate and relevant *Shariah* opinion regarding the total operations of a particular IFI, it is absolutely essential that the reviewer is cognizant of the intricacies regarding the structure, operations, transactions, and other related activities of that particular IFI. The planning will enable the *Shariah* reviewer to determine that the transactions and products of the IFIs, which need to be approved by the SSB, are undertaken according to their requirements (Hassan Scott 2009).

The next phase of the *Shariah* review concerns the implementation of the planned procedures, as discussed previously. At this step, *"the Shariah reviewer needs to make a judgment on the level of understanding of the IFI's management regarding the commitment and the control procedures for adherence to the Shariah rulings"* (Besar, Sukor, Muthalib, & Gunawa,

2009). After this, the *Shariah* review is in many ways similar to the review procedures undertaken by an auditor (Haji Besar et al. 2009). The *Shariah* reviewer, at this stage, will peruse the contracts, agreements and transactions as recorded by the IFI in order to determine whether they violate the *Shariah* mandates. The *Shariah* review will also include reviews of other vital information in the IFI-like circulars, such as minutes of meetings, operating and financial reports, and policies and procedures (Shafi et al. 2010). An effective *Shariah* reviewer, thus, is recommended to consult and work with other external auditors.

There is a requirement for all reviews by the *Shariah* reviewers to be properly documented in the appropriate working papers. When the review is completed, the *Shariah* reviewer is to discuss the findings with the management of the IFI, and suggest any remedial actions that need to be taken. The final step in the *Shariah* review, as recommended by AAOIFI, is the proper filing and recording of all relevant conclusions, and the generation of the *Shariah* review report. This report will then be read at the IFI's annual general meeting, and subsequently published in its annual report (Omar 2009).

In this regard, a number of associated studies were found in the existing body of literature. For instance, Rahman, (2008) analyzed and evaluated the requirement for a *Shariah* audit as a complementary function to the mechanisms of *Shariah* compliance that are already implemented. Furthermore, the study made mention of some hurdles that ought to be addressed to adequately ensure a *Shariah* audit can be effectively implemented - in that a *Shariah* audit should be undertaken systematically as part of the IFIs' mechanisms of corporate governance.

Kasim et al, (2009) empirically analyzed, in the Malaysian context, the gap between the actual methods of practice of *Shariah* auditing and the desired methods of practice. It found that a gap exists between the two concepts in terms of specific issues. Notwithstanding the fact that this study cannot hope to bridge the existing gap, it does indicate that the function of *Shariah* auditing has not been taken seriously as a tool which can have a positive impact for Malaysia's IFIs, despite its potential to monitor *Shariah* compliance.

Kaseb (2010) analyzed the level of harmony between the practices in the *Sukuk* market in Malaysia and the *Shariah* guidelines, by utilizing a qualitative method technique. The study confirmed the view from the existing literature, and from interviews with *Shariah* advisors, that the regulators ought to review and update the current guidelines so that there is more clarity and a more comprehensive guidance of *Sukuk*, to strengthen and facilitate the issuance of *Sukuk* in a definite way. As an example, a *Shariah* advisor ought to be provided with the tools, or with the guidelines to clear legislative requirements, to closely monitor and check the way in which the *Sukuk* issuer intends to place the monies, prior to using the fund in the defined asset.

The function of *Shariah* advisors in the issuance of *Sukuk* was described by ISRA (2013). The study indicated that, in the event of neglecting to properly scrutinize any documentation, this might lead to *Shariah* non-compliance, and, to some extent, might have adverse legal findings impacting on *Sukuk* issuance. Accordingly, *Shariah* auditors ought to provide a continued level of supervision that perpetually upholds the due diligence of transactions, contracts, and procedures. Thus, it is imperative that a *Shariah* advisor is truly competent and able to scrutinize the issuance-related documentation, through a thorough and individual examination of all the available documents.

Ahmed, Islam & Ariffin (2015) analyzed the relationship between the legitimacy of *Sukuk* and *Shariah* auditing. Their study's results affirmed the existence of this relationship, and showed that most *Sukuk* in the financial institutions are subject to a *Shariah* auditing report, indicating they had carried out their duty legitimately and accurately; whereas a small number of reports concerning *Shariah* auditing indicated that the duties were not performed accurately and with legitimacy. When examination of *Sukuk* is extended to two *Shariah* auditing reports or more, it is deemed to indicate the effective role by *Shariah* auditing, in that in the performance of their duty, their work was legitimate and accurate.

## *Shariah* Auditing by the *Shariah* Supervisory Board

As per the principles of *Shariah*, the IFIs are primarily involved with the development of financial products in order to cater to the requirements of a variety of interested parties. It is very important, therefore, that these IFIs can innovate and operate within the domain of the principal mandates of the *Shariah*. Thus, any Islamic financial company or institution must be properly supervised according to the rules of the *Shariah*. This safeguard, or system of checks and balances, is only possible if the Islamic banks have a legitimate controlling body (Lahsasna 2010). It is essential that these financial institutions find a *Shariah* board consisting of experts who are well versed in *fiqh muamalat* (*Shariah* scholars who have the requisite specialized knowledge of Islamic laws for business transactions). Such a board can then guide the operations and transactions of the financial institution, according to the mandates of the *Shariah*. Malaysia, along with many other Islamic countries, has enacted laws to govern and aid in the development and realization of such *Shariah* committees. Hence, the *Shariah* board undoubtedly constitutes the integral and most influential part of any IFI (Malik 2010).

The main duty of the *Shariah* board's members is to oversee the operations of a particular institute, and govern the proper development of its Islamic financial products. They also ascertain whether such activities and investments are compliant with the principles of *Shariah*. The board has to undertake its own audit in order to determine whether any of the operations developed involve any element which is prohibited (*mashbuh*) by the rules of *Shariah*.

IFIs are therefore mandated to develop operating procedures which make certain that none of their business activities or investments are implemented without the prior approval of their *Shariah* Board. The managements of such financial institutions are required by law to update and seek approval of the *Shariah* Board members regarding the actual businesses undertaken, and the investments made by their banks. The management must, in this way, ensure adherence to the preapproved practices by the *Shariah* Board (Ahmed et al. 2013). Therefore, IFIs, which have financial instruments and services, must be overseen by an independent *Shariah* Board comprising a minimum of three *Shariah* scholars having the requisite specialized knowledge of Islamic laws for transacting, or *fiqh al-muamalat*, in order to comply with the principles of *Shariah*. The scholars must also possess knowledge of modern business practices and economics. The main role of these experts, or scholars, is to ensure that the financial institution's business activities, services, and other operations, are compliant with the rules of *Shariah*. The *Shariah* Board is therefore required to give an independent certificate of the financial institution's *Shariah* compliance (Malik 2010).

The routine implementation of *Shariah* mandates by the concerned *Shariah* board members is a role that has two parts. Firstly, they have a great responsibility to understand the complexities of the sophisticated and modern world of finance, and ascertain whether a proposal for a new type of financial venture or product is in agreement with *Shariah*. Secondly, they act as investigators or watchdogs to continually review the *Shariah* compliance of the financial operations undertaken by the IFIs.

According to DeLorenzo (2010), the supervision and required advice on a financial operation in the context of *Shariah* should be introduced in the initial phase. In this first phase a review of the relevant elements of a business proposal or contracts can be undertaken to determine whether any modifications are necessary. Subsequently, as the product is realized or the practice implemented, *Shariah* mandates should be used as a guideline for continual monitoring with the aid of routine audits. Such audits can be accomplished using various means like visits to sites, reviews of documents, or consultation with the concerned management at periodic intervals.

## Risks of *Sukuk*

In recent times, a rapid growth in the issuance of *Shariah* compliant corporate and sovereign Islamic *Sukuk* has been witnessed, so much so that the *Sukuk* industry is a thriving multi-billion dollar market (Vishwanath & Azmi 2009). Other options of conventional types of derivative instruments, such as detachable options and credit derivatives, and interest rate swaps in the Islamic capital markets (ICMs), are not available, as these are prohibited in accordance with the principles of *Shariah* (Tariq & Dar 2007). Accordingly, the considerations and requirements of risk management for competitiveness ought to be a compelling force to enable the *Sukuk* structures to be further developed, and to allow *Shariah*-compliant options to the traditional derivatives on offer. In the absence of further in-depth development of *Sukuk* structures, the Islamic financial markets may not develop many emerging economies into their full potential (Saidi, Scacciavillani & Prasad 2009).

The usages of Islamic *Sukuk*, which conform to Islamic principles, pose special risks and challenges (Talahma 2015). As a consequence, an efficient system of risk management in IFIs has assumed particular importance, as these institutions try to cope with the challenges of globalization (Makiyan 2008). This, however, requires the development of a suitable regulatory framework and new financial instruments (*Sukuk*) to provide an enabling operational environment for Islamic finance (Di Mauro, Caristi, Couderc, Maria, Kaur Grewal & Zaheer 2013). Unfavorable risks affect the competitiveness of the pricing of *Sukuk* assets (Tariq 2004, Ahmed 2011b). Therefore, the innovation of *Sukuk* essentially involves a higher exposure to certain market and financial risks. Thus, *Sukuk* may have multiple risks, and these include market risks, credit and counterparty risks, *Shariah* risks, operational risks, and institutional rigidity. The next sections briefly highlight the *Shariah* risks which are particularly associated with *Sukuk*.

## *Shariah* Risks

*Shariah* risk is a distinctive operational risk in relation to IFIs (Van Greuning & Iqbal 2008, Ginena 2014). Archer and Haron (2007) referred to it as a *Shariah* compliance risk and defined it as, "the risk of non-compliance resulting from a failure of an Islamic bank's internal systems and personnel". Ba¨lz (2008) uses the term *Shariah* risk, and defined it as "the chance that an Islamic financing transaction is challenged on grounds that it does not comply with Islamic law".

In accordance with the above-mentioned definitions of a *Shariah* risk, it is a type of operational risk, in that it is a risk of financial losses that may confront an IFI as a consequence of *Shariah* non-compliance of its principles in relation to business activities, as deemed by the SSB, or by any other relevant authority having jurisdiction. This definition does not include non-material or non-financial losses, as these types of losses are associated with quantifying any monetary damages (Ginena 2014). Nevertheless, Muslims believe that losses on the spiritual front will diminish the blessings of God, and will consequently impact on the financial position of the IFI (Muhamad 2011). However, it is very difficult, if not impossible, to quantify these losses. *Shariah* risk, if not managed appropriately, may reduce the confidence of stakeholders, such as customers, shareholders, depositors, and employees, who realize that the institution is not living up to its commitments (IDB & IFSB 2007).

At times, a *Shariah* risk may lead to compliance and legal risks (Lahsasna 2014). For instance, any IFI that makes a declaration in its articles of association of adherence to the principles of *Shariah*, yet does not live up to its declaration, may find itself confronting lawsuits from various stakeholders adversely affected by the false claims, or by the institution failing to commit to its claims (Ginena 2014). As another example, there may be doubt in court concerning the interpretation of *Shariah* clauses, and whether there is unenforceability in secular law jurisdictions of *Shariah* contracts (DeLorenzo, & McMillen 2007), which can negatively impact the market discipline (IFSB 2007b). Furthermore, it is possible a *Shariah* risk can become a compliance risk. For instance, in the event of failure of an Islamic financial institution to set up proper arrangements of internal *Shariah* governance mechanisms, it can lead to compliance risk and compliance failure, despite the institution being required by the regulator to be compliant.

**Table 2 Events and causes (internal and external) of *Shariah* risk**

| *Shariah* Risks | | | |
|---|---|---|---|
| Internal Causes | | | External Causes |
| People | Processes | Systems | External Events |
| -Fatwa risk<br>- Falsification<br>- Guideline violations<br>- Unapproved product, transaction or legal documentation<br>- Insufficient resources<br>- Inadequate training<br>- Negligence<br>- Mis-communication<br>_Un-segregated duties<br>_ Loss of key player<br>_ In organization | -Unclear processes, policies, procedures, or responsibilities<br>-Inadequate internal *Shariah* governance arrangements or tools<br>- Insufficient disclosure and transparency<br>-Use of charity account, profit distribution, and segregation of funds | - Process and system accounting mismatch<br>- Inadequate product modules<br>- Poor reporting<br>- Unapproved software<br>- Inexperienced vendor<br>- Non-timely vendor support<br>- Non-user friendly system<br>_ System mistakes | - Fatwa risk<br>- Inexperienced *Shariah* advisory firm<br>- Conflict of interest between auditing, consulting and legalizing duties.<br>- Inadequate/lack of sharia governance regulations<br>_ Unclear laws and regulations |

Source: Ginena (2014)

In such a scenario, an IFI may receive fines for contravening those regulations, which could ultimately lead to the loss of its license to operate. Among the external *Shariah* risks are the hiring of inexperienced *Shariah* advisory board members, and possible conflict of interests. The first is related to the recruitment of *Shariah* advisory board members who aren't well versed in the process of providing such services. This may result in introducing a *Shariah* mistake, which otherwise would have been easily avoided if an experienced person is hired instead. The latter refers to the possibility of offering multiple-conflicting services, such as issuing *fatwas,* auditing, and consulting in parallel.

*Shariah* risk is also seen in poor governance and ambiguous laws and regulations surrounding the subject. The importance of a regulator's role in ensuring *Shariah* governance is attested by previous studies, and recognized by institutions (Ahmed 2011a, IDB & IFSB, 2007) given the instability that may result. The effectiveness of the regulators is dependent on the ability of IFI to establish an adequate *Shariah* governance measure that is capable of addressing *Shariah* risks (IFSB 2007a). Any inadequacy in the *Shariah* governance and regulations, or complete absences of the same, would potentially lead to a *Shariah* risk.

The issuance of *Sukuk* without legitimate approval, or pursuing a transaction without appropriate documentation, is another contributor to *Shariah* risk. *Sukuk* that are issued without SSB's approval could potentially lead to public disapproval and withdrawal from the instrument. In addition, both the SSB and legal counsel must scrutinize each other's documentation, according to respective validation criteria, to ensure no contradictions to *Shariah* tenets which may invalidate the *Sukuk* contract are found. A non-existent, or unapproved, legal documentation is a *Shariah* risk which raises questions on *Sukuk* legitimacy. The importance of *Shariah* governance arrangements or tools cannot be undermined, as it could have a dreadful effect. Without practical *Shariah* governance arrangements, *Shariah* compliance controls are unlikely to be setup. The establishment of these structures without the appropriate tools to perform the tasks would also result in similar failure. Hence, the role of regulatory bodies here in ensuring that Islamic financial institutions have established suitable arrangements, and are rightly equipped, cannot be undermined (Hasan 2012).

One of the key legitimacies of *Sukuk* is in the extent of their disclosure and transparency. Insufficient disclosure and transparency would result in stakeholders being unaware of any potential *Shariah* violations, thus making an uneducated judgement in investment. Hasan (2012) found that SSBs' annual reports to stakeholders lack basic transparency requirements on facts such as the number of meetings held, resolutions passed, products approved, and so on. Haniffa and Hudaib (2007), on the other hand, found that, from seven Islamic banks' annual reports over the period 2002-2004, only one had reported the remuneration paid to its SSB. Collectively, any lack in the reports, and the inaccuracy or inadequacy of information presented in them, can lead to misinformed judgments, which can lead to *Shariah* risk.

Pursuant to the requirements of the Malaysian Islamic Financial Services Act of 2013, all IFIs are to comply at all times with tenets of *Shariah*. It also incumbent on IFIs when they become aware of a non-complaint *Shariah* activity to notify the central bank immediately. In order to rectify the situation, the IFI is to desist from carrying on such non-compliant activities within a period of 30 days of becoming aware of the non-compliance, and during this period, submit a plan to remedy the situation (BNM 2010). It is deemed an offence for any person to contravene these guidelines, and the sanctions include a conviction and a fine not exceeding 25 million ringgit (approximately $8 million), or a term of imprisonment not exceeding eight years, or both imprisonment and a fine (Ginena 2014).

The principles of Islamic finance place a great emphasis on strong corporate governance values and structure, transparency as well as disclosure of information, and strict adherence to *Shariah* principles (Laldin 2013). Therefore, *Shariah* risks can be managed via a proper *Shariah* governance framework, which can be installed in all jurisdictions and includes the adoption of an approach of mutual respect (Ahmad & M Khatun 2013). Accordingly, IFIs ought to have adequate *Shariah* compliance mechanisms for policies and procedures pertaining to the approval of products and activities.

## *Shariah* Risks on *Sukuk*

The *Shariah* risk is the loss of the value of the asset as a result of the issuers' breach of its fiduciary responsibilities with respect to compliance with the tenets of *Shariah* (Izhar 2010). For example, if *Sukuk* are based on a hybrid of *Ijarah* and *Istisna* assets, *Ijarah* must always be more than *Istisna* in the pool; otherwise *Sukuk* deeds will dissolve. Thus, generally speaking, a *Shariah* compliance risk must be defined as a rate of return foregone in comparison to the market rates, as a result of complying with *Shariah* law (Tariq 2004). Moreover, fixed rate *Sukuk* face serious market risks. So, to match the market requirements of *Sukuk* to a floating rate, and the *Shariah* requirements of rents to a fixed rate, the *Ijarah Sukuk* are based on a master *Ijarah* agreement with several subordinate *Ijarah* agreements. However, investors could still face a profit rate risk to a certain extent, and, since the originator can only guarantee the fixed return on the underlying asset pools, the issue of floating rate returns still remains contentious, particularly in pooled or hybrid *Sukuk*. Therefore, the association of *Shariah* supervisors with *Sukuk* issues will further increase investor confidence (Tariq, & Dar 2007). In this regard, a number of related studies in the existing literature were found. For instance, Tariq (2004) analyzed the variety of risks underlying the corporate *Sukuk* and Islamic sovereign structures, and made a comparison to the underlying risk of traditional instruments of fixed income with the underlying the structures of *Sukuk*. The study revealed that the novel financial instruments bring with them the previously recognized financial risks. Due to an increase in the convergence of conventional markets and Islamic finance, and the globalization of these financial markets, the effect of the indirect rate of interest rate and other financial risks obliges IFIs to develop their techniques of Islamic financial risk management. Some of the derivatives are inherently not aligned to the principles of *Shariah*, due to the uncertainty involved, which equates to *gharar*. Notwithstanding this, the study referred to the opportunity to broaden the embedded options functions to better fit the needs of the considerations of the principles of *Shariah* that underpin the *Sukuk* certificates.

Tariq & Dar (2007) studied the risks of *Sukuk* as a financial tool and the role *Sukuk* play in the development of debt markets and the mobilization of resources in an emerging economy. The findings of their study indicated an absence of refinement of the structures of *Sukuk* with an inherent lack of mechanisms for risk management.

A study was undertaken by Shafii et al. (2010) which examined the role of *Shariah* auditing in IFIs in reducing *Shariah* compliance risks. Their findings indicated that the IFIs' risk of non-compliance can be mitigated by way of a *Shariah* compliance audit. A *Shariah* committee has the responsibility to convey their opinion as to whether the operation of the IFIs is fully compliant with the principles of *Shariah*, and to help inform decisions they may well rely upon. It is this very information, provided by an audit performed on the various aspects of an IFI's operations, which will help inform these decisions; this includes reporting, documentation, and, to the extent to which there is a separation and control process and duties that involve the system, the involvement of its employees in the operations and the documentation involved.

In analyzing the associated *Sukuk* problems and risks in the capital market, Nanaeva (2010) reviewed the IFIs' level of competitiveness and conducted an empirical analysis of the value of risk of *Sukuk* and conventional bonds in order to present a complete picture to any potential investors in *Sukuk*. The study revealed that, after an average of 10 days, the *Sukuk* value-at-risk has a level of confidence of 99 per cent, which is higher than the conventional bonds' value-at-risk. His findings indicated that most *Sukuk* investors hold on to their Islamic securities until the date of maturity, in other words, not bearing in mind the everyday market risks, and this analysis ought to be a warning for the issuers of *Sukuk*.

The fundamental concept of *Sukuk*, and the implications of the risk of default and its rating, were examined by Zakaria et al. (2012). The sources of data included documentation, observation, and texts, specifically those from agencies such as Standard & Poor's, Malaysia's Securities Commission (SC), the Malaysian Rating Corporation Berhad (MARC), Rating Agency Malaysia (RAM), and the analysis by the authors on the subject matter. Their study indicated there is a continual issuance growth across countries. However, the *Sukuk* issuance may also promote a risk of default and, therefore, there ought to be a credit rating assessment for *Sukuk* to determine their future repayment prospects. Despite the issuance of *Sukuk* being associated with asset security, any negative passage of the assessment of credit rating would indicate a risk of default.

Casper (2012) studied *Shariah* compliance, and the SSBs' role and corporate governance in the context of institutions in Europe. The author claimed there is no uniformity in the interpretation of the principles of *Shariah*. Accordingly, there is a risk that a product's *Shariah*-conformity will be contested, and this then constitutes a *Shariah* risk. Furthermore, it is not appropriate to put in place a requirement for either the issuers or the investor to bear the entirety of the risk of non-compliance.

El Shazly & Tripathy (2013) studied the forms of the components of Islamic financial instruments' risk, and then devised a simple model taking into account some associated risk factors of *Ijara Sukuk*. The disclosure of any such findings ought to be made transparent, and an assurance given that information is readily accessible to alternate entities at differing levels. The study also noted the need for an examination of instruments of risk in order ascertain their accuracy, and for improvement to occur.

A study of the determinants of the performance of risk and return in the structure of the GCC *Sukuk* market, which covered a nine-year period from January 2005 until June 2013, was undertaken by Rauf & Ibrahim (2014). Through sampling their study, they proved the existence of a relationship between the different type of risks and the total rate of return. The findings of the study indicated that according to the *Sukuk* NASDAQ Index, on a sectorial basis in GCC, 91 percent of the GCC *Sukuk* returns could be accounted for by GSKI, whilst 93 percent of the corporate GCC *Sukuk* returns were explained by the GSKF Index, and 92 percent of the GCC *Sukuk* returns could be accounted for by the GSKC Index. This variance is due to a number of risks: the dollar rate risk; *Shariah* compliance risk; maturity risk; credit risk; reinvestment risk; liquidity risk; interest rate risk; and inflation risk.

Lahsasna (2014) studied the significant elements relating to the risk of non-compliance of *Shariah* in Islamic finance, and expanded this study to examine the causative factors for the occurrence of risk in the operations of IFIs. The study revealed that the causes ought to be carefully addressed by the IFIs in order to minimize the risk of *Shariah* non-compliance, otherwise there is a risk the non-compliance will be a frequent occurrence, and this situation may adversely affect the income and the credibility of the bank.

Ahmed, Islam, Zuqibeh & Alabdullah (2014) examined the risks confronting the instruments of the IFIs. They did this by determining the mechanics and application of these instruments with respect to Islamic investment and financing. The study's findings indicated there are some challenges and risks requiring timely solutions for the development and sustainability of the Islamic capital market (ICM). In order to do so, there is a necessity for close cooperation between financial experts, *Shariah* scholars and the senior level of management on the one hand, and further interaction amongst *Shariah* boards on the other.

By studying the mechanisms of the governance of *Shariah*, it was determined that the *Shariah* risk of non-compliance poses a real threat to Islamic banks and their stakeholders, with the likely consequences of non-compliance being financial losses, liquidity problems, higher costs - leading to possible bank runs - financial instability, and industry smearing, and ultimately could lead to a bank's failure (Ginena 2014). Their study also placed an emphasis on *Shariah* risk implications, outlined examples of such events, and incorporated them into the operational risk causes of the Basel Committee on Banking Supervision (BCBS), with the development of a tool for measuring the risk of *Shariah* non-compliance.

Abdullah, Yazid, Abdullah & Kamarudin (2014) examined the risks involved with infrastructure projects' funding from the perspective of *Sukuk* issuance. Their study assessed the risks in relation to the issuance of *Sukuk* for the funding of infrastructure projects and provided information to stakeholders to enable them to address the issues related to the funding of infrastructure projects.

In their study, Mizushima & Mizushima, (2014) analyzed the relationship between *Shariah* governance and corporate governance, and the way in which those concepts of governance are dealt with at IFIs. Their study analyzed *Shariah* compliance risk by examining two cases in relation to *Sukuk* issuance. These cases have been identified as:

1. The issuance of *Sukuk* in the context of Malaysia on the basis of the Islamic contract of *Bai Bithaman Ajil* (BBA) and *Murabahah Sukuk*, which are in compliance with the principles of *Shariah* and are instruments of fixed-income, with features resembling conventional market bonds. Despite approval being granted by the *Shariah* Advisory Council of both regulatory bodies i.e. the Securities Commission of Malaysia (SC) and the Bank Negara Malaysia (BNM) which is Malaysia's central bank, the usage of Malaysia's version of the BBA and *Murabahah* was not accepted anywhere else. Irrespective of this divergence, SC and BNM continued to permit the use of BBA and *Murabahah*, and Malaysia's *Sukuk* market began to move towards more universally accepted Islamic structures. Also, the utilization of BBA and *Murabahah* began to wane at a considerable rate as more counterparties turned away from their usage. In fact, a recent survey conducted by Rating Agency Malaysia on the issuance of *Sukuk* shows the practice of BBA *Sukuk* issuance is virtually non-existent. Notwithstanding this finding, the practice of issuance of *Murabahah Sukuk* continues, and this may be due to their structure evolving to become more universally acceptable by *Shariah* scholars.
2. In 2011, US investment bank Goldman Sachs announced a proposal to issue a program of *Sukuk* issuance in the order of $2 billion dollars. In setting up the program, Goldman Sachs registered the program with the Irish Stock Exchange. It then established a special-purpose vehicle (SPV) in the Cayman Islands. By way of background, HSBC had earlier successfully issued *Sukuk* in the order of $500 million in a market environment in which the demand exceeded supply for premium rated *Sukuk*. However, the Goldman Sachs plan ran into controversy with analysts and Islamic scholars questioning whether the US investment bank was adhering to the religious principles of *Shariah*. There were two issues that received wide ranging attention in connection with this issue of compliance with the principles of *Shariah*, namely, whether the structure of *Murabahah* that Goldman Sachs opted for met the standards set by the requirements of *Shariah,* and, secondly, whether the *Sukuk* proceeds would be used to fund activities deemed as non-*Shariah* compliant. There was also a level of concern as to whether or not the *Sukuk* proposed by Goldman Sachs had received the endorsement of *Shariah* scholars. Indeed,

> some scholars stated that the *fatwa* had already been issued, whilst others involved reported that they had not signed off on the *fatwa*, and this was in contradiction to the statements from Goldman Sachs and its advisors.

Ahmed et al. (2015) studied the effects of the risk of *Shariah*-compliance in the Malaysian context on the IFIs' *Sukuk* legitimacy, and examined the essential factors that have a significant impact on *Sukuks'* legitimacy. Their findings indicate a negative relationship exists between *Sukuk* legitimacy and *Shariah* compliance risks, indicating there is a significant effect of the risk of *Shariah* compliance impacting on the rate of increasing the levels of legitimacy.

## *Shariah* Documentation

The documentation for *Sukuk* is often split into two categories: capital market documents, and *Shariah* transaction documents (Ali 2011). The designation is, of course, imprecise, because all *Sukuk* documents must be *Shariah* compliant, and they can also all be said to be capital market documents, given the nature of the tool being issued (Mohamad & Razif 2013). However, the terminology does serve to split the understanding of *Sukuk* documentation into documents which should follow the norms of the capital market in relation to custody, documents, payment, and administration generally, which form the core of a *Shariah*-compliant transaction. It is assumed that the *Sukuk* documentation will follow proper transparent processes, and with the main contracts comprising clauses without any presence of ambiguity (Van Wijnbergen & Zaheer 2013). Accordingly, it is crucial that the documentation involved in *Sukuk* issuance does not contain any inconsistencies or loopholes which could deprive the *Sukuk* investors of the rights promised to them in the offering circulars (Kaseb 2010). In adopting best business practices, contracts are required to be transparent and enforceable, in order to protect the interests of the parties involved. Similarly, *Shariah* endorses only those contracts which are free from excessive uncertainty and speculation in the contract or transaction (*gharar*) (Van Wijnbergen & Zaheer 2013).

There have been a few ill-fated attempts to standardize the *Sukuk* documentation (Ali 2011), and the lack of success has been predictable. This is because *Sukuk* are structured instruments and, as such, several considerations invariably arise when structuring *Sukuk* (Khnifer 2010a). As previously indicated, they also need to be *Shariah* compliant, and pronounced as such by *Shariah* scholars, and the difficulty is that scholars can have differing views on what is, and is not, permissible. The core principles of Islamic finance are universal, and very simple, but more peripheral or detailed application of those core principles requires knowledge of Islamic jurisprudence, or *fiqh*. A *Shariah* Board ought to be able to give more attention to the above-mentioned illustrated tasks. All documentation should be thoroughly checked to ensure compatibility with *Shariah*, and, therefore, it will have compliance (Yean 2009). Thus, any mistake, or even negligence, might lead to difficulties in issuing the *Sukuk*, due to incompatibility with such compliance. Whatever structure is used, the *Shariah* transaction documents will need to be reviewed by the *Shariah* scholars providing the *fatwa* for the *Sukuk*, because those documents underpin the essence of the *Sukuk* for *Shariah* compliance.

Nowadays, to become an integral part of an economic system, the IFIs need to have a variety of *Shariah* documentation to meet all the requirements of an Islamic *Sukuk*, such as purchase agreements, lease agreements, servicing agency agreements, purchase undertakings, and so forth, and it is the role of a SSB in a financial institution to find the optimum solution for each *Sukuk* contract (Hasan & Sabirzyanov 2015).

A set of responsibilities ought to be carried out by a SSB, including advising on documentation, structuring, and all aspects of *Sukuk*, such as matters dealing with *Shariah* pronouncement made on the basis of the reasoning for the pronouncement, in addition to the structure and mechanisms of the *Sukuk* issue (SCM 2014). Moreover, *Shariah* principles, and its concepts used in the *Sukuk* issue, should be complied with, as recommended by the *Shariah* Advisory Council (SAC) (BNM, 2007). Furthermore, *Shariah* matters should be compatible with the documentation of the *Sukuk* issue. Finally, there is a requirement for an assurance that all conditions related to *Sukuk* are complaint with *Shariah* on the one hand, and matters that are not consistent with the concepts and principles are raised, and do not receive endorsement by the SAC on the other hand, until such time as the inconsistencies are remedied (ISRA 2013). Ideally, IFIs are expected to disclose the following information in their *Shariah* pronouncement:

(i) Structure and mechanism;
(ii) Documentation (including purchase agreements, lease agreements, servicing agency agreements, purchase undertakings, substitution undertakings, declaration of trusts, cost undertakings, agency agreement and certificate purchase agreement (Ahmed et al. 2013).

(iii) *Shariah* approval, in that the *Shariah* Supervisory Board (SSB) ought to grant approval for the issuance of a *Sukuk* in accordance with the conditions, including a time limit of 14 business days for offering or inviting to subscribe or purchase *Sukuk* (SC 2011). In addition, the form related to the approval issued by the SSB programmers should be granted, and comply with the guidelines that refer to the terms and conditions provided by the issuer. In the event of non-compliance with the terms and requirements required by the SAC, the SSB can impose further conditions and obligations to be undertaken until such time as the non-compliance is satisfactorily rectified, and approval is obtained from the SSB (Lahsasna 2014).

In the existing body of literature, some studies have examined the pronouncement of the AAOIFI regarding the *Shariah* compliance issues of *Sukuk* structuring, the future implications of issues, and the impacts of structuring (Lahsasna & Idris 2008). Their study indicated the AAOIFI announcement placed an emphasis on the role and the association of the SSBs in the *Sukuk* documentation provision and implementation.

Kaseb (2010) examined and compared the *Shariah* guidelines and Malaysia's practices in the *Sukuk* market, as to whether there was adherence to the guidelines. The study involved a technique of qualitative research, with face-to-face interviews conducted with advisors of *Shariah*, and its findings revealed that more clarification concerning effective legal documentation on products in the Islamic capital market (ICM) is required. The study also contended that the regulators ought to review and enhance the current guidelines, so that there is more clarity, and that the guidelines provide wide-ranging *Sukuk* guidance, in order to make it easy for the process to be strengthened for the issuance of *Sukuk* to be made in a definite way.

A study conducted by Ali (2011) examined the developments in the *Sukuk* market by way of referring to its structures and the associated documentation. The study demonstrated that it is the documentation that underpins the *Shariah*-compliant transactions. Accordingly, to utilize a *Sukuk* structure it is necessary for *Shariah* scholars to review the *Shariah* transaction documents, and in doing so, these scholars can provide the *fatwa* for the *Sukuk*, as the documentation is an essential element for *Shariah* compliance of the *Sukuk*. The study also claimed that for *Sukuk* investors, the *Shariah* transaction documentation is the principal documentation, as it enables disclosure of all essential information that a prospective investor would require to base their decision on whether or not to invest in a particular *Sukuk*.

A study of the structure of a variety of instruments traded discussed the crucial emerging issues from an overview of major defaults of *Sukuk* (Van Wijnbergen & Zaheer 2013). Their study analyzed four recent major *Sukuk* defaults as a consequence of the 2007 worldwide credit crisis. The findings indicated that Islamic securities mostly comprise two types: *Ijarah, and Musharakah*, and contended that all *Sukuk* issuance documentation ought not have any loopholes or inconsistencies which could take away the rights offered to the *Sukuk* investors in the offering circulars.

Ahmed et al. (2015) examined the relationship between the legitimacy of *Sukuk* and the *Shariah* documentation in IFIs. The findings indicated that *Shariah* documentation is significantly associated, in that it increases the level of legitimacy of *Sukuk*. Accordingly, there is a strong positive relationship between *Sukuk* legitimacy and *Shariah* documentation, as noted by the resulting positive value. Accordingly, this provides a useful insight for IFIs to enhance their level of disclosure of *Shariah* documentation in the respective reports of the SSBs concerning Islamic *Sukuk*, as an enhanced level of disclosure of *Shariah* documentation is an anticipated step to take, not only to differentiate *Sukuk* from other Islamic financial products, but also to differentiate them from their counterparts.

## The Role of the *Shariah* Supervisory Board

In line with *Shariah* principles, IFIs are engaged in product development activities to cater for the needs of a wide range of parties. It is essential for these financial institutions to innovate and operate within the ambit of the principles of *Shariah* law. Hence, the need for supervision is an integral part of any IFI. The safeguard to ensure IFIs operate in accordance with the tenets of *Shariah* is due to a legitimate control body overseeing the financial institution (Lahsasna 2010). It is, therefore, vital for such financial institutions to form a *Shariah* Supervisory Board (SSB) consisting of *fiqh muamalat* experts to guide their operations and transactions in accordance with the rules of *Shariah*. Malaysia and several other countries have passed laws to govern the formation and functions of the SSB Therefore, the SSB is undoubtedly the most important and influential entity in any IFI (Malik 2010).

The role of the members of the SSB is to review the operational activities of the IFIs, to supervise the development of Islamic products, and to determine the *Shariah* compliance of these activities and investments. The SSB has to undertake its own independent audit in relation to any of the operations involving any element that is prohibited, or *mashbuh*, by *Shariah*. Furthermore, Islamic banks ought to adhere to the best practices of corporate governance. In addition, in applying the best practices of corporate governance, the SSB can provide an extra layer of supervision for the IFIs, with the SSB having both supervisory and consultative functions. As *Shariah* scholars on the SSB carry a great level of responsibility, it is important that only scholars of a high caliber are appointed to the SSBs.

It is a requirement for Islamic banks to establish operating procedures to ensure that neither business activities nor investments are undertaken without being approved by the SSB. An IFI's management is required to periodically report and certify to the SSB that the actual business activities undertaken, and the investments, conform to the forms pre-approved by the SSB. IFIs offering products and services must comply with Islamic rules, and, therefore, be governed by a SSB that acts as an independent supervisory body comprised of at least three *Shariah* scholars with specialized knowledge of the Islamic laws for transactions, *fiqh al muamalat*, a knowledge of modern business practices, and a sound understanding of economics. They are responsible primarily for ensuring that business activities, services offered, and other bank operations, comply with the *Shariah* principles. The SSB is required to issue a certificate of *Shariah* compliance independently (Malik 2010).

The day-to-day application of *Shariah* by the SSBs is a two-fold duty. Firstly, in the increasingly complex and sophisticated world of modern finance, the members of the SSB ought to endeavor to ascertain whether or not any proposals for new operations or products comply with the rules of *Shariah*. Secondly, they act to a large extent in an investigatory role in reviewing the operations of the Islamic banks to ensure that they comply with the principles of *Shariah* (Qureshi 2011).

According to De Lorenzo (2010), *Shariah* supervision and advice ought to be included at the earliest stages, to ensure that any elements of the proposed business contracts requiring modification to comply with *Shariah* principles and precepts are captured and remedied early in the process. Moreover, once a product is launched, *Shariah* supervision may take the form of ongoing monitoring through periodic audits. Such audits may be undertaken by way of site visits, reviews of documentation, or through regular intervals of consultation with the IFIs' level of management.

It is essential that all dealings in business must avoid activities deemed as *haram*, as such activities are not in accordance with the rules of *Shariah* and negatively impact on compliance. As an example, Muslims are required to work in activities deemed as *halal,* meaning lawful or permitted. So far as *Shariah* is concerned, it is "a body of legal principles derived from *Qu'ran*, the teachings of the prophet Mohammed (Peace Be Upon Him) and interpretations of those teachings by Islamic jurisprudential scholars" (Masudi 2005). In general, *Shariah* seeks to bring benefits to individuals and to the community, and its laws are designed to protect these benefits and to facilitate the improvement and perfection of the conditions of human life on earth (Kamali 2009).

As for doubtful deeds, these are matters that are neither distinguishable as being *halal* nor *haram*, thus, not many people recognize them or know their ruling. Scholars, however, can reach a ruling regarding such matters by applying a suitable text or *qias* (analogy) or *istishab* (accompanying). So if the scholar were to come across a matter in which it is not immediately obvious as to whether it is *halal* or *haram*, then the scholar would attempt to classify it as one of the two, with the appropriate evidence. If the scholar is able to classify it under *halal*, it is considered as such. Such matters may not be free of doubt even then, and if it is so, then it is safer to determine it as adhering in accordance with the Prophet's advice, as "he who avoids doubtful deeds has achieved purity in his religion and his reputation." As for those matters that are considered as unable to classify, *mujtahed,* whether or not the scholar ought to rule it to as *halal* or *haram*, or refrain from ruling (*al-twaquf*), is still a tenuous question (Al Nawwawi: Vol. 11/27, 16/111).

It is imperative for the Islamic world to find alternative financial models that are both Islamic *Shariah* compliant and free of *riba*. As the tenets of *Shariah* encompass all aspects of life, Muslims should follow the requirements of the rules of Islamic law which are also extended to cover all aspects of life, and not restricted, or limited to certain areas, particularly finance and banking. In leaving any ambiguity, and not complying with Islamic *Shariah,* IFIs can tarnish the reputation of the Islamic financial industry, due to controversy, especially in the institutions that deal with both systems (traditional and Islamic). This has an effect on Muslim customers, in the event a company is committed to comply with the law, though they may still have a minor number of activities that do not meet the requirements of *Shariah* (Abdul Rahim 2008). According to Jamal (2002), it has been mentioned before that *Imam al-Bukhari* recorded this *Hadith* in the book *al-Buyu*, implying that when it comes to trade, there are a considerable amount of doubtful activities; for example, when professionals carry out fraudulent activities. Therefore, Muslims must be careful with all commercial activities; otherwise, one should avoid any which are doubtful (Ahmed, Islam & Al-Harthy 2013).

*Shariah* supervision is the single most important element that distinguishes between the operations of a conventional institution and an IFI. It is the only way of certifying that its services, operations, and products are actually *Shariah*-compliant. In the emerging Islamic financial sector, therefore, *Shariah* supervision has to be considered a significant factor in influencing *Shariah* compliance and elevating the practices of the IFIs worldwide to meet the objectives of compliance.

In essence, *Shariah* supervision is the process of ensuring that operations, financial products, or services, comply with Islamic legal precepts and principles, either by conforming to, or by not violating, a recognized Islamic legal norm (Delorenzo 2010). Ideally, *Shariah* supervision should be a part of an Islamic product or service throughout the whole period it is offered, including its development and launch. Thus, at the stage of development and research, drafting contracts or offering memorandums, *Shariah* supervision, in one form or another, should be an active participant.

According to the AAOIFI Governance Standard for Islamic Financial Institutions (GSIFI) No. 1, an SSB is an independent body of specialized jurists in *fiqh muamalat*. AAOIFI has stated that SSBs shall consist of at least three members. The role of the SSB covers five main areas: (1) certifying permissible financial instruments through *fatwa* (ex-ante *Shariah* audit); (2) verifying that transactions comply with the issued *fatwa* (ex-post *Shariah* audit); (3) calculating and paying *Zakat*; (4) disposing of non-*Shariah* compliant earnings; and (5) advising on the distribution of income or expenses among shareholders and investment account holders. The SSB issues a report to certify that all financial transactions comply with the above-mentioned principles.

In the context of Malaysia, the Islamic Banking Act (IBA) 1983 provided the provision for the establishment of a *Shariah* Advisory Board as a requirement of granting a license to an IFI. Furthermore, in reference to the IBA 1983, the Malaysian Accounting Standards Board has issued "Financial Reporting Standards - i" (FRS-i). The purpose of the standard is to provide a guideline which is *Shariah* compliant, as well as applicable in the

Malaysian context, in order to address accounting issues and practices in Malaysia (MASB 2004). In addition, Bank Negara Malaysia (BNM) provides further guidelines issued on the Governance of *Shariah* Committee through the "Garis Panduan Shariah 1" (GPS-1). The BNM/GPS1 came into effect from 1 April 2005, whereby all IFIs are regulated and supervised by the BNM and are required to comply with all the requirements as outlined in the guideline. The report is often an integral part of the annual report of the companies who are under *Shariah* compliance.

The SSB plays a very important role, since many organizations, including banks, have their own separate board of *Shariah*, and this will facilitate and give the public confidence in their transactions. SSBs have a direct relationship to business activities. Scholars and index providers who define the different *Shariah* strategies can be considered as major contributors, as the most qualified *Shariah* scholars, and this will show the importance to an organization to have the SSB (Derigs, & Marzban 2009). It is imperative that SSBs consist of Muslim scholars, and their main objective is to check to ensure that banking practices are aligned, or can be aligned, with the principles of *Shariah* (Grassa 2013). The SSB continues to evaluate banking practices through extensive meetings and discussions, whereupon the level of *Shariah* process of implementation in IFIs is expected to continue to improve.

In the existing body of literature, a number of studies were found to support the above-mentioned discussion. For instance, AAOIFI (2008) studied the observations and difficulties raised concerning *Sukuk* issuance. The study recognized that the SSBs' role is not merely to issue a *fatwa* on the permissibility of the *Sukuk* structure after having examined all the applicable contracts and documentation associated with the actual transaction. Their role is broader than that, in that the SSBs have oversight of the actual process of implementation, and ensure that at every stage, the operation complies with the guidelines and requirements of *Shariah*, as duly noted in the *Shariah* standards.

A study examined broadly any controversy and problems concerning *Sukuk*, and specifically, the observations made by the *Shariah* Board of AAOIFI and its resolutions (Yean 2009). The study determined that the SSBs have a more crucial role to undertake. Accordingly, the SSBs ought to be involved in the structure of the transactions, including providing guidance in the drafting, reviewing, and approval of the documentation, to ensure compliance of *Shariah* transactions, ensure the fit of the documentation with the requirements, and the desired outcomes of consistency, certainty, and transparency, of the process of enforceability of these transactions.

In that regard a study, in the Malaysian *Sukuk* market context, examined the SSBs' role and the IFIs' practices prior to, and after, the issuance of *Sukuk*. The study claimed that *Shariah*-related challenges emerged directly after the issuance of *Sukuk* had taken place, in that the practices may not adhere to the SSB *fatwa*. Indeed the study indicated that the majority of *Sukuk* customers sought a simple structure similar in nature to conventional products, with the minimal levels of liability, risk, and cost.

A study undertaken by Casper (2012) examined the SSBs' functions and *Shariah* compliance on corporate governance in the context of institutions in Europe. Casper recommended that potential investors and holders of *Sukuk* ought to obtain independent advice, and proposed that in examining whether products comply with the principles of *Shariah,* this can be done by consulting their own *Shariah* advisors, or a comparable source which is reliable. As part of the process of discovery, an investor is often aware, and acknowledges that the prospective yield of profit of a product which is *Shariah*-compliant might be at a lesser rate than that of the market standard.

## *Shariah* Supervisory Board Procedures in *Sukuk* Issuance

In general, the members of SSBs are a group of experts in *Shariah* who are delegated to give guarantees that instruments and products used in the Islamic financial industry are comparable to the *Shariah* aspects, which usually consist of the capital market, *Takaful* and banking (ISRA 2013). Organizations involved with the Auditing and Accounting for Islamic Financial Institutions (AAOIFI) would have noted the following definition of a Governance Standard in relation to the *Shariah* Board of an Islamic finance institution as: "specialized jurists, particularly in *fiqh muamalat* and Islamic Finance, entrusted with the duty of directing, reviewing and supervising the activities related to Islamic finance in order to ensure that they are in compliance with Shariah rules and principles".

Following the *Sukuk* guidelines issued by the SC (2011), a *Shariah* Board has to be either a committee that meets the standards registered under the guidelines of *Shariah* advisors, or an Islamic institution or a bank approved by Bank Negara Malaysia to carry out advice from *Skim Perbankan Islam Shariah* advisors, or "The Islamic Banking Scheme". In this respect, the procedures start from the inception of the *Sukuk* until such time as their issuance, the related part in directing to the intended product and then reviewing the product, and consequently, the supervision of the product's execution, for the purpose of effectively ensuring that it is compatible with the standards and requirements recommended by *Shariah*.

Thus, the responsibilities and role of the SSBs are not only limited to stakeholders, but they cover other important religious obligations that are to be upheld. In this regard, SSBs play an important role in the issuance of *Sukuk* that should be concurrent with the product, starting from the moment of providing advice on the product. Based on this, the SSBs' role is to ensure there is due diligence through their continued and permanent supervision, procedures, and transactions. Here, the important role of the SSBs lies in two stages related to *Sukuk* issuance: pre-*Sukuk* issuance, and post-*Sukuk* issuance (Lahsasna & Lin 2012). In relation to pre-*Sukuk* issuance**,** *Shariah* committees play an important and significant role (Ahmed et al. 2013). The whole process regarding *Sukuk* relies on this stage, in that any negligence or failure at this point can lead to a bad reaction in the long term for the entire procedure of *Sukuk*. In the pre-issuance stage, there are four main tasks that ought to be taken into consideration:

(i) There ought to be compatibility between the *Sukuk* structure and the *Shariah* rules. Any proposed diagrams and transaction flows by the arrangers have to be clearly understood by *Shariah* committees, and moreover, to identify *Shariah* issues in order to prepare and submit solutions to the interested parties (Machmudi 2008). One of the important matters that should be tested at this stage is the compliance with all building blocks and terms in accordance with the principles of *Shariah*. For instance, it is important for a building block to be able to ensure the *Sukuk* structure's capital or return; when for example using *musharakah*, *wakalah bi al-istithmar*, or *mudarabah*, as essential contracts. In the same vein, dealing with purchase undertakings, liquidity facilities, or sale undertakings, there is a requirement for these to be constructed and arranged in such a way so that in the final analysis, it leads to a guarantee, and ensures there is a return on capital (ISRA 2013).

(ii) Auditing procedures are to be utilized by way of checking the conditions and terms in the documents regarding *Sukuk* issuance (Al-Maghlouth 2009). These documents should be checked accurately by *Shariah* committees in order to ensure that there are no conditions contrary to any principle in *Shariah* (Besar, Abd Sukor, Abdul Muthalib & Gunawa 2009). The important issues requiring checking are:

a) There is a facility description with a guarantee that the description and its illustration submitted is accurate and compatible with the approved aspects of the *Shariah* committees.
b) There is an underlying asset or assets with a guarantee that the asset(s) used in *Sukuk* issuance are compatible with the *Shariah* requirements (Tariq & Dar 2007).
c) That for the utilization of proceeds, a guarantee is given that there is an obvious statement on the outcome of the *Sukuk* that they are to be used only in activities compliant with *Shariah* requirements, in addition to ensuring that the returns submitted on the list are totally compatible with *Shariah* requirements (Dusuki 2010b). This part is very important, especially if the activities of the issuer are inconsistent with the requirements of *Shariah*.
d) That a designated account is used to guarantee that only *Shariah* compliant accounts will be taken into consideration.
e) The purchase price is also a very important consideration, and needs to be carefully observed (ISRA 2013). This importance has been noted in several countries. For example, in Malaysia, with respect to *Sukuk* issue, the structure of *Sukuk* based on *mu`awadah* contracts in *Guidelines on Sukuk*, issued by the Securities Commission of Malaysia, admitted the following points. In the instances of *Sukuk bai` bithaman ajil, Sukuk Murabahah, Sukuk Istisna,* and *Sukuk Ijarah,* these are processes involving the purchase and sale of an underlying asset or assets. When investors purchase an underlying asset, or assets, the purchase price is to comply with the purchase price, and must not exceed 1.51 times the market value of the asset. Alternatively, in the scenario whereby the market value of an asset cannot be ascertained, a fair value or any other value must be applied. This admission protects all relevant parties who are involved in the *Sukuk* issuance from incompatibility with the real price against the underlying asset.
f) *ATa`widh* contract is a compensation contract, and is meant as a guarantee that the compensation rate is compatible with the decision made by a competent authority, like a *Shariah* advisory council in a central bank (BNM 2007).

(iii) There is to be an audit undertaken of the legal documentation to guarantee that all conditions and terms in such documents do not conflict with the principles of *Shariah*, as there are differing types of legal documentation in the issuance of *Sukuk*. There actually needs to be an accurate examination through *Shariah* committees to guarantee that there are no items incompatible with *Shariah* guidelines (Muhamad Sori, Mohamad, & Shah 2015).

(iv) There is to be a guarantee, given that the admission (decision) of the *Shariah* committee is understood and implemented by the issuer (Ahmed et al. 2013). However, this is a difficult task, especially as there are so many issuers that are only focused on, and are familiar with, traditional banking training, while there is a lack of knowledge about the issuance under the *Shariah* requirements. Thus, it is extremely important that the *Shariah* committee be aligned with the *Shariah* knowledge of the issuer of the *Sukuk*, so that the issuer might implement and fulfill the decisions accordingly (ISRA 2013).

Finally, the *Shariah* committee ought to give more attention to the above-mentioned tasks, with all documentation being checked to make sure of its compatibility with *Shariah* compliance (Yean 2009). Thus, it is important in the pre-issuance stage to detect any mistake, or even negligence, as not detecting these problems might well lead to difficulties in issuing the *Sukuk* due to their incompatibility with such compliance.

With respect to post-*Sukuk* issuance, it is important for the SSB/*Shariah* committee to audit or review the *Sukuk* issued. Several vital tasks need to be undertaken at this stage (Ahmed et al. 2013). Firstly, there should be a guarantee that *Sukuk* returns are used according to activities which are compatible with *Shariah* requirements. Secondly, there should also be a guarantee that the status of the *Sukuk* issuer is maintained according to the requirements of *Shariah* compliance (Al Elsheikh & Tanega 2011). This principle is suitable, and can be applied where the issuer is a company that has mixed activities, whereas at the same time as *Sukuk* issuance, the company has to declare *Shariah* compliance through the authorities which have the right to grant this status to companies that are listed in the capital market. The Securities Commission in Malaysia, for example, announces whether or not companies listed in the Bursa Malaysia' status are in line with *Shariah* compliance (Sabli & Noor 2012). Malaysia's Securities Commission undertakes this procedure bi-annually, in May and November. If the status of some, or any, of these companies is changed, the *Shariah* committee has to investigate the status of the *Sukuk*, and make decisions whether or not the *Sukuk* can be considered, and this depends on its compliance with *Shariah* (Ahmed et al. 2014). This matter is important, especially if changes have occurred because of primary activities of the company and not because its financial ratio exceeds the compliance benchmark (ISRA 2013).

## *Shariah* Supervisory Board as Moderator

There has been tremendous development witnessed in the field of Islamic *Sukuk* during the last decade or so. It is also during this period that attention has started to be paid to it as a discipline, and different areas are now being researched. However, it is also a fact that the discipline of Islamic *Sukuk* and its issuance has not been given proper attention so far by the regulators, or by the practitioners and academicians (Lahsasna, et al. 2014). As a result of this situation, there is a lack of literature examining the legitimacy of *Sukuk*. The literature available has shown the determinants deemed as variables when examining *Sukuk* as a dependent one (See Wilson 2004, Tariq & Dar 2007, Lahsasna & Idris 2008, Wilson 2008, Rahman 2008, Howladar 2009, Yean 2009, Usmani 2009, Kasim et al. 2009, Khnifer 2010b, Herwany & Febrian 2010, De Lorenzo 2010, Shafii et al. 2010, Kaseb 2010, Nanaeva 2010, Ali 2011, Zakaria et al. 2012, Kantakji 2012, Casper 2012, Hidayat 2013, Van Wijnbergen & Zaheer 2013, Ahmed et al. 2013, El Shazly & Tripathy 2013, Abdulmalik 2013, Abdullah et al. 2014, Mizushima & Mizushima 2014, Azmat et al. 2014b, Ginena 2014, Ahmed et al. 2014, Rauf & Ibrahim 2014, Lahsasna 2014, Zulkhibri 2015, Aloui et al. 2015). However, to date, no previous study has investigated nor chosen the role of the SSB as a moderating variable on the relationship between determinants and *Sukuk* legitimacy.

The current study has two main justifications for a new area of examination. The first is related to the reason why the current study has chosen a moderating variable, while the second justification shows why the SSB is suitable to be a moderating variable on the relationship between determinants and the legitimacy of *Sukuk*.

The first reason for selecting a moderating variable is that, as argued by Baron and Kenny (1986), Holmbeck (1997), and Frazier Tix, and Barron (2004), when the relationship between an independent variable and a dependent variable is poor or inconsistent, a moderating variable can be established to strengthen or weaken such a relationship, and to explain when, or for whom, an independent variable affects a dependent one.

Secondly, the rationale for determining the SSB as being suitable to be a moderating variable, is that the SSB is one of the most important governance mechanisms of IFIs to ensure there is compliance with the principles of

*Shariah*. Therefore, the role of the SSB as a moderator on the relationship between determinants and *Sukuk* legitimacy could be used to enhance and strengthen the role of the SSB towards *Sukuk* legitimacy. Furthermore, the choice of the SSB as a moderating variable for the current study is justified, as the SSB has a positive impact as assured by several studies in the literature. For example, Yean (2009), Laldin (2008), Lahsasna (2010), Rahail (2011), Usmani (2008), Kantakji and O'haj (2010) all demonstrated that a SSB is an important variable that has its significant effect on the determinants of legitimacy. Furthermore, a study undertaken by Ahmed et al. (2013) showed that the SSB plays an important role concerning *Shariah* auditing for Islamic financial instruments. Moreover, to assure that the SSB is sound to be utilized as a moderating variable, a set of interviews were carried out for the current study, as further explained in Chapter Five. In summary, this study selected an SSB as a moderator for two reasons: firstly, based on the literature, it can be considered that the SSB has a high influence on *Sukuk*, and secondly, there is a lack of studies about the relationship between *Shariah* advisory boards and *Sukuk*. Thus, the current research chooses the SSB as a moderating variable on the relationship between the determinants and *Sukuk* legitimacy.

## Summary

There is a lack of literature examining the legitimacy of *Sukuk*. The literature review has identified the determinants (pricing, type of structure, *Shariah* auditing, *Shariah* risks and *Shariah* documentation), and these determinants have been utilized in this study as independent variables, whilst *Sukuk* has been set aside as the dependent variable to determine its legitimacy in relation to the determinants. In addition, there is a lack of studies examining the relationship between the SSB and *Sukuk*, as well as there being no previous studies examining the SSB as a moderating variable in the relationship. Therefore, this study extends the past studies through the examination of these new aspects. In summary, Chapter Three provided details of the theoretical foundational aspects related to the present study of these concepts, and analyzes the relevant theoretical and empirical studies. The earlier part viewed the foundation and conceptualization of legitimacy of *Sukuk*. Furthermore, the chapter presented a general review of the related literature for pricing, type of structure, *Shariah* risks, *Shariah* auditing, and *Shariah* documentation. This was followed by a discussion on the *Shariah* Supervisory Board (SSB) as the moderating variable, and presented the theories chosen to underpin this research endeavor.

# CHAPTER 5

# RESEARCH BACKGROUND

## Research Problem

The issue of *Sukuk* legitimacy has been one of the foremost issues of ICM (Kettell 2010, Saripudin, Mohamad, Razif, Abdullah, & Rahman 2012, Maiyaki 2013), thanks to the differing schools of thought and points of view among scholars (Salman 2014). There is a fundamental requirement for the structure of *Sukuk* to follow the structure set by Islamic finance in order to be qualified as *Shariah* compliant (Chik 2012, Saeed & Salah 2014). However, evidence concerning the current practices by Islamic banks worldwide suggests that the majority of financing operations are not based on equity, instead they take the form of debt-like instruments (Aggarwal & Yousef 2000, Wajdi & Abdullah 2006, Mehmet 2007).

*Sukuk* investors have an inherent right to information on the use of their investments, the nature of underlying assets, and other particulars that would otherwise be redundant in conventional investments (Krichene 2012). As Islamic-based financial institutions accomplish their operations based on *Shariah* principles and rules, it is anticipated that there will be no disparity in the practices of disclosure with respect to the legitimacy of Islamic financial instruments. This point of view ties in with the notion that both culture and religion might impact upon accounting procedures and practices (Baydoun & Willett 2000, Gambling & Karim 1991, Hamid, Craig & Clarke 1993). The transparencies in the disclosures are important to ensure the legitimacy and the extent of *Sukuk* compliance with *Shariah* principles, which enables a conscious investment decision to be made by the investors. However, despite being noted as a method of legitimizing Islamic instruments, the actual practice of disclosing information on the extent of *Shariah* compliance is seen to be lacking (Salman 2014).

One of the factors that influences the legitimacy of *Sukuk* is the pricing (Ra'fatt 2015, Kantakji & O'haj 2010, Usmani 2007, Omar, Azmi, Noor, & Meera 2010, Al-Bashir 2008, Wilson 2008). However, *Shariah* scholars and

Muslim economists have yet to identify an alternative to the interest rate as a readily available indicator of profitability (Kantakji 2003, Al-Bashir 2008). Hence, in the absence of Islamic-compliant benchmarks, the conventional usury-based benchmarks are adopted to determine *Sukuk* pricing (Selim 2008). This view is justified in taking into consideration the early development stage of the modern Islamic finance (Usmani 2002, Kantakji & O'haj 2010), which permits the use of conventional mechanisms. Despite the justification, the majority of studies claimed that the use of the conventional benchmark, the London Interbank Offered Rate (LIBOR) as a reference and guideline (Kantakji 2003, Mirakhor & Zaidi 2007) is undesirable from the *Shariah* perspective. Therefore, this is a major challenge to Islamic financial instruments' valuation, which raises the question of the legitimacy of *Sukuk,* and hence, requires disclosure accordingly. (Usmani 2007, Wilson 2008, Nanaeva 2010, Herwany & Febrian 2010, Aloui, Hammoudeh, & Hamida 2015).

Muslim investors, in particular, are always looking for investment opportunities, and in doing so, seek to invest in businesses with good corporate governance and management processes which are *Shariah* compliant (Srairi 2015). The ultimate aim for Muslim investors, in particular, is to take full advantage of the probability of making a profitable investment with an adequate rate of return, while being in compliance with *Shariah* (Rahman 2015). Of late, many of these investors have expressed an interest in the fiduciary rating, as the rating can give an indication of the performance and the structural nature of *Sukuk*, and the risks that investors take into consideration when entrusting monies to particular investment managers (Naifar & Mseddi 2013). However, there are two underlying problems with this rating practice as far as *Sukuk* is concerned.

The first, lies in how IFIs communicate the belief to investors that *Sukuk* is comparable to a conventional asset, rather than it being distinctive regarding the regulations of disclosure and transparency (Ahmed, Islam & Alabdullah 2014). Investors who are familiar with conventional securities naturally prefer it if the *Sukuk* carry a similar structure, rather than representing a new unknown realm (Wilson 2008, Hanifa, Masih, & Bacha 2014). Therefore, despite the fact that the Islamic *Sukuk* specialists rating agency in Malaysia, or global risk-rating agencies like Standard and Poor's, are ready to rate *Sukuk* to provide assurance to investors (Wilson 2012), the rating criteria used are not unique to *Shariah*-compliant securities like *Sukuk* (Ahmed et al. 2014)."

The second problem is related to the classification of the rating. Rating agencies place *Sukuk* into two categories: asset-backed, and asset-based, *Sukuk*. This classification has an effect on the legitimacy and compliance of *Sukuk* (Yean 2009). Asset-backed *Sukuk* is significantly more compliant with *Shariah* principles, in comparison to the asset-based *Sukuk* (Hidayat 2013). Asset-backed *Sukuk* is also less risky than asset-based *Sukuk* (Khnifer 2010b), and backing an asset-based *Sukuk* could lead to a default of the *Sukuk*. According to Usmani, about 85% of outstanding *Sukuk* in the market had failed the *Shariah* compliance test, as they were found to be asset-based, and not asset-backed with the guaranteed return of the face value of the *Sukuk* on maturity without transfer in asset ownership to *Sukuk* holders.

*Shariah* risk is one of the essential and unique operational risks of IFI that affects *Shariah* compliance (Ginena 2014). *Shariah* risk, if not appropriately managed, can reduce the confidence of stakeholders, such as customers, shareholders, depositors, and employees, who realize that the institution is not living up to its commitments (IDB & IFSB 2007). *Sukuk*, like conventional bonds, are exposed to credit risk. According to Khan and Ahmed (2001) credit risk refers to the risks that occur due to the failure of a business partner to timely and fully meet its obligations in accordance with the agreed terms. It also refers to the likelihood of an asset or loan becoming irredeemable because of default, or delay in settlements (Tariq & Dar 2007). Investors need to be informed of the types of *Sukuk* categories to enable a fact-based investment decision. Previous studies have revealed that reducing Sukuk's *Shariah* risk is an important element that could increase its compliance with *Shariah*, and enhance *Sukuk* legitimacy (Nanaeva 2010, Shafii, Salleh, & Shahwan 2010, Casper 2012, Lahsasna 2014, Ginena 2014, Mizushima & Mizushima 2014, Abdullah, Yazid, Abdullah & Kamarudin 2014). However, as knowing any potential risk linked to the investment implies that the investors are assuming a quasi-equity type of risk, which isn't preferable for investment, *Sukuk* documentation is seen as totally silent in disclosing the information (Haneef 2009).

*Shariah* principles, and its concepts, used in *Sukuk* issue should be complied with, as recommended by the *Shariah* Advisory Council (SAC) (BNM 2007). It needs to be ensured that all conditions related to *Sukuk* are compliant with *Shariah* on one hand, and matters that are not consistent with the concepts and principles are endorsed by the SAC on the other hand (ISRA 2013). Thus, to ensure compliance and adequate documentation disclosure, *Shariah* auditing needs to be conducted. *Shariah* auditing is one of the essential and unique components of corporate governance that oversees the IFI business conduct, to ensure that all transactions are fully compatible and in compliance with *Shariah* (Rahman 2008, Casper 2012). Numerous studies have revealed that disclosing information for a transparent, *Shariah*-compliant documentation in the reports, is an important element which enhances the legitimacy of Islamic financial instruments (Haniffa & Hudaib 2007, Maali, Casson & Napier 2006, Lahsasna 2014). However, despite being recognized as a potential monitoring tool for *Shariah* compliance, the *Shariah* auditing function has not been taken seriously (Kasim Ibrahim, Hameed & Sulaiman 2009, ISRA 2013).

To ensure compliance with *Shariah,* every IFI operating in Muslim communities ought to place an emphasis on transparent business activity disclosure (Sulaiman & Willett 2003). As *Sukuk* are formulated based upon *Shariah* principles, the *Shariah* Advisory Council (SAC) within the Central Banks has made a requirement that its *Shariah* Committee is to be consulted for *Sukuk* issuance matters (Yean 2009). Accordingly, to give assurance of *Sukuk* legitimacy, Malaysia's SAC has set a condition that the *Sukuks*' legal documents, and the structure of the *Sukuk* are to be examined, and, if found to be in order, to be eligible to receive endorsement from the *Shariah* advisors for the *Sukuk* to be issued (ISRA 2013). This is also a practice that is in line with international standards and expectations. Therefore, *Shariah* advisors can be viewed as providing the moral fiber worldwide for the financial industry, and their advisory role for the aspect of compliance would be at risk without such countenance and guidance (Laldin 2008).

In addition, to guarantee legitimacy and compliance with *Shariah* principles, *Sukuk* ought to be overseen by a *Shariah* Supervisory Board (SSB). The role of the SSB would be to oversee the respective financial institution (Lahsasna 2010). Such a supervisory body should comprise *Shariah* experts (Malkawi 2014) who can guarantee that the IFI's complete their transactions in accordance with the requirements of *Shariah*. It is usual for the SSB to be comprised of *Fiqh Muamalat* scholars (those who understand the rulings relating to economic transactions) to provide guidance concerning the financial transactions and operations pursuant to the rules of *Shariah*. According to Malik (2010), the SSB is without doubt the most significant and influential body in any Islamic financial institution. It can guarantee that *Shariah*-compliance has been achieved, and there is legitimacy of *Sukuk* issuance. With monitoring and review on the *Shariah* operational documents by the SSB, the SSB is able to provide a *fatwa* (a learned interpretation or legal opinion) which authenticates and underlies the approval of the *Sukuk*, thereby providing legitimacy to the *Sukuk* structure and mechanisms used (ISRA 2013). These *fatwas* would inherently validate the legitimacy and compliance of the *Sukuk* to *Shariah* (Rahail 2011). Thus, the role of the SSB as a moderator can be used to enhance and strengthen the validity of *Sukuk* legitimacy.

The aforementioned problems highlight that the fundamental issues with *Sukuk* are in recognizing and justifying its legitimacy. Hence, it is not far-fetched to conclude that, a lack or absence of transparency and disclosure of *Sukuk* legitimacy could negatively impact investment in the *Sukuk* industry. Thus, this study is undertaken to address an urgent review to establish a proven source to authorize and validate *Sukuk* legitimacy. To the best of the author's knowledge, this research endeavor is a ground-breaking study examining *Sukuk* legitimacy, and therefore, there is a pressing need to identify the relationship between the factors mentioned above and *Sukuk* legitimacy.

## Research Questions

Following on from the preceding objectives, the following research questions are presented:

i. Is there any relationship between determinants (pricing, type of structure, *shariah* auditing, *shariah* risk and *shariah* documentation) and *Sukuk* legitimacy?
ii. Does the *Shariah* Supervisory Board (SSB) moderate the relationship between pricing and *Sukuk* legitimacy?
iii. Does the *Shariah* Supervisory Board (SSB) moderate the relationship between the type of structure and *Sukuk* legitimacy?
iv. Does the *Shariah* Supervisory Board (SSB) moderate the relationship between *Shariah* auditing and *Sukuk* legitimacy?
v. Does the *Shariah* Supervisory Board (SSB) moderate the relationship between the *Shariah* risks and *Sukuk* legitimacy?
vi. Does the *Shariah* Supervisory Board (SSB) moderate the relationship between the *Shariah* documentation and *Sukuk* legitimacy?

## The Scope of the Study

The Islamic financial institutions in Malaysia have been chosen, primarily, because these Islamic institutions play a significant role in the development of the Islamic finance industry in the country in general (Sulaiman, Majid & Ariffin 2011). The present study focuses on some of the *Sukuk* selected determinants, which are pricing, type of structure, *Shariah* auditing, the *Shariah* Supervisory Board (SSB), *Shariah* risk, and *Shariah*-related documentation. In order to determine the factors which are important elements for the legitimacy of *Sukuk*, these factors or determinants ought to be taken into consideration in order to improve the legitimacy of the *Sukuk* and make it compatible with *Shariah* principles.

## Definition and Illustration of the Key Terms

This section gives a definition of the study's variables, and this involves the legitimacy of *Sukuk*, its structure and pricing, *Shariah* risk, *Shariah* auditing, the *Shariah* Supervisory Board and *Shariah*-related documentation.

## Legitimacy of *Sukuk*

*Sukuk* legitimacy refers to the authenticity of *Sukuk* structure and mechanisms, documentation, and compliance, in accordance with *Shariah* rules (Ali 2011). Compliance with *Shariah* rules is classified as being free from any *qimar/maysir* (meaning gambling), *riba* (meaning usury), or *gharar* (meaning uncertainty), and any other activities that are non-*Shariah* compliant (Salman 2013).

## Pricing

In order to decide on the benchmarks required, a suitable mechanism for the pricing of services and products is needed, in order to ascertain the sharing ratios for distributing profit amongst the joint venture partners. These conventional benchmarks are utilized by Islamic financial institutions in nearly all jurisdictions, with the jurisdictions being dependent upon these traditional market benchmarking rates (such as LIBOR or EURIBOR) to realize the pricing of the tools for the Islamic financial industry (Ayub 2007).

## Type of Structure

The types of structure of *Sukuk* can be readily classified into two separate categories: asset-based *Sukuk*, and asset-backed *Sukuk* (IFSB guidelines No. 2, 2005). The rating structure is concisely defined in the following subsections:

## Asset-Based *Sukuk*

An asset-based *Sukuk* can be described as an investment certificate in which the aspect of a true sale is not evident. This then means that the underlying assets' legal ownership sits with the *Mudarib*, and only a beneficial ownership is given to the *Sukuk* holders. In such cases, the *Sukuk* certificate holders are not able to sell the asset to another, or to a third party, due to a lack of legal title ownership (Dusuki 2010a, Salman 2013).

## Asset-Backed *Sukuk*

On the other hand, an asset-backed *Sukuk* can be described as an investment certificate that underlies the asset, and has been transferred entirely into the *Sukuk* structure ownership. Crucially, if the original owner who sponsored the creation of the *Sukuk* becomes insolvent, as a consequence of this unfortunate event, it does not put the asset at risk. In addition, should the sponsor fail to carry out their contractual obligations there is a process in place to remedy this situation, through issuing of a special purpose vehicle (SPV). The asset can be sold, and the funds distributed to the *Sukuk* investors (Hidayat 2013, Salman 2013).

## *Shariah* Risk

Any risk arising from *Sukuk* non-compliance with *Shariah* principles and rules is determined by the applicable *Shariah* regulatory councils, so that during the life of the *Sukuk*, any breach in *Shariah* standards can be examined and a determination reached (Afshar 2013).

## *Shariah* Auditing

In relation to auditing, the *Shariah* review examines whether an Islamic financial institution (IFI) follows *Shariah* in all its activities. The *Shariah* review examines the IFIs contracts, agreements, policies, products, transactions, memorandum, and articles of association, financial statements, reports (especially internal audit and central bank inspection), circulars, etc. (AAOIFI 2010, Sultan 2007, Rahman 2014).

## *Shariah* Documentation

The documentation related to *Sukuk* is often divided into two categories: capital market-related documents, and *Shariah* transaction documents.

However, the designation into the two categories is not always precise, given there is a requirement for all *Sukuk*-related documents to be *Shariah* compliant, and, given the characteristics of the tool being issued, they can all be viewed as capital market documents (Ali 2011).

## The *Shariah* Supervisory Board

The *Shariah* Supervisory Board is set up by a financial institution (usually an Islamic bank or an Islamic insurance company) to advise and certify certain financial products (Saeed 1996).

## Special Purpose Vehicle

A Special Purpose Vehicle (SPV) is an entity formed by a company or government for a particular project or task, with legal status that makes its obligations secure even if the parent company goes bankrupt. The actions of the SPV are usually very tightly controlled, and it is only allowed to finance, buy, and sell assets, or typically, to hold assets, and not to make a profit.

# CHAPTER 6

# RESEARCH METHODOLOGY

As Chapter Three summarizes, previous study in the literature describes in detail the research design and methods that are used in the study. The theoretical framework which forms the main basis of this research is outlined and discussed in detail. The theoretical framework specifies all the constructs adopted in the study, and depicts their relationship to one another. This is followed by the hypotheses development section, which clarifies and verifies the main constructs of the study, with supporting literature and rationalizations, to form the hypotheses of the study. Then, the chapter presents the research methodology, which includes the design of the study, sampling data collection methods, and data analysis techniques.

## Research Framework

The theoretical framework of this study provides the underlying structure in relation to the dependent variable (*Sukuk* legitimacy), and the independent variables (pricing, type of *Sukuk* structure, *Shariah* risks, *Shariah* auditing and *Shariah* documentation). Logically, the theoretical framework is developed to describe the relationships among the identified variables by way of a thorough literature review survey. The research hypotheses were then developed to answer the study's research questions.

The hypotheses of this study were developed by examining the direct relationship between the determinants represented by pricing, type of *Sukuk* structure, *Shariah* risks, *Shariah* auditing, *Shariah* documentation, and *Sukuk* legitimacy. In addition, the hypotheses were also developed based on examining the moderating effect; namely the *Shariah* Supervisory Board (and specifically the influence from the members appointed to the Board and committees). The current study chose these five essential independent elements (factors) to represent the determinants for certain reasons. Firstly, such determinants are important factors influencing the legitimacy of *Sukuk*, and, furthermore, they are suitable to be chosen and tested in Malaysia, as *Sukuk* play a significant capital-raising role in the Malaysia's economy through the initiatives of real sector development, as well as Malaysia's significant *Sukuk* market growth, which can be used as leverage to create a major competitive advantage in the Asian region, as well as a global competitive market over other countries. In addition, the Malaysian government recently established a fund to enable *Shariah* scholars to research and develop the *Sukuk* market, in order to provide a suitable platform for the consideration of *Shariah* compatibility of newly created Islamic markets and financial instruments. Secondly, in the previous studies undertaken in the Malaysian context, there is a recommendation from the researchers (Dawood 2008, Azmat et al. 2014a, Lahsasna 2014, Zulkhibri 2015) for increasing a level of awareness to be made, and diligence to be applied to the importance of complying with the principles of *Shariah*. For Muslim investors, compliance with the *Shariah* requirements in business transactions is an important issue, as a transaction compliant with the principles of *Shariah* emphasizes the purity of the income earned and expenditure incurred. On the other hand, however, non-compliance has a negative impact on the revenue of a firm, as revenue earned from illegal disclosure of *Shariah* compliance can only be considered for charitable purposes, or for donations. Accordingly, the legitimacy of *Sukuk* and its provision represents a rare valuation that can satisfy the requirements of Muslim investors and their desire for dealing with *halal Sukuk* products, as well as providing the basis to gain a competitive advantage.

In line with the research objectives, and based on the theory of indebtedness and the institutional theory, which are discussed in Chapter Three, the following theoretical framework is developed. The relationship between pricing, type of *Sukuk* structure, *Shariah* risk, *Shariah* auditing and *Shariah* documentation with *Sukuk* legitimacy is shown in the following figure, Figure 4.1.

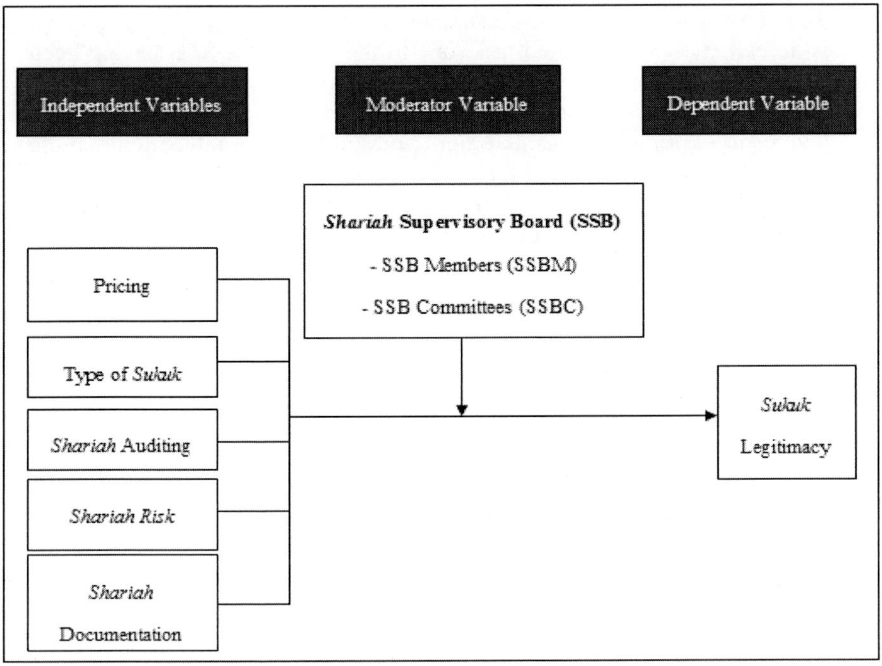


Figure 4.1: Schematic Diagram of Research Framework

## Underpinning Theories

*Shariah* compliance, as a concept, applies a standard criterion which focuses on the activities of Islamic institutions. As such, subject to certain conditions, IFIs whose activities are not contrary to *Shariah* principles will be considered *Shariah*-compliant securities (*Sukuk*) (SC 2011). On the other hand, IFIs will be classified as being associated with *Shariah* non-compliant securities if they are involved in the following core activities: *riba* (interest); *shubuhat*, gambling; gaming; the sale of non-*halal* products or related products; manufacture or sale of tobacco-based products or related products; and other activities deemed non-permissible according to *Shariah*. The *Shariah*-compliant view provides the basis for this study of *Sukuk* legitimacy. The *Shariah*-compliant view asserts that controlling some characteristics and determinants, which are strategic and capable, leads to a competitive advantage, and superior performance of the IFIs to allow more compliance with *Shariah* rules (Ahmed et al. 2013).

To study the determinants of *Sukuk*, and their relationship with legitimacy, is an extremely complicated task, due to the role of the SSB having been examined from a number of different theoretical perspectives, which, in turn, has led to various competing theories dealing with the determinants and *Sukuk* legitimacy. Thus, in order to provide a concise illustration of the related Islamic and business theories to support its theoretical framework, this study used two underlying theories: the theory of indebtedness; and the institutional theory. By doing so, the relationship between the dependent and independent variables can be assessed by way of introducing a moderating variable.

## The Theory of Indebtedness

There is a set of concepts in *Shariah* screening, capital, and money market instruments, and a validation of contracts that are looked upon when fulfilling the demand from customers, fund managers, and dedicated IFIs for *Shariah*-compliance of the available products, and for due consideration to be given in the formulation of new products and financial tools. Furthermore, several *Shariah* advisors have different viewpoints regarding the legitimacy of Islamic financial tools in the Islamic finance sector. One of the convincing opinions is the theory of indebtedness (*Al-Mithaq*). The indebtedness theory has been commonly used in Islamic finance as well as in research based on *Shariah* compliance. The theory was formulated from the work of a few authors (Rosly 2007, Ahmed 2012). The central idea of the indebtedness theory is that it is based on the assumption that that a human's existence is explained by the debt he owes to his Creator, and his subsequent enslavement to His law as a means of repayment. It means that it requires humans to manifest the Covenant (*Al-Mithaq*) by way of submitting their desires to His will (i.e., the *Shariah*) in absolute true willingness. Similar theory is also shared by Greenberg (1980), defining indebtedness as a 'state of obligation to repay another'. He believes that indebtedness is conceived as a psychological state of having motivational properties, such that, the greater the magnitude of indebtedness, the greater the arousal, and hence, the stronger the ensuing attempt to deal with or to reduce indebtedness. It is predicted on the existence of a norm of reciprocity that people should help those who have helped them, and should not injure those who have helped them.

In general, Islam means *al-Din* (submission), which involves many things that have to do with the meaning of indebtedness. In that regard, one of the meanings of *Din* is indebtedness, which, at its root, is originally an Arabic word. It represents the indebtedness notion that gives the deeper meaning to the rationale for humans being in an economic existence, in *Shariah*. This is because human beings once never existed, but now they do, as humans were created by *Allah* (*Al-Mu'minun* {23}:12- 14). Thus, when a human is in debt, he is supposed to repay his debt, even though *Allah* needs nothing from human beings, as He is definitely the Creator and Sustainer. Nevertheless the debt that person owes must be paid, and eventually such an act is to obey *Allah*.

As mentioned by Naquib Al-Attas, returning or paying debts according to Islamic rules refers to giving oneself up in service, to *Allah*. All acts have to be for *Allah*'s sake, as the Creator, and loyalty has to be towards His prohibitions and commands. Therefore, one lives by the dictates of His law. This is, as far as Islamic rules are concerned, the meaning of human existence in their relationship to their indebtedness to *Allah* the Creator. Consequently, human beings' enslavement to the law of *Allah* is the way humans settle their *dayn*, or debt. Through commandments, and obeying *Allah*, the believer therefore submits their desires to *Allah* willingly. This is the respectful way that they can pay their dues towards *Allah*, the Creator.

Hence, based on the principle of Islamic compliance, business activities and operations managed by human beings are subject to the submission to the Law of *Allah*, and this includes the prohibition of *gharar* (ambiguities), *riba* (interest), *jahala* (fraud) and *maisir* (gambling) in all financial business operations. Therefore, the indebtedness theory (*Al-mithaq*) is extremely fundamental, to illustrate the reasons why believers dutifully observe Islamic rules in the conduct of business and in financial operations (Rosly 2007).

Essentially, as discussed above, the theory admits that all creations have to submit to *Allah*, and complying with *Shariah* rules is no exception. In this study, it is assumed that the SSB is a manifest of the Covenant (*Al-Mithaq*) and by way of submitting its desires to His will (i.e. the *Shariah*) corresponds to an absolute true willingness as an indebtedness of the relationship between them and *Allah* the Creator. Thus, it is assumed that IFIs that have an SSB will follow the rules of *Shariah* to ensure there is validation of *Sukuk* contracts to fulfill the demands of *Shariah* compliance for *Sukuk* holders, as well as providing and disclosing information to the *Sukuk* holders concerning the legitimacy of *Sukuk*. The current study selects the most relevant and practical Islamic *Sukuk* legitimacy in light of the influence of *Shariah* compliance in relation to the IFIs, *Sukuk* holders, customers, and the regulators.

## The Institutional Theory

Meyer and Rowan (1977) stated that institutional theory is extremely useful, because it helps give an explanation as to why an SSB reports the way in which it does. Institutional consistency, as mentioned by Di Maggio and Powell (1991), is a mechanism whereby the practices of an organization are adopted by other organizations facing the same institutional pressures. Moreover, it has been demonstrated that this kind of consistency is based on the source from which such pressures are derived. Kasim (2012) explained that this consistency, essentially, has a relationship with organizational behavior with the regulative and political impacts for certain institutions like policies, and government regulators, further to their regulations. Kasim also illustrated that simulation consistency uses the same set of practices used by successful organizations in order to reduce uncertainty and to normalize consistent means of complying with the norms and expectations of professional bodies, and society in general.

Based on the above, the structure of consistency includes three ways through which organizations can be changed to become like others. This change can come about by legislation and rules imitating best practices, and by being compatible with social traditions and expectations. Scott (2001) provided reasons for compatibility being an enhancement for legitimacy. That compatibility also alleviates the risk of threats, and in taking this stance, additional resource might become available.

Research by DiMaggio (1998) explained that institutional theory has much to contribute to the study of religious organizations, focusing on the idea of ritual, symbolic understandings, and legitimacy. According to him, institutional theory is relevant, and similar to the objectives of religious organizations, as normal business organizations tend to concentrate more on 'rational actors', an image focusing on profit maximization. Osman, Alwi, Mokhtar, Ali, Setapa, Muda, and Rahim (2015) studied corporate image in Islamic banks based on institutional theory. The study found that institutional image, such as being Islamic, humble, and trustworthy, will lead towards other values and images of performance. Aziah Abu Kasim (2012) utilized institutional theory to underpin the examination of the disclosure of *Shariah* compliance, as reported by the SSBs in the annual reports of *takaful* (cooperative system of reimbursement) companies in Malaysia. The findings of the study indicated a similarity in the reports of the *Shariah* Boards, not only in relation to the Bank Negara Malaysia guidelines, but also to that of other *takaful* companies. Furthermore, the concept of isomorphism drawn from institutional theory is useful, and is used in the

*Shariah* Board reports. Ahmed, et al. (2014) mentioned that institutional theory is useful for disclosure practices in the pronouncement of *Shariah* in IFIs. He noted two essential reasons. It relies on, and uses, institutional theory, because the concept of consistency is derived from such theory, as well as a clear similarity among all IFIs, including the generation of reports by the *Shariah* Boards, and guidelines from the central banks. Therefore, the current study relies on these two essential reasons, and uses institutional theory to underpin the discussion on its findings, because there is a clear similarity among IFIs, including the pronouncements of the SSBs and the guidelines of the central banks, as well as the concept of consistency derived from such theories.

## Hypotheses Development

The study's model incorporates many relationships which have not been previously studied in a thorough way. Therefore, in order to examine the model, a set of hypotheses is constructed and tested. These hypotheses are also based on previous research results. The hypotheses state the nature of influence of one variable on another. Fifteen main hypotheses have been developed and formulated in order to reflect the relationships depicted in the framework. These formulated hypotheses can be utilized to examine the direct relationship between the determinants, which have been identified as: the pricing; type of *Sukuk* structure; *Shariah* risks; *Shariah* auditing; *Shariah* documentation; and *Sukuk* legitimacy. As mentioned above, the current study has chosen these determinants further to the recommendations of the previous studies undertaken in the Malaysian context. Moreover, this study's hypotheses were also developed based on the moderating effect of the *Shariah* Supervisory Board (SSB).

### The Relationship Between Pricing and *Sukuk* Legitimacy

Pricing is one of the most important factors impacting on the legitimacy of *Sukuk* (Wilson 2008, Usmani 2009, Herwany & Febrian 2010, Ahmed et al. 2014, Aloui et al. 2015). For instance, the market views of *Shariah*-compliance might be in danger of being damaged in the event of a change in opinion by scholars, and might adversely affect investors' confidence in supporting the instrument impacting on pricing (Jadwa 2009). *Shariah* scholars and Muslim economists have not come up with an alternative to the interest rate as a readily available indicator of profitability (Al-Bashir 2008). Hence, LIBOR has been utilized as a pricing benchmark, and has become part of the practice in IFIs, as well as a reference guide leading to long-term investment pricing (Kantakji & O'haj 2010). The majority of previous studies admit that the method of distancing pricing from conventional benchmarks is a major challenge in the Islamic capital market, as pricing has an effect on the *Shariah*-compliance of Islamic financial instruments (Kantakji 2003, Wilson 2008, Usmani 2009, Nanaeva 2010, Herwany & Febrian 2010, Ahmed et al. 2014, Aloui et al. 2015). Accordingly, such studies found that the pricing benchmark is a significant and important factor in contributing to, and enhancing, legitimacy. The factors for computing the pricing benchmark ought to be free from interest rates, non-real economic activities, and non-*halal* activities, such as indices of derivatives of financial instruments (Omar et al. 2010). However, it should be duly noted that, whilst it is permissible to use LIBOR as a pricing benchmark, it is not correct to rely upon it for the determination of returns (Kantakji & O'haj 2010).

Fitri (2007) evaluated the working function of pricing adopted by the Islamic banks in order to define the pricing of the *Ijarah* and *Murabaha* products, which were recommended by Islamic financial institutions in Malaysia. He also revealed that, in the environment of the dual banking systems in Malaysia, there is a necessity for a new pricing standard for the commodities of the IFIs. Wilson (2008) indicated that the use of the LIBOR benchmark in *Sukuk* pricing is not suitable, as per the opinion of Islamic scholars, and suggested benchmarking corporate *Sukuk* against performance indicators of financial companies. Jobst et al. (2008) critically analyzed the industrial practices in *Sukuk*, made a comparison of them with the replication efforts made, and found that a lesser amount of research was undertaken concerning the ways in which innovation and development of *Shariah*-oriented products could be generated.

In contrast, another study (Usmani 2009) provided support for the argument for an immediate cancellation of the practice of *riba* by the IFIs. This advances the argument that the usage of interest rates as a benchmark for *halal* products is not a desirable practice. Furthermore, the values and philosophy of an Islamic economy are not promoted and, therefore, there is no effect on the distribution system. Also, ISRA (2013) utilizes the Capital Asset Pricing Model (CAPM) to estimate the pricing model in order to ascertain whether a direct link exists between the market risk of projects or businesses and their required rate of returns. It has been established that the Islamic pricing model is more stable than the KLIBOR alternative. Ahmed et al. (2014) described the significance of the pricing mechanisms and rating on *Sukuk* as essential elements that have a significant impact on *Sukuk*. Their study found that the selected influencing factors need prompt solutions for the sustainability and development of the *Sukuk* market and the *Sukuk* structure. This requires close cooperation among *Shariah* scholars and financial experts. Also, an empirical study undertaken by Aloui et al. (2015) argued that the linkages between the *Shariah* stocks and *Sukuk* GCC markets are regime-dependent, and the *Shariah* stock market volatility reacts asymmetrically to events in the *Sukuk* market. Additionally, this study provided evidence for the assertion that changes in the GCC *Sukuk* price index have a significant impact on the probability of transmission across regimes. More specifically, in the Malaysian context, Ahmed et al. (2015) found that the pricing had a statistically significant and positive effect on the legitimacy of *Sukuk* in Malaysia, because there is an influence from pricing on the structure and legitimacy that is applied by the IFIs. Based on this literature, the following hypothesis has been developed:

*H1:* *There is a positive relationship between the pricing and the legitimacy of Sukuk.*

## The Relationship between *Sukuk* Legitimacy and the Type of Structure

In general, in accordance with the IFSB guidelines No. 2, 2005, the structure of *Sukuk* can be classified into two differing categories: asset-based instruments; and equity-based instruments. The category of *Sukuk* structure is considered a significant factor impacting positively on the *Sukuk* (Godlewski et al. 2014). In accordance with the findings of Usmani, 85 percent of the outstanding *Sukuk* had failed a test for *Shariah*-compliance. The *Shariah*-compliance failure was attributed to the fact that the *Sukuk* were not asset-backed; they were asset-based. Therefore, these asset-based *Sukuk* did not have a guaranteed return of the *Sukuk* face value at maturity without a transfer of ownership of the asset to the holders of the *Sukuk* (MARC 2010). Following on from the financial crises in relation to subprime mortgages, this led to *Sukuk* default, to a rise in the level of ownership in the underlying asset, and for the requirement to categorize and rate asset-based and asset-backed *Sukuk* (Hidayat 2013).

The rating agencies delineate and treat asset-backed and asset-based *Sukuk* differently, further to a rating methodology for an asset-backed security's chosen application for *Sukuk* transactions (Haneef 2009). In a similar way to the conventional market bond benchmark, *Sukuk* do have exposure to credit risk. In relation to credit risk, this can arise further to the point of failure of the *Sukuk* holder to fully meet their obligations of the agreed terms in a timely manner. A credit risk also refers to the probability of a loan or an asset becoming impossible to regain due to a delay in settlement or a default (Tariq & Dar 2007).

In examining the literature, previous studies have determined that the types of *Sukuk* structures differ significantly between the asset-backed and asset-based *Sukuk*, both from a *Shariah* and a market standpoint, with the ability to influence the level of positivity of the legitimacy of the *Sukuk* (Haneef 2009, Howladar 2009, Khnifer 2010a, Hidayat 2013, Alia et al. 2013, Shabana 2013, Abdulmalik 2013, Azmat et al. 2014a). In that regard, an enhancement of the legitimacy of *Sukuk* will have an added impact.

In addition, Howladar (2009) determined that the framework for an asset-based *Sukuk* appears only to satisfy the pattern of an agreement with a great deal of sophistication, which eventually points to an Islamic equivalent of an unsafe traditional bond. In the same vein, Haneef (2009) mentioned that asset-backed *Sukuk* are more efficient when offered in comparison to asset-based ones. Khnifer (2010b) examined three *Sukuk* issuances: the asset-based *Tamweel Sukuk* Limited (TSL); the asset-backed *Tamweel* residential mortgage backed securitization (RMBS); and the asset-backed issuance of East Cameron Gas (ECG), which had defaulted. The findings indicated that asset-backed *Sukuk* have more risk and may lead to default. Hidayat (2013) examined the structures of the asset-based and asset-backed *Sukuk* from the *Shariah* perspective. It found that the asset-backed *Sukuk* structure is more compliant to *Shariah*, both in form and substance, than the asset-based structure. In the same vein, Alia, et al. (2013) examined the performance between the *Shariah* residential mortgage-backed securities, and the conventional securities issued by Cagamas, with the equal issuance year, rating grades, and maturity period. This study found that *Shariah* mortgage-backed securities did indeed perform better than its conventional mortgage-backed securities, with a much better rate of investment return to the investors. Shabana (2013) examined both asset-backed and asset-based *Sukuk* operations. The findings outlined the differences between the asset-backed and asset-based *Sukuk*; especially on the issue of true ownership. Abdulmalik (2013) explained the consequences of default in each case of asset-based and asset-backed *Sukuk* by analyzing these differences, from both a *Shariah* and a market standpoint. The study revealed the position that an asset-backed *Sukuk* is more in line with the principles of *Shariah*, and provides more protection to the *Sukuk* holders in case of default. Azmat et al. (2014a) examined the factors affecting an issuer's choice of *Sukuk* structure in comparison to the conventional financial instruments. The study found there are some significant differences concerning the issuer's choice determinants between the Islamic and the conventional bonds, which can be attributed to the specific characteristics of *Sukuk*. More recently, a study undertaken by Ahmed et al. (2015) examined the effects of the rating (type of structure) on the legitimacy of *Sukuk* in Malaysia, as the type of structure is an important element impacting upon the *Sukuk*. Importantly, the study found that asset-backed *Sukuk* have a greater impact on the enhancement of *Sukuk* legitimacy and have shown to comply more with the rules of *Shariah* to increase the legitimacy of *Sukuk* in comparison to asset-based *Sukuk*. Accordingly, the study makes the following hypothesis:

*H2:* *There is a positive relationship between the type of structure and the Sukuk legitimacy.*

## The Relationship between *Shariah* Auditing and *Sukuk* Legitimacy

*Shariah* auditing is one of the essential and unique components of both Board dynamics and overall quality of corporate governance mechanisms, overseeing an IFI's business conduct to ensure that all transactions are extremely compatible with the conditions and terms of the principles of *Shariah* (Rahman 2008, Casper 2012). Therefore, *Shariah* auditing has to be considered a significant factor in the emerging Islamic financial sector. There is a consensus from the previous studies in the literature that illustrate and admit that the effectiveness of *Shariah* auditing can be achieved based on the experts' (*fiqh al-muamalat*) level of expertise, and their knowledge of Islamic laws for transactions (Malik 2010, Lahsasna 2010, Kaseb 2010, ISRA 2013, Ahmed et al. 2013, Nabil 2013). Diversities of viewpoint have been outlined in the findings of the previous studies concerning the effectiveness of *Shariah* supervision. Some studies have determined that *Shariah* supervision ought to be undertaken systematically, as part of the corporate governance mechanism of the IFIs, in order to complement the *Shariah* compliance mechanisms (Rahman 2008). On the other hand, from another perspective, the previous studies demonstrate that the provision of continuous *Shariah* supervision and perpetual due diligence of transactions, and procedures can lead to a better and particular outcome than routine audits alone. Such a viewpoint proposed that a large board of auditing is more effective than a small-sized *Shariah* Board, and for an increased level of supervision of *Shariah*-compliance a larger *Shariah* Board size ought to be considered (Yean 2009, Casper 2012). In contrast, other studies (Kasim et al. 2009, ISRA 2013) argued that the *Shariah* auditing function has not seriously made an impact in IFIs in Malaysia, despite its potential as a monitoring tool for *Shariah* compliance. A study undertaken by Kaseb

(2010) found that to improve the current level of *Shariah* auditing, a more clear and comprehensive *Sukuk* guidance is required, to facilitate and strengthen *Sukuk* issuance in a concrete way. In support of this claim, one empirical study found that there is positive relationship between *Shariah* auditing and the legitimacy of *Sukuk (*Ahmed et al. 2015). Based on these findings, the following hypothesis has been developed:

*H3:* *There is a positive relationship between the levels of Shariah auditing and Sukuk legitimacy.*

## The Relationship between *Shariah* Risks and *Sukuk* Legitimacy

A *Shariah* risk is one of the unique operational risks of the IFIs affecting the *Shariah*-compliance of products (Ginena 2014). A *Shariah* risk is a crucial issue impacting on the legitimacy (compliance) of *Sukuk*, and may influence adversely the audaciousness of investors to support the instrument and can ultimately impact upon *Sukuk* pricing (Jadwa 2009). Unfavorable risks affect the competitiveness of the pricing of *Sukuk* assets (Tariq 2004, Ahmed 2011b). *Shariah* risks, if not managed appropriately, may reduce the confidence of stakeholders such as customers, shareholders, depositors and employees, who realize that the institution is not living up to its commitments (IDB & IFSB 2007). *Shariah* risks can also negatively affect the market discipline (De Lorenzo & McMillen 2007).

The previous studies revealed that reducing the *Shariah* risks for *Sukuk* is an important element, whereby increasing *Shariah* compliance structure through the promotion of the role of *Shariah* advisors ought to enhance *Sukuk* legitimacy (Nanaeva 2010, Shafii et al. 2010, Casper 2012, Lahsasna 2014, Ahmed et al. 2014, Ginena 2014, Mizushima & Mizushima 2014, Abdullah et al. 2014).

Shafii et al. (2010) found that an increase in the level of *Shariah* auditing leads to a reduction of *Shariah*-compliance risks in IFIs. Therefore, it follows that *Shariah* risks facing IFIs can be mitigated through *Shariah*-compliant auditing. This is also evidence that an increase in the level of *Shariah* risk will lead to a reduction in *Shariah* compliance. Nanaeva (2010) conducted an empirical analysis of *Sukuk* risks and problems, and their competitiveness in the capital market, in order to present potential *Sukuk* investors with a detailed breakdown. The study found that an average value-at-risk of *Sukuk* at 99 percent confidence level is higher than the value-at-risk of conventional bonds. However, Navaeva also found that most *Sukuk* investors hold onto the Islamic securities until their date of maturity, and do not take into consideration the market risks. This analysis ought to act as a warning for *Sukuk* issuers. Accordingly, for *Sukuk* with higher levels of risk there ought to be an incentive to control and monitor the *Sukuk*, and this function will act to enhance their legitimacy. Other researchers (Tariq 2004, Tariq & Dar 2007) found that derivatives are inherently against *Shariah* considerations because of the uncertainty associated with them, which amounts to *gharar*. Therefore, there is a possibility of extending the functions of embedded options to fit the needs of *Sukuk* certificates and *Shariah* considerations. Zakaria et al. (2012) argued that the implication of the risk of *Sukuk* defaults and their rating is a negative migration of the credit rating assessment, and would indicate default risk. Therefore, the default risks of *Sukuk* need to undergo a credit rating assessment of their future payment prospects. That then means, when *Sukuk* have a higher rate of risk, a lowered level of effectiveness is inferred, whether on the structure, or rating, of *Sukuk*. Moreover, Casper (2012) and Lahsasna (2014) determined that an increase in the level of *Shariah* non-compliance risks in Islamic financial operations will adversely affect the credibility of the banks involved. These studies mentioned that the IFIs ought to mitigate the level of risk of *Shariah* non-compliance, otherwise *Shariah* risks will have a negative impact on the *Shariah* compliance of products. Rauf and Ibrahim (2014) empirically investigated the determinants of return and risk performance in the GCC *Sukuk* market structure, and the authors revealed there is variance to the *Sukuk* index due to the maturity risk, and the *Shariah*-compliance risk. El Shazly and Tripathy (2013) examined the forms of risk components in Islamic financial tools, with a focus on *Ijara Sukuk*. It was noted that the risks still needed to be studied for accuracy, and for the improvement of *Shariah* compliance of financial instruments. Ginena (2014) and Abdullah et al. (2014) argued that the absence of disclosure and transparency in Islamic banks can lead to *Shariah* non-compliance, and the unintended consequences of higher costs, financial losses, liquidity problems, bank runs, industry smearing, and financial instability, which could ultimately lead to a bank's failure. Thus, *Shariah* risks are considered to be a significant factor affecting the legitimacy of *Sukuk*. Mizushima and Mizushima (2014) examined the *Shariah* compliance risk of *Sukuk* by examining two cases: *Bai Bithaman Ajil* (*BBA*); and *Murabahah Sukuk* in Malaysia. The findings indicated that *BBA* were not accepted elsewhere, due to the increased exposure of *Shariah* risks causing disagreement amongst *Shariah* scholars, leading to a decline in demand. The study indicated there is a negative relationship between the level of *Shariah* risk and *Shariah* compliance, thus, more risks will lead to a reduction in the level of legitimacy. Ahmed et al. (2015) examined the relationship between *Shariah* compliance risks in *Sukuk* in the Malaysian context. The result confirmed that *Shariah* risks have a significant and negative effect on the legitimacy of *Sukuk*. The current study predicts that reducing the level of *Shariah* risks will lead to increasing the level of legitimacy of an Islamic *Sukuk*. In order to reduce the level of risk, close cooperation is required among the senior-level of management, financial experts, and *Shariah* scholars on one hand, and more interaction among *Shariah* Boards on the other. Thus, the study hypothesizes that:

*H4:* *There is a negative relationship between the level of Shariah risks and the Sukuk legitimacy.*

## The Relationship between *Shariah* Documentation and *Sukuk* Legitimacy

The literature in relation to *Sukuk* puts forward a proposition that IFIs, through the promotion of the effectiveness of the legitimacy of *Sukuk,* might help alleviate the *Shariah* non-compliance problems by monitoring and controlling *Sukuk* structures, in order for a variety of *Shariah* documentation to meet all the requirements of *Sukuk* (Kaseb 2010, Ali 2011, Khnifer 2010b, Van Wijnbergen & Zaheer 2013, Ahmed et al. 2013, Lahsasna 2014).

Accordingly, there ought to be compliance with *Shariah* principles, and its concepts for the issue of *Sukuk*, as recommended by the *Shariah* Advisory Council (SAC) (BNM 2007). Additionally, an endorsement should be given that all conditions related to *Sukuk* issuance are in compliance with the principles of *Shariah*. However, any matters not found to be consistent with the concepts and principles should be noted, and not receive endorsement by the SAC (ISRA 2013). A thorough examination of the documentation should be made to ensure their compatibility and compliance with *Shariah* principles (ISRA 2013). Thus, any mistake, or even negligence, might lead to difficulties in issuing the *Sukuk*, due to the incompatibility with such compliance. Therefore, through the mechanism of the SAC, compatible *Shariah* matters can be determined to ensure legitimacy of the documentation of the *Sukuk* issue. Haniffa and Hudaib (2007) and Maali et al. (2006) claimed that IFIs can make use of improved levels of disclosure in the *Shariah* Board reports, and this disclosure is an important Islamic financial tool. It is through an increased level of disclosure of *Shariah* documentation in these reports that important elements emerge; a decrease in the level of problems of non-compliance with *Shariah*, and an enhancement in legitimacy of Islamic financial instruments (Haniffa & Hudaib 2007, Maali et al. 2006, Ahmed et al. 2013, Lahsasna 2014).

Kaseb (2010) examined the relationship between *Shariah* guidelines and the practices in the Malaysian *Sukuk* market. The result found there should be the regulation of effective legal documentation on the products in the Islamic capital market. He also noted the regulators ought to review and improve the current guidelines, and facilitate and strengthen *Sukuk* issuance in a concrete manner. This finding indicates that effective legal documentation has a positive effect on *Sukuk* issuance. Lahsasna and Idris (2008) argued that the implications of the AAOIFI pronouncement on the *Shariah* compliance issues of *Sukuk* structuring have an impact, and, therefore, there are implications for future issues. They also noted that the SSBs have a role in the documentation and implementation of *Sukuk.* Ali (2011) examined the *Sukuk* market by referencing the structures and documentation. The findings indicated that the *Shariah* documentation is the key document for *Sukuk* investors, because it discloses all material information that an investor needs to inform their decision as to whether to invest in *Sukuk* or not. Thus, the *Shariah* documentation is considered to form the core of *Shariah*-compliant products, and having this core of information increases the clarity of compliance of *Shariah* documentation, and, therefore, its legitimacy. Van Wijnbergen and Zaheer (2013) examined the recent major defaults in relation to *Sukuk* in the aftermath of the worldwide credit crisis that engulfed the world in 2007. They argued that all the documentation concerning *Sukuk* issuance (*Musharakah* and *Ijarah*) were without any inconsistencies or loopholes which could deprive the *Sukuk* investors of the rights promised. Ahmed et al. (2015) examined the relationship between *Shariah* documentation and *Sukuk* in the IFIs. Their study indicated that there is a good relationship between the *Shariah* documentation and *Sukuk* legitimacy, as evidenced by the positive value in the results. Therefore, improved levels of disclosure of *Shariah* documentation in the *Shariah* Board reports of Islamic *Sukuk* are very useful for IFIs. Therefore, the present study predicts that increasing the level of disclosure of *Shariah* documentation will be associated with increased levels of *Sukuk* legitimacy. Accordingly, the study hypothesizes that:

*H5:* *There is a positive relationship between Shariah documentation and Sukuk legitimacy.*

## The Effect of the *Shariah* Supervisory Board as a Moderator in the Relationship between the Determinants and *Sukuk* Legitimacy

The role of the *Shariah* Supervisory Board (SSB) as a moderating variable on the relationship between the determinants and *Sukuk* legitimacy could be used to enhance and strengthen the role of the SSB towards *Sukuk* legitimacy. Furthermore, the SSB has been selected as a moderating variable by the current study, due to its positive impact, as assured by several studies in the literature. For example, Yean 2009, Laldin 2008, Lahsasna 2010, Rahail 2011, Usmani 2008, and Kantakji 2012, demonstrated that the SSB is an important governing body that significantly impacts upon the determinants of legitimacy. Furthermore, a study undertaken by Ahmed et al. (2013) showed that the SSB plays an important role in relation to *Shariah* auditing for Islamic financial instruments. Moreover, to assure that the SSB is sound to be utilized as a moderating variable, a set of interview questions were crafted, and interviews undertaken by the current study, which confirmed the validity of the SSB as a moderating variable. This concept will be explained further in Chapter Five.

Empirical evidence in corporate governance suggests that Board size can affect controlling, monitoring, and the level of disclosure (Akhtaruddin, Hossain & Yao 2009, Chaganti, Mahajan, & Sharma 1985). Whilst there is no restriction on the number of SSB members and committees, the perfect number should be between three and seven members. The common number of SSB members in an IFI is three members, which is in line with the SC and AAOIFI standards. Increasing the number of members appointed to an SSB would provide more effective monitoring and more consistency with the rules and principles of *Shariah*. According to Chen and Jaggi (2000), a larger size of Board may decrease the possibility of information asymmetry. In addition, a higher number of members appointed to the Board may also reduce uncertainty, and may alleviate the problem of a lack of information (Birnbaum 1984).

Drawing insights from institutional theory, conformance due to regulatory pressures, such as the SC guidelines, demonstrates a coercive isomorphism. According to institutional theory, there are three forms of drivers that create isomorphism in organizational strategies, structures and processes - which are coercive, normative, and mimetic (DiMaggio and Powell 1983). Coercive occurs from influences exerted by those in powerful positions, while normative drivers ensure that organizations conform in order to be perceived as partaking in legitimate actions (Sarkis, Zhu & Lai 2011).

Institutional theory proves that the regulatory pressures are needed on the *Shariah* Boards to control and monitor the operations of IFIs, due to the possibility of non-*Shariah* compliant risks (Aziah Abu Kasim 2012, Ahmed et al. 2014). Legitimacy disclosure on *Sukuk* in IFIs seems to develop in much the same manner as other disclosure practices, that is, a tendency to comply with rules rather than with principles. IFIs are complying to meet minimum regulation requirements in fear of having their eligibility to offer *Sukuk* disapproved by SC. Since there is high legitimacy in *Sukuk* moderated by the SSB, *Sukuk* operators are also seen as inclined to conform towards adherence to the norms, which is attributed as normative isomorphism under institutional theory. Therefore, with the SSB playing the role of the governing body which moderates the *Sukuk* compliance to *Shariah*, institutional theory asserts that, due to the coercive nature, and the tendency to compete and comply, IFI's would be managing *Sukuk* operations in a *Shariah*-compliant manner. Consequently, all the *Shariah* pronouncements, and guidelines to professional bodies, would consist of identical content (declaration requirements) which is ultimately transparent and *Shariah*-compliant.

On the other hand, institutional theory is also in line with the concept of covenant in Islam which is known as *Al-Mithaq*. *Al-Mithaq* is deemed as a formal alliance or agreement made by God with humanity in general. It is a promise that mankind has with God, that implies adhering to, and fulfilling, what this bond entails. The concept of epistemology is not merely theoretical to Muslims, but influences the thought and behavior in individuals and the society at large. Therefore, all practicing Muslims and scholars regard Islamic epistemology based on the *Qu'ran, Hadith*, and Islam, of great importance. According to Al-Attas (1979) "The function of knowledge in Islam is to know God so that humankind may serve and worship Him". The essence of being a Muslim is encompassing the spiritual, moral, and conceptual, development is brought about by Islamic epistemology during the period of the Prophet (PBUH). In upholding the *mithaq*, the basic meaning of this word is to incline away from falsehood, towards that which is true. The relationship between God and believers is conceived in terms of a covenant, which establishes certain rights and obligations. The core of this agreement is that God binds mankind to serve God, to the exclusion of any other being [1:5, 24:55, 51:56], and in return, gives the promise of material and spiritual success. In the *Qu'ran*, chapter 13, verse 22 Allah says, "And those who are patient seeking the consideration of their Lord; and they uphold the *salat* (worship), and they spend from what We have bestowed upon them secretly and openly, and they counter evil with good; these will have an excellent abode". This *mithaq* brings about an indebtedness theory. The indebtedness theory is extremely fundamental, to illustrate the reasons why believers dutifully observe Islamic rules in business conduct and financial operations (Rosly 2007).

And [mention] when your Lord took from the children of Adam - from their loins - their descendants and made them testify of themselves [saying to them], "Am I not your Lord?" They said, "Yes, we have testified". [This] - Lest you should say on the day of Resurrection, "Indeed, we were of this unaware" (Surat Al-Araf, 172).

All of a believer's actions are predominantly and solely meant for Allah's sake, and such obedience is shown by avoiding His prohibitions and complying with His commands. This is, as far as Islamic rules are concerned, the meaning of human existence in its relationship of indebtedness to Allah the Creator. The indebtedness theory admits that all creations have to submit to Allah, and complying with *Shariah* rules in the aspect of economy is no exception to this rule. Thus, in any daily dealings, a believer must ensure compliance with *Shariah*. Similarly, in *Sukuk* management, the SSB, being the governing body, needs to demonstrate the requirement of compliance as a factor to certify the nature of *Sukuk* to be deemed as *Shariah* compliant. Thus, the SSBs ought to be involved in the structure of the transactions, including providing guidance in the drafting, reviewing, and approval of the documentation for compliance of *Shariah*. This moderator role, much like the coercive isomorphism in institutional theory, would ensure that all transactions and documentation comply with the requirements, therefore enabling a desired outcome of consistency, certainty and transparency, in the process of *Sukuk* management. The need to certify and market *Sukuk* as *Shariah* compliant may be used as a tool to pressure the SSB in following higher *Shariah* compliant levels, and consequently, enhance *Sukuk* legitimacy. The *Shariah*-compliant view asserts that controlling some characteristics and determinants, which are strategic and capable, leads to a competitive advantage and superior performance of the IFIs. Following normative isomorphism, the rest of the IFIs and professional bodies are expected to follow the norm, by being and offering a fully *Shariah*-compliant *Sukuk*.

The Board and committee size is likely to affect its ability to control and review all the transactions of the IFIs to ensure their operations are in compliance with *Shariah* rules and principles (Rahman & Bukair 2013). In addition, the ability of members of the SSB to monitor the institution's activities impacting on the well-being of the members of society is much higher, with more members appointed to the Board (Akhtaruddin et al. 2009, Chaganti et al. 1985). With more members, the collective knowledge and experience of the SSB is increased, which, consequently, leads to greater legitimacy of *Sukuk*.

In summary, the SSB is the instrument of pressure that is predicted by the present study to have a positive impact on legitimacy and performance of *Sukuk*, because the *Shariah* Board is the only entity in the IFIs that has the right to endorse the independent certificate of *Shariah* compliance on the *Sukuk* structure. The philosophy and interpretation behind choosing the SSB as a moderating variable in the relationship between the determinants and the legitimacy of *Sukuk* is that the *Shariah* committee has the right to make decisions about compliance or non-compliance of business activities in the IFIs. In examining a committee of directors, the committee has no choice other than to obey the decisions made by the SSB concerning legitimacy of transactions and operations. Thus, any decision made by the SSB is an instrument of pressure on the Board of directors to align the interests to that of the *Shariah* committee with the *Sukuk* holders, and this action will consequently enhance the level of *Sukuk* performance. The current study uses two variables as moderators: the number of SSB members (SSBM), and the number of SSB committees (SSBC). These two variables have an impact on the relationship between the determinants and *Sukuk* legitimacy. From the discussion above, the following ten hypotheses have been formulated:

*H6:* *The effect of pricing on Sukuk legitimacy is strong when the collective knowledge and decision-making of the Shariah Supervisory Board Members (SSBM) is stronger.*

*H7:* *The effect of pricing on Sukuk legitimacy is strong when the collective knowledge and decision-making of the Shariah Supervisory Board Committee (SSBC) is stronger.*

*H8:* *The effect of type of structure on Sukuk legitimacy is strong when the collective knowledge and decision-making of the Shariah Supervisory Board (SSBM) is stronger.*

*H9:* *The effect of type of structure on Sukuk legitimacy is strong when the collective knowledge and decision-making of the Shariah Supervisory Board Committee (SSBC) is stronger.*

*H10:* *The effect of Shariah auditing on Sukuk legitimacy is strong when the collective knowledge and decision-making of the Shariah Supervisory Board Members (SSBM) is stronger.*

*H11:* *The effect of Shariah auditing on Sukuk legitimacy is strong when the collective knowledge and decision-making of the Shariah Supervisory Board Committee (SSBC) is stronger.*

*H12:* *The effect of Shariah compliance risk on Sukuk legitimacy is strong when the collective knowledge and decision-making of the Shariah Supervisory Board Members (SSBM) is stronger.*

*H13:* *The effect of Shariah Compliance Risk on Sukuk Legitimacy is strong when the collective knowledge and decision-making of the Shariah Supervisory Board (SSBC) is stronger.*

*H14:* *The effect of Shariah documentation on Sukuk legitimacy is strong when the collective knowledge and decision-making of the Shariah Supervisory Board Members (SSBM) is stronger.*

*H15:* *The effect of Shariah compliance risk on Sukuk legitimacy is strong when the collective knowledge and decision-making of the Shariah Supervisory Board (SSBC) is stronger.*

## Research Methodology

As mentioned in the earlier chapters, the current study aims to examine the influence of the chosen determinants (pricing, type of structure, *Shariah* risk, *Shariah* auditing and *Shariah* documentation) on the legitimacy of *Sukuk*. Furthermore, different data collection methods are discussed, focusing on the reasons for choosing particular methods. The discussion on choosing these methods is followed by the discussion of the method utilized for collecting data, as well as the different approaches employed to analyze the information. In this chapter, the research methodology is presented. Data was obtained from primary and secondary sources.

The main issues discussed in the following sections are the research design, variables, interview question development process, the sampling design, the data collection procedure, the statistical methods and the analysis of the data.

Finally, a brief discussion on the reliability and validity of the instruments is presented. For many years, most research procedures have been based on a quantitative approach in conducting and obtaining scientific understanding. A quantitative non-experimental research approach is based on the collection and analysis of numerical data, which is usually obtained from questionnaires, real data, tests, checklists, and other formal paper-and-pencil instructions

(Gay & Airasian 2003). A quantitative research approach entails more than just using numerical data; it also involves stating both the hypotheses to be examined and the research procedures to be implemented in the study.

## Research Design

Mixed method studies are those that combine the quantitative and qualitative research techniques, methods, approaches, and concepts, into a single study (Brewer & Hunter 1989, Patton 1990, Tashakkori & Teddlie 1998, Onwuegbuzie & Johnson 2004, Lin & Loftis 2005, Driscoll, Appiah-Yeboah, Salib & Rupert 2007, Creswell & Garrett 2008). Howe (1988) conjectured the use of different paradigms, i.e. pragmatism in which the major tenet of this concept is that quantitative and qualitative approaches are compatible, and thus, researchers could use both approaches in their researches. This method gathers up the strengths and weaknesses from both approaches into a single study in order to help the researchers to better answer a research question (Brewer & Hunter 1989, Creswell, PlanoClark, Gutmann & Hanson 2003, Johnson & Onwuegbuzie 2004, Creswell & Garrett 2008) and expand one's understanding of the method they undertook (Watson 1990, Onwuegbuzie & Leech 2004, Lin & Loftis 2005).

Since the research world is becoming increasingly more interdisciplinary, dynamic and complex, the evolution of mixed method studies is widely received, and becoming more commonplace in the social and behavioral sciences. Scholars from various disciplines (e.g. Brewer & Hunter 1989) have emphasized the use of a more integrated methodological approach, focusing on the need for the researcher to combine methods in their studies. This is because mixed method studies enable researchers to develop a conceptual framework (Onwuegbuzie & Leech 2004) by validating quantitative results by means of linking information extracted from the qualitative phase of the study, and vice versa (Madey 1982). Other advantages of mixed method studies include that it:

1. enables researchers to be more flexible and holistic in their investigative techniques (Onwuegbuzie & Leech 2004);
2. helps to improve communications among researchers from different paradigms as they attempt to advance knowledge (Watson 1990, Maxcy 2003), and thus, provide a more workable situation, as they can put together insights and procedures from both approaches to produce a superior product (Johnson & Onwuegbuzie 2004);
3. helps to bridge the schism between quantitative and qualitative research (Onwuegbuzie & Leech 2004);

4. allows the researcher to mix and match designs that best offer the chance of answering their specific research questions (Johnson & Onwuegbuzie 2004).

Mixed method research is defined as research in which the investigator collects and analyses data, integrates the findings, and draws inferences using both approaches (qualitative and quantitative) in a single study (Tashakkori & Creswell 2007). Table 4.1 below shows the strengths and weaknesses of all three competing methods, which indicates why the approach of the mixed method research is applied here, given that it offers strengths that make up for the weakness by solely applying the qualitative or quantitative method.

**Table 1: Strengths and Weaknesses of Common Research Methods**

| Issue | Qualitative | Quantitative | Mixed Method |
|---|---|---|---|
| Understanding the context | √ | X | √ |
| Directly hearing voice of participants | √ | X | √ |
| Generalizing the findings | X | √ | √ |
| The results are more easily influenced by the researcher's personal biases. | X | √ | √ |

√: Strengths X: Weakness

## Population and Sampling for a Quantitative Study

A population is the total number of cases that conform to some designated specifications; which could be people, events, or things of interest to the researcher (Sekaran 2003, Churchill 1987). In this study, the target population is defined as the Islamic *Sukuk* issued by the Islamic Financial Institutions (IFIs) in Malaysia.

Sampling is defined as the process of obtaining information from a subset (a sample) of a larger group (the universe or population) (McDaniel & Gates 2001). In addition, Lynn (2012), and McDaniel and Gates (2001), defined a population as the totality of units or people about whom the researcher needs to obtain information. A population is a complete group of people that constitute a community, a society, an organization, or anything that may have some common criteria. Sampling allows the researcher to identify some vague characteristics concerning the population. When the target population holds the same characteristics, only a small sample is required to conduct a study. However, collecting data, or testing every element, is sometimes impossible in terms of time, cost, and other factors, including a lack of human resources (Sekaran 2003). Alternatively, data collection can be successful by limiting the study of the population to sampling some of its members. Subsequently, certain generalizations can be completed based on the whole population.

A significant consideration in the sample design is the choice of the sample size. Larger samples provide greater accuracy, but require greater costs. A common approach in choosing the sample size is to specify the desired precision. Then, the optimal sample size that allows for the level of accuracy required can be determined. Random sampling is based on a given population, and is obtained using a probability formula. The use of this technique is to select subjects that could enable the researcher to obtain complete suitable generalizations from a sample of any given population. Finally, the researcher must be careful to avoid generalization of the results that may assume a broad view to other groups of individuals.

The population of this study is *Sukuk* issuance under the Exempt Regime in Bursa Malaysia. SC and BNM have been listed as *Sukuk* on the Bursa Malaysia list under the exempt regime in accordance with section 229 (1) and section 230 (1) of the Capital Markets and Services Act 2007 (CMSA). In order to enhance the level of transparency for investors, offers providing valuable profiling opportunities for issuers of the instruments are of significance. The population size in this study consists of 82 *Sukuk* approved by the SC and registered in the Bursa Malaysia, and this represents a full sample for eleven consecutive years for the period from 2005 to 2015 (see Appendix A). This period was chosen as the first available *Sukuk* data under the exempt regime in Bursa Malaysia in 2005. Therefore, the entire population was able to be studied without having to take smaller samples for the analysis. According to Sekaran (2003) successful research is possible with samples as small as 10 to 20 in size. Given the small population frame of the study, census population techniques were employed to select the sample (Cooper, Schindler & Sun 1998). According to Cohen (1988), if there are five independent variables in the study, and the sample size is only 20, the $R^2$ value has to be 48 percent and above to be significant (at .05), and if it is lower, it will not be significant.

The primary source of the sample *Sukuk* is from the required Bursa Malaysia *Sukuk* reports and requirements (announcements, offering memorandum, principal terms and conditions, *Shariah* pronouncement, and rating reports) for internal and external users. Furthermore, this research endeavour comprised the 82 listed *Sukuk* reports under the exempt regime in Bursa Malaysia. Thus, the types of information available in relation to *Sukuk* legitimacy ought to be relatively consistent in nature.

## Sampling in the Qualitative Study

This study uses a purposive sampling technique to select the respondents for a study which utilized a qualitative analysis (Teddlie & Tashakkori 2009). This technique is applied by selecting the members of *Shariah* Supervisory Boards (SSBs) in the IFIs. The total selected sample size for the qualitative study was seven members, and these respondents were selected due to their level of experience and basic knowledge of *Fiqh Al-Mua'malat*, along with its application in Islamic banking.

## Research Instruments

In this study, the data was collected from secondary data (the *Sukuk* reports) and from primary data (the interview protocol). The *Sukuk* reports and requirements (announcements, offering memorandum, principal terms and conditions, *Shariah* pronouncement and rating reports) were adopted as units of analysis for this study, and these elements were used for testing the level of disclosure of *Sukuk* legitimacy (Ahmed et al. 2014). In relation to this study's interview, the interview questions were formulated by the researcher and forwarded to experts for validation. Furthermore, the adaptation of the items in the instrument was guided by the theoretical framework of the study, and the instrument solicited for information was related to the influence of the determinants on *Sukuk* legitimacy.

### Instruments for the Quantitative Study

The quantitative method employed in this research involved an inquiry into an identifiable problem with the aim of producing statistical data. Once obtained, the data can then be analyzed using statistical techniques. The aim is to use a set of population parameters to formally test the theory and the study's hypotheses. Babbie (1995) defined the method used in this research as the quantitative method, whereby the numerical representation and manipulation of observations are undertaken for the purposes of describing and explaining the phenomena that those observations reflect. Many studies have used an increasing number of individuals drawn from the population and selected in a controlled procedure. As such, quantitative methods provide a base upon which to produce formal inferences concerning populations. By contrast, qualitative methods often provide important insight into the factors underlying quantitative findings.

The research is designed in such a way that the research problem is identified at the outset. The statement of the main problem is followed by the research questions, the objectives of the study and the hypotheses. The methods of collecting data, which include a secondary data method, are also explained. The *Sukuk* reports have been used for testing the level of disclosure with regards to *Sukuk* legitimacy. The researcher considers that the *Sukuk* reports are a communication tool together with the surroundings (Ahmed et al. 2014). The reason for selecting the *Sukuk* reports to analyze the legitimacy of *Sukuk* is due to their availability. In other words, *Sukuk* reports form a method for gaining a better insight into social relationships.

## Instrument for Qualitative Study

A qualitative study is a process of inquiry with the goal of understanding a social phenomenon or a human problem from multiple perspectives, where it may also be called a multi-angular process. The quantitative and qualitative methodologies share things in common, particularly when examining some of the phenomena. Both approaches deal with data, which normally break the flow of events in the social world, and selectively focus on such issues like attitudes, utterances, actions, functions, or behaviors, of individual respondents. Additionally, "at the same time, the two approaches bring distinctive qualities to the research process" (Cupchik 2001). The constructivist perspective suggested several things which can advance the abstract approach to qualitative data collection (Onwuegbuzie & Johnson 2006). Since the process is ultimately interpretive, one only requires it for coherence in the analysis, and that ought to be enough to justify the authenticity of the basis of the qualitative setting in any research study (Creswell & Garrett 2008). For this study, the second instrument is in-depth interview sessions conducted with seven members of *Shariah* Supervisory Boards (SSBs). This process is a purposeful interaction, in which one person obtains data from the respondents based on the literature reviews and the advice from experts. It is through interviews that researchers are able to obtain important data they cannot acquire from the questionnaire alone (Gay & Airasian 2003).

Qualitative interviews have been described as purposeful conversations or active interactions between two or more people that result in co-constructed contextually-based results (Denzin & Lincoln 2003). Merriam (2001) mentioned that the use of interviews as a data collection method is ideal when analyzing behavior, feelings, or how people interpret the world around them, when it cannot be readily observed. The interview method is also useful when there is interest in past events that are impossible to replicate. Furthermore, interviews can be described as structured, semi-structured, or unstructured. Structured interviews usually contain carefully worded questions administered to participants, verbatim, in a predetermined order. These interviews are often used with survey instruments or when data is required from numerous researchers (Fisher & Stenner 2011).

A semi-structured or guided interview is used to extract data from all the respondents. Merriam (2001) stated that these interviews are guided by a list of questions or issues to be explored, but neither the exact wording nor the order of the questions is determined ahead of time. This format allows the researcher to respond to the situation at hand, grasp the emerging worldview of the respondents and gain new ideas on the topic. Moreover, this format also allows further probing due to the fact that participant responses are directed (Lindlof & Taylor, 2002).

A semi-structured interview technique is the most flexible of the interview techniques. Hitchcock and Hughes (1995) stated that this type of interview enables the researcher to probe and expand the answers of the interviewee by altering the sequences to overcome a common tendency for interviewees to anticipate questions. This format is flexible, and enables the researcher to test the limits of the respondents' knowledge (Cohen, Manion & Morrison 2000). The aim of using the interview method in the current study is to investigate whether the variables of pricing, rating, *Shariah* auditing, *Shariah* compliance risk, and *Shariah* documentation, can improve the level of legitimacy for *Sukuk*. The interview questions comprised seven semi-structured interview questions directed to 10 members of the SSB. Important questions were asked when deemed necessary during the session. Interview questions are provided in the Appendix B4.

## Data Collection Methods

This study's data comprises quantitative and qualitative data, which will be collected through the procedures discussed in the following subsections.

## Data Collection for the Quantitative Study

There are two types of data that might be collected by any business or management-related research; namely secondary data and primary data. The secondary data collection approach makes use of all sources that are available to a researcher to obtain the necessary information to analyze a research problem. Using the typology coined by Saunders, Lewis and Thornhill (2007), secondary data can be categorized as documented data, which includes written (e.g., journals, books, and reports) and non-written (e.g., television programs and CD-ROMs) data.

Data collection methods are an integral part of the research design. Data can be collected in several ways, in different settings, or from different sources (Sekaran & Bougie 2010). For this study, the researcher used the primary and secondary sources to complete this study, and to solve the problem in order to meet the study's objectives. In comparison, secondary sources are represented by information gathered from sources that already exist.

A variety of sources were used to collect the data for this study. The main basis of data was the *Shariah* report of the *Sukuk* issuing company. Sources include Bursa Malaysia and the Securities Commission (SC) website. The data collected regarding the literature review was obtained from various sources, such as books, articles, journals, and websites. Such a gathering of comprehensive datasets augers well for an inclusive analysis to be made, and ultimately best positions the researcher for desirable results.

## Data Collection for the Qualitative Study

While the previous section elaborated on the collection of quantitative data, and the procedure that has been followed to collect it, the current section explains more about the qualitative data that was collected by using the approach of mixed modes of interview (a semi-structured interview method and an e-mail interviewing method).

### Semi-Structured Interview

The secondary data collection approach used in this research, as mentioned above, was to conduct interviews. According to Sekaran (2003), another method of collecting data is to establish a group to interview, to obtain information from the respondents concerning the issue of interest. Collis and Hussey (2009) defined an interview as a method of collecting data in which participants are asked questions to find out what they do, think or feel. However, according to Saunders et al. (2007), there are three categories of interview; namely, structured, semi-structured, and unstructured, interviews.

Structured interviews are used in descriptive research to obtain quantitative data, whereby the researcher uses questionnaires based on a predetermined and standardized, or identical, set of questions. The researcher can elect to read out each question and then record the response on a standardized schedule, usually with pre-coded answers. The second category of interview is the semi-structured interview; this is non-standardized and used in explanatory studies whereby the researcher has a list of themes and questions to be covered. Therefore, these interviews may vary from one interview to another. The last category of interview is the unstructured interview, or in-depth interview, which is usually used in exploratory studies, to explore a general and/or new area in which the researcher is interested, in-depth.

Generally, the use of the interview as a data-collecting method has several advantages. Firstly, the use of the interviews boosts certainty. The direct contact between the researcher and the interviewee allows the interviewer to explain the main purpose of the study more freely, thus the researcher is able to clarify any doubt and avoid any misunderstanding of the concepts, or the questions put forward (Oppenheim 1998).

Secondly, it allows the interviewer to introduce and ask questions that are more complex, and to ask follow-up questions which would not be achievable in the questionnaire method of data collection. Furthermore, the researcher is able to take into account nonverbal communication, such as the feelings, behavior, attitudes, and facial expressions, of the interviewee. Therefore, it may allow a higher degree of confidence in the replies, compared with questionnaire responses (Collis & Hussey 2009).

The decision to choose a particular type of interview as a data collection method depends on the research objectives (Leedy & Ormrod 2001). The current study applied the semi-structured interviews to validate the results obtained by the quantitative study. Semi-structured interviews might be able to solicit elements that need to be further explored, and to explain themes that have emerged from the use of a quantitative data collection. Moreover, semi-structured interviews are used not only to disclose and understand the 'what' and the 'how' of a phenomenon, but also to place more emphasis on exploring the 'why' (Saunders et al. 2007).

In the current study, semi-structured interviews have the maximum degree of flexibility among the other qualitative methods, as these types of interview are capable of reaching the specified senior-level of managers more effectively than the survey approach (Leedy & Ormrod 2001). In addition, semi-structured interviews are widely recommended as a means of validating findings obtained from the use of a questionnaire (Wass & Wells 1994). In the Malaysian context, it is recommended that the researcher uses the semi-structured interview technique as a means of data collection, beside a survey of real data to conduct business and management-related research. Such a technique is extremely successful in Malaysian IFIs, where members of the SSB like to talk, rather than to complete a questionnaire. Thus, the current study has utilized the semi-structured interview as a confirmatory study to confirm and validate the results that emerged from the quantitative analysis.

**E-Mail Interviewing**

In the past two decades, several studies have emerged in library and information science (LIS) that employ qualitative research methods (Meho 2006). This type of approach has led to a noticeable shift towards studies that rely on observation and interviewing, as opposed to questionnaires or structured interviewing. Exploring the value of e-mail interviewing in qualitative research can be very effective and useful to LIS researchers. This method might well be useful to those people who prefer an online interview rather than face-to-face interaction, and in addition, it would be useful to those who are not easily accessible.

According to Denscombe (2003), the quality of the responses gained through online research is much better than the quality of the same responses produced by traditional methods. Thus, several studies in the literature review (e.g., Curasi 200, Meho & Tibbo 2003, Murray 2004, Murray & Harrison 2004) tend to rely on the two methods; e-mail and face to face interview. These studies found that participants interviewed via e-mail are more focused on the interview questions, because e-mail provides more reflectively dense accounts than its face-to-face counterparts. This does not mean that the quality of face-to-face interviews is lower, but rather highlights the benefits of the e-mail interview to both researchers and the interviewees regarding the factors of time and communication, especially when limited time is available to a prospective respondent, or when there are geographical barriers and boundaries which exclude conducting a face-to-face interview (Karchmer 2001, Murray 2004, Young, Persichitte, & Tharp 1998).

Previous studies in the literature have used e-mail for conducting qualitative, in-depth interviews. It was revealed that e-mail interviewing offers unprecedented opportunities for qualitative research, therefore, it provides access to millions of potential research participants who are otherwise inaccessible (Meho 2006). This method can be employed quickly and inexpensively, and generates high-quality data when handled carefully. Although this method has a number of challenges, many of them were found to be easily overcome, presenting scholars with a new technique for conducting efficient and effective qualitative research. While a mixed mode interviewing strategy should always be considered when possible, semi-structured e-mail interviewing can be a viable alternative to the face-to-face and telephone interviews, especially when time, financial constraints, or geographical boundaries, are barriers to an investigation (Meho 2006).

The use of e-mail for collecting qualitative data will be expanded as the level of access to the internet increases, and, therefore, this method for collecting data will become increasingly prevalent. Few empirical studies have addressed the relevant methodologies, and accordingly, there is need to explore more studies that may implement some techniques to deal with e-mail-based interviews in comparison to telephone and face-to-face interviewing.

Thus, the current study has utilized the e-mail interview technique as a means of data collection, beside a semi-structured interview, to confirm and validate the results that emerged from the quantitative analysis. Such a technique of gathering data via e-mail is extremely successful in IFIs, where members of an SSB are unlikely to be available for face-to-face interviews. This is especially true when time and financial constraints are barriers to an interview being conducted.

## Interview Design

The mixed mode interview (semi-structured interview method and e-mail interviewing method) is considered as one of the most important research techniques, but the majority of previous accounting studies have overlooked this approach. Semi-structured interviews allow the interviewer to ask other questions arising from the dialogue between the researcher and the interviewee (DiCicco-Bloom & Crabtree, Meho 2006). After consultations and discussions with academics in Islamic finance and accounting practitioners, the design of the interview questions was greatly improved. Furthermore, the academicians and practitioners contributed to the enhancement of the design of the interview questions. The interview questions covered most of the issues related to *Sukuk* legitimacy, determinants, and the SSBs. The core questions of the interviews were then supplemented by several sub-questions in order to deeply understand every issue during the interview process (Zikmund 1997).

**Interview Process**

Seven members of an SSB from the Islamic finance sector agreed to participate in semi-structured interviews conducted by telephone, and three members by e-mail interview. In the event that any of the members of the SSB were not able to participate, another institution from the same sector was contacted. A copy of the information letter, interview consent form, contact information form, and the main interview questions, were mailed to each of the members of the SSBs who had agreed to participate. The information letter provided the members of the SSB with a full explanation concerning the aim of the interview. Moreover, the letter contained a declaration guaranteeing the confidentiality of the participants. Following that, the managers were contacted again to set up the interview. Each interview session was confirmed a day before the date of appointment, and was conducted by telephone.

The members of the SSB were selected for the interview because their experience was deemed to be sufficient to reflect the full scope of issues under examination for the current study (Cooper et al. 1998). To keep across case comparability, similar semi-structured questions were utilized for all the interviews. All the interviews were recorded with the participants' permission. The duration of each interview was between 30 and 40 minutes. After introducing himself, the researcher began with the main question which related to *Sukuk* legitimacy, then other main questions and sub-questions were asked. Every participant was encouraged to add any additional issues that the current study had not covered. All the interviewees' enquiries were answered during the interview. At the end of each interview, the participants were asked to give feedback, edit any transcripts, or delete any information they did not wish to be used in any subsequent publications. The process went smoothly, as no information was requested to be deleted during this process. However, only information which referred to the questions of the study was considered.

## Measurement of the Variables

The present study used eight variables: one dependent, five independent, and two moderating, variables. As shown in Figure 2.3 below, the dependent variable is *Sukuk* legitimacy, and the independent variables are: the pricing of *Sukuk*, the type of structure, *Shariah* auditing, *Shariah* risk, and *Shariah* documentation. The two moderating variables are *Shariah* Supervisory Board members, and *Shariah* Supervisory Board committees.

This study has adopted its measurements from the extensive literature review that provided and identified a wide range of measurements. The quantitative method is the basic design for this study. The variables are measured as follows. To analyze the dependent variable the basic design is underpinned by the method of content analysis. A definition of content analysis is that it is "a research technique for the objective, systematic, and quantitative description of manifest content of a communication" (Cooper et al. 1998). When examining a *Shariah* disclosure, many scholars have adopted the method of content analysis for their study. Content analysis has been utilized to examine the nature and the quantity of *Shariah* disclosure (Abdul Rahman et al. 2010, Maali et al. 2006, Gray, Kouhy & Lavers 1995a,b).

Some prior studies have been undertaken to create an appropriate list of social information that IFIs are to disclose. Furthermore, only a few empirical studies have utilized a *Shariah*-compliant disclosure index, specifically in relation to IFIs (Haniffa & Hudaib 2007, Maali et al. 2006). Accordingly, this study is one to lead the way by taking into account three new components that comprise the report of the *Shariah* Board: *Shariah* ruling and considerations; the mechanisms and structure of *Sukuk* legitimacy; and *Shariah* compliance.

This study comprises three parts: firstly, the structure and mechanisms of *Sukuk* legitimacy; secondly, the *Shariah* ruling and considerations; and the thirdly, *Shariah* compliance. This is further to the adoption of the *Shariah* report (pronouncement) and this relates to all information concerning the *Sukuk's* legitimacy evaluation, and measurement of the level of information relating to the disclosure of the legitimacy of *Sukuk*, by way of an indexing procedure of *Shariah* pronouncement in Malaysia's IFIs. Measurement, by way of an index to analyze the level of legitimacy disclosure, is supplementary to the requirement for specified items of information that is predictably provided in the *Shariah* pronouncements. In order to attain this study's objectives, each of the specified items will be obtained from the

*Sukuk Shariah* pronouncement, solely by weight. Indeed, the weighting of each item will be on the basis of the absence, or the presence, of each of the items in the *Sukuk Shariah* pronouncement. If the item was indeed disclosed, then the weighting of the *Sukuk* receives a value of one, and if not disclosed, then a value of zero is given.

Furthermore, this study's indexing method is based on Bursa Malaysia's Islamic *Sukuk* listed reports (pronouncements) to measure and evaluate the disclosure level of information relating to *Sukuk* legitimacy from the specified items of information outlined in the *Sukuk* pronouncements. From the information gathered, the index list comprised 14 items of information relating to the disclosure of *Sukuk* legitimacy information, in the Malaysian context, as accepted by previous studies (Maali et al. 2006, Haniffa & Hudaib 2007) and by the AAOIFI (2012) and the SC (2011), as outlined in Table 4.3. In relation to the structure of the disclosure index, the index was checked against a sample of *Sukuk*. Furthermore, as Table 4.2 demonstrates, the index was categorized into three classifications: *Shariah* ruling and considerations (5 items); mechanism and structure (4 items); and *Shariah* approval (5 items), as adopted from SC (2011).

In examining the *Sukuk*, a maximum number of 14 items were set aside, covering off on the broad themes. To obtain a score for the *Sukuk*, each item's score was first added, and then the total was divided by the maximum of the likely scores, and to obtain the percentage scores the number was multiplied by 100. For this study, the 14 broad theme items corresponded to the maximum possible score for disclosure of the combined number of items. For instance, in the event a *Sukuk* reported 5 out of a possible maximum of 14 items, then the dependent variable score was approximately 36 percent. Accordingly, a variable score of 50 percent would be attained in the event that 7 of the 14 items were reported. Through the examination of a specified item, through the process of division of the number of disclosures of *Sukuk* of that specified item by the total number of items, a calculation was attained for the average score.

**Table 2: Categorization of the List of Items Included in the Classification Index (Legitimacy disclosure of *Sukuk*)**

| | Items | Sources | | | |
|---|---|---|---|---|---|
| | **Structure and Mechanism of *Sukuk* Issue Based on the *Shariah* Principle** | SC, (2011) | AAOIFI., (2012) | Maali et al. (2006) | Haniffa Hudaib (2007) |
| 1 | *Shariah* opinion on the lawfulness of the purchase of assets. | √ | √ | √ | √ |
| 2 | View of the *Shariah* Board on lease of assets. | √ | √ | √ | |
| 3 | Present details of purchase, substitution and redemption undertaking. | √ | √ | | |
| 4 | Appointment of a Servicing Agent | √ | √ | | |
| | ***Shariah* Ruling and Considerations (Important Highlights)** | | | | |
| 5 | Financial Ratio Test (Islamic market index) | √ | √ | | |
| 6 | Utilization of proceeds. | √ | √ | | |
| 7 | Waiver of interest and exchangeable *Sukuk* features. | √ | | | |
| 8 | *Wakalah* Agreement | √ | √ | | |
| 9 | Business Activity Test (non *Shariah*-compliant) alcohol, tobacco, pork-related products, Conventional financial services (banking, insurance, etc.), weapons and defence, and entertainment (hotels, casinos/gambling, cinema, music, pornography etc.) | √ | √ | √ | √ |
| | ***Shariah* compliant (Approval)** | | | | |
| 10 | The view of the *Shariah* Adviser in relation to the prevailing circumstances, the structure and mechanism. | √ | √ | | |

| | | | | | |
|---|---|---|---|---|---|
| 11 | Agreement of the *Shariah* Adviser to approve the documents for the *Sukuk* structure. | √ | √ | | |
| 12 | The legal constraints under which the proposed *Sukuk* is being developed. | √ | | | |
| 13 | View of the *Shariah* Adviser to develop the Islamic *Sukuk* issuance. | √ | | | √ |
| 14 | View of the *Shariah* adviser for the removal of *riba.* | √ | | | |

The price of *Sukuk* is computed according to several benchmarks, and whether it follows the conventional or the Islamic benchmark. A few of the previous studies in the literature depended on the use of such benchmarks (both the Islamic and the conventional) such as LIBOR, KLIBOR, the Dow Jones Islamic Index (DJII), and the Kuala Lumpur Syariah Index (KLSI), as profitability indicators to measure financial performance, or to analyze the risk and return in general, and specifically in the context of Malaysia (Hayat 2006, Muhammad & Mokhtar 2008, Hayat & Kraeussl 2011). Nonetheless, the majority of these studies did not bear in mind, nor mention, the probability of it being undesirable to use the conventional benchmarks for Islamic jurisprudence which might be used by the issuers. Importantly, the present study does not seek to avoid this inattention, and, therefore, seeks to address the limitations of the previous studies.

A pricing benchmark has been chosen as one of the components of *Sukuk* legitimacy (Al-Amine 2008, Wilson 2008, Zulkhibri 2015). In addition, another wave of studies investigated a pricing benchmark as an important indicator to represent the *Sukuk* structure in the area of Islamic finance (Zaidi 2007, Khan 2007, Wilson 2008, Al-Bashir 2008, Nanaeva 2010, Kantakji & O'haj 2010, Rahman et al. 2013, Usmani 2002, Aloui et al. 2015). However, based on the literature in the respected journals relating to economics and corporate finance, the pricing benchmark is considered an important issue in relation to *Sukuk* legitimacy evaluation; in that a pricing benchmark is seen as one of the important elements impacting on a *Sukuk*. More explicitly, a pricing benchmark has been widely recognized and supported by the literature as a choice affecting the legitimacy of *Sukuk*. For example, Ahmed et al. (2015) utilized a pricing benchmark as one of the measurements to determine the relationship between pricing and *Sukuk*. In the same vein, Hayat and Kraeussl (2011) used both Islamic and conventional pricing benchmark measurements for measuring Islamic equity funds' performance.

Thus, in order to measure a pricing benchmark, reports and documents of the *Sukuk* have been utilized. The *Sukuk* reports contain the content on disclosures about the pricing benchmark in relation to the disclosure of the margin of profit. Some *Sukuk* do not disclosure any information about the pricing benchmark, therefore the researcher will contact the respondents personally via telephone. To deal with the issue of confidentiality, respondents were guaranteed that their responses would be treated in the strictest of confidence. A list of their contact numbers is provided in Appendix B3.

An examination of the literature indicates that prior studies found that, in comparing asset-based *Sukuk* and asset-backed *Sukuk* from the *Shariah* perspective, there are some significant differences, due to the types of structure and this has an impact on the legitimacy of *Sukuk* (Haneef 2009, Howladar 2009, Khnifer 2010b, Hidayat 2013, Alia et al. 2013, Shabana 2013, Abdulmalik 2013, Azmat et al. 2014b).

In examining the type of structure as measurement, there have been some empirical studies that have analyzed the structure of *Sukuk* (Dusuki 2010a, Dusuki 2010b, Khnifer 2010a, Hidayat 2013). In relation to the current study, the structure type was measured on the basis of two categories; asset-based and asset-backed *Sukuk*, further to the SC classifications as demonstrated in Table 4.3. Furthermore, a variable which is dichotomous has been utilized for the *Sukuk* structure type; in that an asset-backed *Sukuk* will be rated as the value of '1', and '0' if not asset-backed.

**Table 3: Categorization of the Type of *Sukuk* Structure (SC 2009)**

| **Asset-Based** | | **Asset-Backed** | |
|---|---|---|---|
| Sale-Based | Lease-Based | Partnership-Based | Agency-Based |
| *Murabahah* | *Ijarah* | *Mudharabah* | *Wakalah Bi Istithmar* |
| *Salam* | *Ijarah Muntahiah Bi Tamlik* | *Musharakah* | |
| *BBA* | *Ijarah Mawsufah fi Zimmah* | | |
| *Istisna* | | | |

In relation to *Shariah* auditing, it is one of the necessary functions for the overall corporate governance quality, and for the Board dynamics that oversee the business of the IFIs to make certain that all its operations are particularly compliant with *Shariah* terms and conditions (Rahman 2008, Casper 2012). Prior studies, have found that the efficacy of *Shariah* auditing can be reached on the basis of advice from experts with a high level of knowledge and expertise of Islamic laws in relation to financial transactions (*fiqh al-muamalat*) (Malik 2010, Lahsasna 2010, Kaseb 2010, ISRA 2013, Ahmed et al. 2013, Nabil 2013). A few studies focusing on *Shariah* auditing have utilized content analysis as their method of the study (Haniffa & Hudaib 2007). Several prior studies in the literature were undertaken to develop the appropriate steps for IFI disclosure items for a *Shariah* review (Malik 2010, Lahsasna 2010, Kaseb 2010, ISRA 2013, Ahmed et al. 2013, Nabil 2013). As mentioned previously, several empirical studies have developed a disclosure index to examine *Shariah* annual reports in relation to pronouncements and auditing (Haniffa & Hudaib 2007). Accordingly, to fully examine the *Shariah* risks, the current study has utilized a method of indexing to measure and evaluate the *Shariah* auditing comprised of the *Sukuk*-related *Shariah* reports. In addition, the index is utilized to provide measurement of the required *Shariah* auditing from the specified items of information as presented in the *Shariah* reports. As Table 4.4 below indicates, the index list comprises eight items of information concerning *Shariah* auditing, as adopted from the study by Haniffa and Hudaib (2007). Consequently, this maximum number of eight items for each *Sukuk* represented the maximum score for a possible disclosure for the number of items of *Shariah* auditing. To calculate the average score, this was made through the division of the number of *Shariah* auditing disclosures of a specified item by the total number of items.

In examining *Shariah* risks in a given market, these are risks linked to a possible system failure, and in general, these are as a consequence of less-than-adequate strategies and internal processes. If the potential *Shariah* risks are not adequately managed, this may lead to a situation of lowering the stakeholder confidence level, and adversely impacting on shareholders, customers, employees, and depositors, as the IFI is not able to meet its stated commitments (IDB & IFSB 2007). Importantly, each *Sukuk* structure ought to be *Shariah* compliant from their date of issue continuing on to the date of maturity (Junaid & Muhammad 2010). According to Mehmood (2010), "*Shariah* monitors the whole context of each *Sukuk* transaction". As *Sukuk* are complex and novel structures, they are not fully understood by those operating in the capital market. Furthermore, experts accustomed to working in the traditional financial system are not well versed regarding

Islamic banking and the guiding *Shariah* principles.

**Table 4: Disclosure of the Items of *Shariah* Auditing**

| | Items | Source |
|---|---|---|
| | ***Shariah* Auditing** | Haniffa and Hudaib (2007) |
| 1 | The names of members are provided. | √ |
| 2 | The photographs of the members are provided. | √ |
| 3 | Remuneration of the members has been given. | √ |
| 3 | The report has been signed by all the members. | √ |
| 4 | An examination of all business transactions ex ante and ex post has been undertaken. | √ |
| 5 | Any defects in the products have been specified and detailed. | √ |
| 6 | Recommendation made as to the way in which to rectify any defects in the product. | √ |
| 7 | If a product defect has been reported, whether any action has been taken by management to rectify the product defect. | √ |
| 8 | The distribution of profits and losses complies with the principles of *Shariah.* | √ |

Several studies have examined *Shariah* risks by way of an index measurement method, as the basis of the development of relevant steps to identify and mitigate *Shariah* risks as disclosed by the IFIs (Tariq 2004, Nabil 2013, Ginena 2014). In relation to a disclosure index of *Shariah* risks, several empirical studies have analyzed and developed a disclosure index (Nanaeva 2010, Rauf & Ibrahim 2014). In this way, measurement of the *Shariah* risks can be made on the basis of the contents of the *Sukuk* requirements and reports such as those providing principal terms and conditions, an offering memorandum, announcements, rating reports, and *Shariah* pronouncements, as these documents provide useful information in relation to *Shariah* risks. It is implied that information in relation to risks is present in the *Sukuk* requirements provided by the SSBs, as well as other authorities.

In order to evaluate the *Shariah* risks, and to measure these risks, this study utilized an assessment grid method to analyze the risks mentioned in the *Sukuk* reports. There are seven items of information relating to *Shariah* risks included on the *Sukuk* index list, as adapted from Ginena (2014) and as discussed in Chapter Three. In addition, the *Shariah* risks presented in the *Sukuk* reports were ascertained from the selected items of information, and were measured by way of the index.

A risk assessment grid relating to the principles of *Shariah* is utilized to evaluate *Sukuk's Shariah* risks, as indicated in Table 4.5. This is established by way of firstly assigning a score from one to ten (with one being lowest and ten being highest) for each event in relation to two significant dimensions: the likelihood (L) of the occurrence of an event; and the potential for its adverse impact (I) on the *Sukuk*. As some of the events can be more damaging in comparison to others, consideration of the impact on *Sukuk* is taken into account. Subsequently, to obtain a score of risk (R) the results for events I and L are multiplied.

**Table 5: *Shariah* Risk Assessment Grid**

| | ***Shariah* Risks** | **Risk Assessment** | | |
|---|---|---|---|---|
| | Case Identification | Likelihood (1-10) (L) | Impact (1-10) (I) | Risk Score (R) |
| 1 | Inexperienced *Sukuk Shariah* Advisory | - | - | - |
| 2 | Inadequate/lack of *Shariah* governance regulations | - | - | - |
| 3 | Unapproved product, transaction or legal documentation | - | - | - |
| 4 | Inadequate internal *Shariah* governance arrangements or tools | - | - | - |
| 5 | Poor reporting | - | - | - |
| 6 | Use of profit distribution and segregation of funds | - | - | - |
| 7 | Insufficient *Shariah* risk disclosure and transparency | - | - | - |
| | Overall *Shariah* risk score | - | - | - |

The main distinguishing element between conventional financial, and Islamic, tools is the documentation itself (Ahmed et al. 2013). *Sukuk* are structured instruments, and as such, it is essential that a thorough examination of their structure is made to fully understand the documentary components. In examining the characteristics of *Sukuk*, their documentation is often divided into what are known as 'capital market documents' and '*Shariah* operational documents' (Ali 2011). It is expected that IFIs will disclose detailed information concerning unlawful or forbidden operations (Maali et al. 2006). Further to Maali et al. (2006), other studies, such as Haniffa and Hudaib (2007), have found that IFIs and their insights assist in improving the level of disclosure in relation to Islamic financial instruments in the *Shariah* Boards' report. These studies indicated that an improvement in the level of *Shariah*-compliance disclosure is predicted to differentiate between the various Islamic financial products themselves, and will also differentiate between the traditional financial institutions' products. As mentioned previously, disclosure in *Shariah* reports is made by the SSBs concerning the documentation related to *Sukuk* contracts. To analyze the level of disclosure, some researchers examining *Shariah* documentation have utilized content analysis for their methods of research (Lahsasna & Idris 2008). Several prior studies were undertaken to develop an appropriate list of documentation that ought to be disclosed by the IFIs. However, only a small number of empirical studies have developed and utilized a disclosure index specifically relating to *Sukuk* documentation (Lahsasna & Idris 2008, Kaseb 2010, Ali 2011, Van Wijnbergen & Zaheer 2013).

Following on from this study's objectives, each specified item was acquired from the *Sukuk*-related *Shariah* reports. The weighting of each item was made on the basis of the absence, or the presence, of each item examined in the report. In the event there was disclosure of the item, then a weighting of 'one' was attributed to the *Sukuk*; however, in the event there was no disclosure, then the value of 'zero' was given. As mentioned previously, for this current study, a method of indexing was employed to measure and evaluate the *Sukuk*-related *Shariah* documentation in the *Shariah* reports, with the index measuring the required *Shariah* documentation from the specified items of information, as outlined in the *Shariah* reports. As Table 4.6 indicates, the index list comprised 13 items of *Sukuk* documentation, as adopted from the prior literature (SC 2011, AAOIFI 2012). Accordingly, a maximum possible score of the items for each of the *Sukuk* was 13.

The average score was attained through the division of the number of *Shariah* disclosure documents in relation to a specified item by the total number of items.

**Table 6: List of *Shariah* Documentation Items Disclosed**

| | Items | SC (2011) | AAOIFI (2012) |
|---|---|---|---|
| | ***Shariah* Documentation** | | |
| 1 | *Wakalah* Agreement | √ | √ |
| 2 | Sale and Purchase Agreement | √ | √ |
| 3 | Closing Date Deed of Surrender | √ | √ |
| 3 | Cash Settlement Purchase Right Deed | √ | √ |
| 4 | Commodity *Sukuk* Investment Agreement | √ | √ |
| 5 | Purchase Order | √ | √ |
| 6 | Issuer Undertaking | √ | √ |
| 7 | Form of Letter of Acceptance and Offer | √ | √ |
| 8 | Buyer Agency Letter | √ | √ |
| 9 | Obligor Undertaking | √ | √ |
| 10 | Purchaser Undertaking | √ | √ |
| 11 | Lease Agreement | √ | √ |
| 12 | Grant of Rights to Services Agreement | √ | √ |
| 13 | Sub-Grant of Rights to Services Agreement | √ | √ |

The size of a Board is likely to impact on its capacity to monitor, review, and control, all of the IFIs' transactions, to ensure their operations are in compliance with *Shariah* rules and principles (Nathan 2012, Rahman & Bukair 2013, Grassa 2015a). Such information ought to be disclosed in the annual report for shareholders to be more confident in dealing with the IFIs. Besides this, detailing the activities and disclosing the number of meetings held annually ensures that the board members are aware of the activities of the organizations, and this is in line with *Shariah* requirements. The other issue is the necessity of SSB members being independent from the banks' management, as reported by Karim (1990). Chapra and Ahmed (2002) proposed that the existence of decentralized SSB members for each country will ensure there is a level of independence from the institutions' level of management. Empirical evidence in corporate governance suggests that the size of a Board can affect controlling, monitoring, and the level of disclosure (Akhtaruddin et al. 2009, Chaganti et al. 1985). Whilst there is no restriction on the number of members appointed to an SSB, the ideal number should be between three and seven members. Indeed, the common number of SSB members in IFIs is three, and this number is in line with BNM and AAOIFI standards. A greater number of members appointed to a SSB or to *Shariah* committees would provide more effective monitoring, and would be more consistent with the principles of *Shariah*. According to several researchers (Chen & Jaggi 2000, Grais & Pellegrini 2006, Farook, Hassan, & Lanis 2011), a larger size of committee may reduce the possibility of information asymmetry. Therefore, in appointing more members to a committee there is an expectation of a reduction in the level of ambiguity, and a reduction in the lack of information. Thus, measurement of this moderating variable is based on the numbers of members appointed to the SSB, and the existing numbers of SSB committees.

**Table 7: Operationalization of the Moderating Variable of the SSB**

| **SSB** | **Operationalization** |
|---|---|
| Number of members | Dichotomous; 1 for the number of SSB members above the median of 3.0 otherwise |
| Number of committees | Dichotomous; 1 for the number of SSB committees above the median of 2.0 otherwise |

## Data Analysis Techniques

The current study has employed mixed method data collection, by using quantitative and qualitative methods as two main methods to analyze the data. An analysis of the quantitative data was made utilizing the Partial Least Squared (PLS) approach, and the qualitative data was examined using a thematic analysis approach.

The next sections will elaborate further on the methods of data analysis adopted for this research endeavor.

### Quantitative Data Analysis

This section describes the manner in which the data has been measured. The data was collected from *Sukuk* reports, and analyzed using the Partial Least Squared (PLS) approach. Furthermore, the tools of Structural Equation Modeling (SEM) and bootstrapping in Smart-PLS software version 2.0 M3 were used as the statistical techniques for the analysis in this study, and in order to determine the relationship amongst the variables. The use of PLS has certain advantages which makes it ideal for this study, whereby it is useful for the purposes of prediction, and it does not require as large a sample size as other causal modeling techniques (Urbach & Ahlemann 2010). As such, PLS is a second generation regression method which combines confirmatory factor analysis with linear regression. In addition, the purpose of the data analysis is to test the goodness of data in terms of reliability and validity (assessment and measurement model), hypothesis testing (assessment of structural model), moderating effect, and the overall fit of model (goodness of fit analysis). Hence, it is feasible to implement the structural and measurement model at the same time, and reduce the error variance according to the study by Fornell and Cha (1994). The data collection was processed through different statistical techniques, as outlined in the following five subsections.

## Descriptive Statistics

The Statistical Package for Social Science (SPSS) is widely used as a program for statistical analysis in social science. It is a technique utilized to analyze various data results, such as descriptive analysis and factor analysis. Hence, in this study the first phase of the data analysis was carried out via a SPSS statistical technique by using data screening and descriptive analysis. Descriptive statistics are used to provide some simple synopses about measurements and population. The descriptive statistics will be used to summarize and describe the basic features of the data gathered from the study, such as the frequency, percentage, means, standard deviations, and range.

## Structural Equation Modeling (SEM)

Structural Equation Modeling (SEM), using the partial least square (PLS) approach, was used to test the research hypotheses. SME is a family of statistical models that seek to explain the relationships amongst multiple variables. According to Lu, Lai and Cheng (2007), SEM has become a preferred data analysis method for empirical research in relation to operations management, with researchers lately identifying this new statistical model as the appropriate method to adopt. In addition, Shah and Goldstein (2006) indicated that researches that utilize SEM as the primary analytic tool have frequently made an appearance in main journals in relation to operations management (Lu et al. 2007).

**Table 8: Rules of Thumb for Model Evaluation**

| | Validity Type | Criterion | Guidelines |
|---|---|---|---|
| Measurement Model | Internal Consistency | Composite Reliability (CR) | CR> 0.7 (exploratory study) CR> 0.8 (advance research)<br>CR < 0.6 (lack reliability) |
| | Indicator Reliability | Indicator Loadings | An item's loading is to be > 0.7 and significant at least at the 0.05 level. |
| | Convergent Validity | Average Variance Extracted (AVE) | AVE is to be >0.50. |
| | Discriminant Validity | Cross Loading (the Fornell-Larcker Criterion) | An item's loading of each indicator is highest for its designated constructs. The square root of AVE of a construct should be greater than the correlations between the construct and other constructs in the model. |
| Structural Model | Model Validity | (R2 ) | -0.67substantial<br>-0.333moderate<br>0.190- weak |
| | | Path Coefficients | At least a value of 0.100 and at a significant value of 0.05. |

Source: Hair, Ringle & Sarstedt (2011)

The method of Partial Least Square (PLS) is a second generation multivariate technique that can examine simultaneously the measurement model (the relationship between constructs and their corresponding indicators) and the structural model (the relationship among constructs), using it to reduce the error variance (Sang, Lee & Lee 2010). The latent constructs scores are used to run the ordinary least square regressions for each construct, to determine the estimates of the structural model relationships, which are the path coefficients. It also creates loading between the reflective constructs and their indicators, and gives weight between the constructs and coefficients of the multiple determinations (R2) for dependent variable, as cited by Sang et al. (2010). Table 4.8 summarizes the validity guidelines of the measurement model and the structural model evaluation.

The structural model can only be analyzed after the measurement model has been validated successfully. In PLS, a structural model can be evaluated using the coefficient of determination (R2) and the path coefficients.

**The Structural Model**

The following model indicated sufficient discriminant and convergent reliability and validity and, therefore, the data analysis could commence by utilizing the hypotheses generated to examine the constructs, as outlined in the structural model. In accordance with Chin (1998), a structural model is associated to the relationships between the individual constructs.

It denotes as hypotheses in the theatrical framework, or the style of study, as postulated by the researcher (Sang et al. 2010). A structural model makes mention of the causal relationships between the constructs within the model. It consists of an estimate of the path coefficients that reveals the advantages of the hypothesized relationship (the relationship between the dependent and independent variables) and the R2 value which identifies the forecasting strength of the model (the amount of variance explained by the independent variables) (Sang et al. 2010).

**Bootstrapping Model**

As stated by Chin (1998), samples of bootstrapping are built based on re-sampling, which is a substitute from the original sample. This process produces a sample comprising exactly the same number of units as the original sample. The numbers of re-samples need to be specified at the same time. The significant levels for loading, weights, and path coefficients, can be figured out by way of the bootstrapping method.

After PLS evaluations have been carried out with several data set partitions, the t-values can be computed from it, and indications as to which of the relationships between independent and dependent variables are more significant than others. Therefore, there are two conditions to show whether the hypothesis is significant: a p-value below 0.01 and a t-value more than 2.33; and a p-value below 0.05 and a t-value more than 1.65.

**Moderating Effect**

A moderation analysis can be applied to detect the moderating effect of the SSB (moderator variable) on the relationship between the determinants (predictor variable) and the *Sukuk* legitimacy (criterion variable). To test the possibility of such an effect, the predictor and moderator were multiplied to create an interaction construct (predictor x moderator) to predict criterion. To investigate the moderating effect, this study has estimated the influence of the predictor on the criterion (path a), the direct impact of the moderating variable on the criterion variable (path b), and the influence of the interaction variable on the criterion variable (path c) is meaningful, independently of the size of the path coefficient (a) and (b) (Fairchild & MacKinnon 2009).

**Hypothesis Testing**

Smart PLS 2.0 software was used to develop a structural model for hypothesis testing. The coefficient paths were produced using a bootstrapping which essentially is a re-sampling using available observation. The bootstrapping, which results in a larger sample, is claimed to model the unknown population (Henderson 2005). Bootstrapping enables greater subsamples to be drawn from the original sample, with substitution. The t-value with coefficient paths of above 1.96 is implies that it is significantly different from zero at a significance level of 5% (α= 0.05; two-sided test). The 5% level is acknowledged to be sufficient by previous studies (Feuerverger, Stigler, Fuchs, Bentley, Bird, Höfling & Kadane 2008), with a justification that a p-value at 5% of confidence provides stronger evidence to accept hypotheses that are related to the perception of respondents in social science studies. Thus, researchers accept the 5% level as a reasonable sample size, and agree that it has ability to detect effect-sizes that are of interest.

**Qualitative Data Analysis**

Unlike quantitative data, there are no standardized methods of analyses that are specific to qualitative data because of their nature (Saunders 2003).

Bryman (2006) indicated that clear-cut rules about how qualitative data analysis should be carried out have not been developed further. Therefore, there are several qualitative research traditions and approaches, with the result that there are also different strategies to summarize the data collected (Saunders 2003).

Although different approaches are not mutually exclusive, they can be combined, such that it can be argued that the thematic analysis approach is the best one to be used in this study. The interest, or emphasis, of thematic analysis is more on the content of the speech and on what is said, rather than how it is said (Riessman 2004). The analysis of the qualitative data starts after the quantitative data collection has been completed. The data obtained from the interviews is processed and analyzed following a number of steps. Firstly, the recordings are listened to carefully, and then the contents are transcribed in writing. Each participant's response is written on a separate sheet of paper. Processing and analyzing interviews normally takes time because there is a requirement to listen to the recordings very carefully, before they are transcribed into writing, then read and re-read repeatedly (Drever 1995). Therefore, the transcribed data is read carefully to accurately identify the topic area related to the study's aim. Each question's responses is put together and rewritten on different sheets of paper so that all the answers to a particular question are grouped together. Categories of the responses to each question are developed and the relevant data placed under each category. The responses are then described in terms of topics or categories, and quotes used to illustrate them. To take care of this issue, in this study the interviewees were provided with a list of the interview themes in advance prior to the interview being conducted. The rationale behind this procedure is to promote validity and reliability by enabling the interviewees to consider the information requested, thus allowing the interviewees to assemble supporting organizational documentation from their files (Saunders 2003). With regards to qualitative data, manual qualitative data analysis has been applied to analyze the data gathered from the interviewees during the mixed mode interviews (semi-structured and e-mail interviews).

## Summary

This chapter has discussed the development of this study's theoretical framework, and the hypotheses to be tested. This chapter has clarified the relationship under investigation in this study, as well as outlining the theoretical foundation for the study. Based on previous research, the chapter has illustrated that the independent variables (the pricing of *Sukuk*, type of structure and *Shariah* risks, *Shariah* auditing and *Shariah* documentation) and the moderating variable, are hypothesized to have an effect on the dependent variable (*Sukuk*). In the earlier discussion, the methods used to conduct this study, and the variables, along with the measurements, were presented. This study will be conducted based on primary and secondary data collection. In this chapter, the population/sample and the data collection processes were discussed, including the differing statistical techniques utilized for processing the data collected. The following chapter will discuss the results of the research.

# CHAPTER 7

# RESEARCH FINDINGS (BASED ON QUANTITATIVE DATA)

## Introduction

In the previous chapter, the theoretical foundation for the study, in which the theoretical framework, hypotheses development, and methods used to conduct this study, as well as the variables, along with the measurements, were highlighted, was discussed. This chapter reports the data analysis and hypotheses testing of the study. The Partial Least Squared (PLS) Method, a covariance-based Structural Equation Modelling (SEM), was used to analyze the data collected from secondary sources. The descriptive analyses of determinants and *Sukuk* legitimacy are presented by using Statistical Package for Social Sciences (SPSS) version 2.0 software. Finally, the structural model assessment was performed, and the summary of hypotheses testing was concluded, together with the model fit assessment.

## Population versus Sample

This study was done through a census using *Sukuk* which were issued by IFI, which is listed at Bursa Malaysia under the exempt regime for the period between 2005 and 2015. The *Sukuk Shariah* reports (*Shariah* pronouncements) issued by the SSB were the main source of data. The *Shariah* report is issued for *Sukuk* only once by the SSB. Each report signifies the approved procedures of Islamic *Sukuk* issued by SSB, which contains a complete data serving the current study for the purpose of measuring its variables; determinants, legitimacy, and *Shariah* Boards; where such reports also consist of useful data for other related variables. The use of secondary data based on IFI *Shariah* statements in the *Shariah* pronouncements (which deal with *Sukuk* characteristics, *Sukuk* legitimacy and SSB) is done for several reasons: a) due to the ease of data availability; b) its reliability as it is *Shariah* pronouncements that are required by law;

and c) it is issued by the *Shariah* advisory council authority in the Central Bank.

## Descriptive Statistics

Descriptive statistics provide some information concerning the distribution of scores on continuous variables (Jaggi 2003). This section presents the descriptive analysis of the research variables; dependent, independent, and moderator, variables for the 82 Islamic *Sukuk* listed at Bursa Malaysia, using descriptive statistics (mean, standard deviation, minimum, and maximum). In this study, PLS was used with a bootstrapping option for 500, re-sampling for each of 82 samples. This means that each reported statistically significant value for PLS is based on 41,000 bootstrapping resamples (82 data sets times 500 re-samples). Bootstrapping estimates the empirical sampling distribution of a parameter by re-sampling from a sample with replacement. However, each re-sample has the same number of elements as the original sample. Therefore, the bootstrap method has the advantage of modelling the impacts of the actual sample size, and offers a viable alternative (Fan & Wang 1996).

Based on the results of descriptive statistics, the dependent variable, which is *Sukuk* legitimacy, showed that the level of legitimacy of *Sukuk* was 62%, representing the average of *Sukuk* with *Shariah* disclosure, with a standard deviation of 0.189. Furthermore, the minimum and maximum value indicated that *Sukuk* legitimacy is 33% and 89%, respectively. In addition, the descriptive analysis for determinants shows that: pricing has an average of 57.3% with standard deviation of 0.497; the type of structure has an average of 58.5% with standard deviation of 0.495; Shariah risk has an average of 11.0% with standard deviation of 0.050; and *Shariah* auditing has an average of 58.0% with standard deviation of 0.221, followed by *Shariah* documentation having an average of 46.7%, with standard deviation of 0.283.

For the moderator variable (SSB), the descriptive analysis results are as follows: SSBM analysis (mean = 2.56, SD = 1.68), the minimum and maximum reported that SSBM is 1.00 and 8.00, respectively. As for SSBC analysis (mean = 1.51, SD = 820), the minimum and maximum reported that SSBC is 1.00 and 4.00, respectively. Table 5.1 shows a summary of the descriptive statistics of the dependent, independent, and moderator, variables.

**Table:1 Descriptive Statistics of all Variables**

| Variables | Mean | Std. Dev | Minimum | Maximum |
|---|---|---|---|---|
| *Sukuk* Legitimacy | .620 | .189 | .33 | .89 |
| Pricing | .573 | .497 | .00 | 1.00 |
| Type of Structure | .585 | .495 | .00 | 1.00 |
| *Shariah* Risk | .110 | .050 | .02 | .24 |
| *Shariah* Auditing | .580 | .221 | .32 | .89 |
| *Shariah* Documentation | .467 | .283 | 1.00 | 9.00 |
| SSBM | 2.56 | 1.68 | 1.00 | 8.00 |
| SSBC | 1.51 | .820 | 1.00 | 4.00 |

## Descriptive Statistics (Frequency) SSB

In this section, Table 5.1 presents descriptive analysis of an SSB, which is the moderator variable on the relationship between determinants, and *Sukuk* legitimacy of 82 *Sukuk* listed under the exempt regime in Bursa Malaysia. The SSB variable has two categories, namely the number of members in an SSB (SSBM) and the number of committee members (SSBC). An SSB consists of no fewer than three members from the *Shariah* Board. Members of an SSB have several meetings in a year to assess the legitimacy of *Sukuk* structure, by reviewing transactions and operations of IFI. In addition, some IFIs appoint *Shariah* committees, which may be one *Shariah* committee member or more, to review financial transactions.

Table 5.2 describes the percentage of SSB members in IFI for *Sukuk* issuance. The descriptive statistic showed that only 49 *Sukuk* have fewer than three members of the SSB which equals to 59.8%, while 33 *Sukuk* (40.2%) had three or more members of the SSB. The descriptive statistic showed that most of the *Sukuk* in Malaysia IFIs have SSB members numbering fewer than three.

**Table 2: Statistics (Frequency) SSB and SSBC**

| **SSBM** | **Frequency** | **Percent (%)** | **SSBC** | **Frequency** | **Percent (%)** |
|---|---|---|---|---|---|
| Fewer than 3 | 49 | 59.8 | 1 to 2 | 69 | 84.1 |
| Above 3 | 33 | 40.2 | 3 to 4 | 13 | 15.9 |
| Total | 82 | 100.0 | Total | 82 | 100.0 |

Table 5.2 describes the percentages of the number of *Shariah* committees (SSBC) on *Sukuk*. The descriptive statistic showed that 69 *Sukuk*, or 40.2%, have fewer than three *Shariah* committees, and 13 *Sukuk* have three *Shariah* committees, which equals to 15.9%. The descriptive statistic showed that most of the Islamic *Sukuk* in IFIs had a number of *Shariah* committee members lower than three.

## Descriptive Statistics on *Sukuk* Legitimacy

Table 5.3 reports *Sukuk* legitimacy in Islamic institutions. The analysis shows that the percentage of *Sukuk* legitimacy was between 0.33% and 0.89%, whereas the descriptive statistics revealed that 0.33% represents the lowest level of *Sukuk* legitimacy which appeared in a *Shariah* report. On the other hand, the table also revealed that the highest level was 0.89. The current study divided *Sukuk* legitimacy into three levels; low (0.33 – 0.49), medium (0.50 – 0.75), and high (0.76 – 0.89). These levels converted from real data to the form of index, in order to determine the level of legitimacy, as shown in Appendix C. These levels represent the legitimacy disclosure in the *Shariah* report that was approved by an SSB. There were 27 *Sukuk* that had legitimacy between 0.33 and 0.49 percent, 31 *Sukuk* which had legitimacy between 0.50 and 0.75 percent and 24 *Sukuk* had legitimacy between 0.76 % and 0.89 %. Based on the content analysis, 29.3% of *Sukuk* issued from 2005 - 2015 conformed to *Shariah* principles. The rest, which stood at 32.9%, were found to have been lacking in *Shariah* conformity.

**Table 3: Statistics of *Sukuk* legitimacy**

| Legitimacy | Level | Frequency | Percent (%) |
|---|---|---|---|
| Valid 0.33 to 0.49 | Low | 27 | 32.9 |
| 0.50 to 0.75 | Medium | 31 | 37.8 |
| 0.76 to 0.89 | High | 24 | 29.3 |
| Total | | 82 | 100 |

## Assessment of Measurement Model

The present study proposed a model which consists of determinants, dependent variables, and moderators. The goodness of measures for all constructs was examined, in order to test their validity. This was done using PLS. The criterion used for evaluating the goodness of variables is construct validity, which included two important components; convergent validity and discriminant validity.

Convergent validity is the degree to which the constructs that are indicators of a specific construct should converge, or share a high proportion of variance in common (Hair, Black, Babin & Anderson 2010). Hair suggested several ways to estimate the convergent validity among construct measures, such as factor loading, average variance extracted (AVE) and composite reliability (CR). The loading for all constructs should exceed the recommended value of 0.50 or higher. Average variance extracted (AVE) which is a mean variance extracted for the constructs loading on a construct, should be above the recommended value of 0.50 (Hair et al. 2010). Discriminant validity is the extent to which a construct is truly distinct from other constructs (Hair et al. 2010). It is indicated by inevitable low correlation between the measure of interest and other measures that are supposedly not measuring the same variable or concept (Heeler & Ray 1972). In order to examine discriminant validity in PLS analysis, there are criteria applied. The square root of each construct's AVE should be greater than the level of correlations involving the constructs. Therefore, to address discriminant validity, the square root of the AVE is compared against the correlations of the other constructs (Fornell & Larcker 1981). As shown in Table 5.4, the calculated square root of the AVE exceeds the inter-correlations of the construct with the other constructs in the model, which ensures adequate discriminant validity.

**Table 4: Discriminant Validity Constructs (Without Moderators)**

| | LG | PR | TYP | SHAUD | SHR | SHDC |
|---|---|---|---|---|---|---|
| **LG** | 1 | | | | | |
| **RR** | 0.589 | 1 | | | | |
| **TYP** | 0.444 | 0.325 | 1 | | | |
| **SHAUD** | 0.751 | 0.342 | 0.424 | 1 | | |
| **SHR** | -0.584 | -0.274 | -0.123 | -0.642 | 1 | |
| **SHDC** | -0.230 | -0.147 | -0.265 | -0.253 | -0.642 | 1 |

Accordingly, Table 5.5 shows the result that the criteria have been successfully fulfilled. Hence, the measurement model of the study demonstrated adequate convergent and discriminant validity.

**Table 5: Discriminant Validity Constructs (With Moderators)**

| | LG | PR | PR * SSBC | SHAUD | SHAUD * SSBC | SHD | SHD * SSBC | SHR | SHR * SSBC | TYP | TYP * SSBC |
|---|---|---|---|---|---|---|---|---|---|---|---|
| **LG** | 1 | | | | | | | | | | |
| **SSBC** | 0.1127 | | | | | | | | | | |
| **PR** | 0.5886 | 1 | | | | | | | | | |
| **PR* SSBC** | 0.1415 | -0.0114 | 1 | | | | | | | | |
| **SHAUD** | 0.7514 | 0.3423 | -0.0042 | 1 | | | | | | | |
| **SHAUD* SSBC** | -0.0312 | -0.0045 | 0.318 | 0.031 | 1 | | | | | | |
| **SHDC** | -0.2299 | -0.1465 | -0.0079 | -0.2528 | 0.0201 | 1 | | | | | |
| **SHDC* SSBC** | 0.0678 | -0.0086 | -0.2964 | 0.0202 | -0.461 | 0.0155 | 1 | | | | |
| **SHR** | -0.5835 | -0.2739 | 0.0174 | -0.6417 | 0.0393 | -0.0241 | 0.0023 | 1 | | | |
| **SHR* SSBC** | -0.01 | 0.0237 | -0.4361 | 0.0501 | -0.5426 | 0.003 | 0.4025 | 0.26 | 1 | | |
| **TYP** | 0.4438 | 0.3247 | 0.0582 | 0.4236 | -0.1579 | -0.2654 | -0.2819 | -0.1233 | 0.1993 | 1 | |
| **TYP* SSBC** | -0.0739 | 0.0582 | 0.3776 | -0.1474 | 0.4653 | -0.2609 | -0.5723 | 0.1459 | -0.2512 | 0.1119 | **1** |
| | **LG** | **PR** | **PR * SSBM** | **SHAUD** | **SHAUD * SSBM** | **SHD** | **SHD * SSBM** | **SHR** | **SHR * SSBM** | **TYP** | **TYP * SSBM** |
| **LG** | 1 | | | | | | | | | | |
| **SSBM** | 0.0468 | | | | | | | | | | |
| **PR** | 0.5886 | 1 | | | | | | | | | |
| **PR * SSBM** | 0.0573 | -0.0084 | 1 | | | | | | | | |
| **SHAUD** | 0.7514 | 0.3423 | -0.0933 | 1 | | | | | | | |
| **SHAUD * SSBM** | -0.0926 | -0.089 | 0.2799 | 0.0171 | 1 | | | | | | |
| **SHD** | -0.2299 | -0.1465 | -0.0558 | -0.2528 | 0.0754 | 1 | | | | | |
| **SHD * SSBM** | 0.0585 | -0.0569 | -0.2282 | 0.0806 | -0.2573 | 0.0381 | 1 | | | | |
| **SHR** | -0.5835 | -0.2739 | 0.1196 | -0.6417 | 0.0918 | -0.0241 | -0.1226 | 1 | | | |
| **SHR * SSBM** | 0.1044 | 0.1455 | -0.2924 | 0.1171 | -0.3905 | -0.1463 | 0.1438 | 0.351 | 1 | | |
| **TYP** | 0.4438 | 0.3247 | -0.0645 | 0.4236 | -0.2087 | -0.2654 | -0.3658 | -0.1233 | 0.3397 | 1 | |
| **TYP * SSBM** | -0.231 | -0.0604 | 0.2056 | -0.2049 | 0.2464 | -0.336 | -0.6709 | 0.2614 | -0.0619 | 0.0858 | **1** |

Note: Diagonals represent the square root of the average variance extracted (AVE) while the off-diagonals represent the correlations among the constructs

## Assessment of Structural Model

The Structural Model represents the relationship between constructs or latent variables that were hypothesized in the research model. Since the primary objective of PLS is prediction (Hair et al. 2011), the goodness of the theoretical model is established by the variance explained ($R^2$) of the endogenous constructs and the significance of all path estimates (Chin 2010).

Structural Model assessment was performed only after measurement model analysis had passed all the recommended criteria. The starting point for judging the structural model was to examine the determination coefficient ($R^2$). In this study, the endogenous variables appear to have $R^2$ value of 0.710 (substantial), suggesting that 71% of the variance in legitimacy can be explained by pricing, type of structure, *Shariah* auditing, *Shariah* risk and *Shariah* documentation. As Table 5.6 shows, the endogenous variables have a high $R^2$ value of 0.772 with the moderator (SSB), and the highest $R^2$ value 0.782 with the second moderator (SSBC), which means that the level of legitimacy is better with moderators, in that the existence of a moderator (SSB) will strengthen and increase the level of legitimacy. According to Cohen (1988), an $R^2$ value of 0.26 and above is considered substantial, which means that the estimated model fits the data very well. Thus, it can be concluded that this study meets this criteria considerably well. The variance explained for endogenous construct is shown in Table 5.6, below.

**Table 6: Variance Explained**

| **Endogenous Construct** | **Variance Explained ($R^2$)** |
|---|---|
| Exogenous Variables -> Endogenous (Legitimacy) | 0.710 |
| Exogenous Variables*Moderator (SSB) ->Endogenous Variable | 0.772 |
| Exogenous Variables*Moderator (SSBC) ->Endogenous Variable | 0.782 |

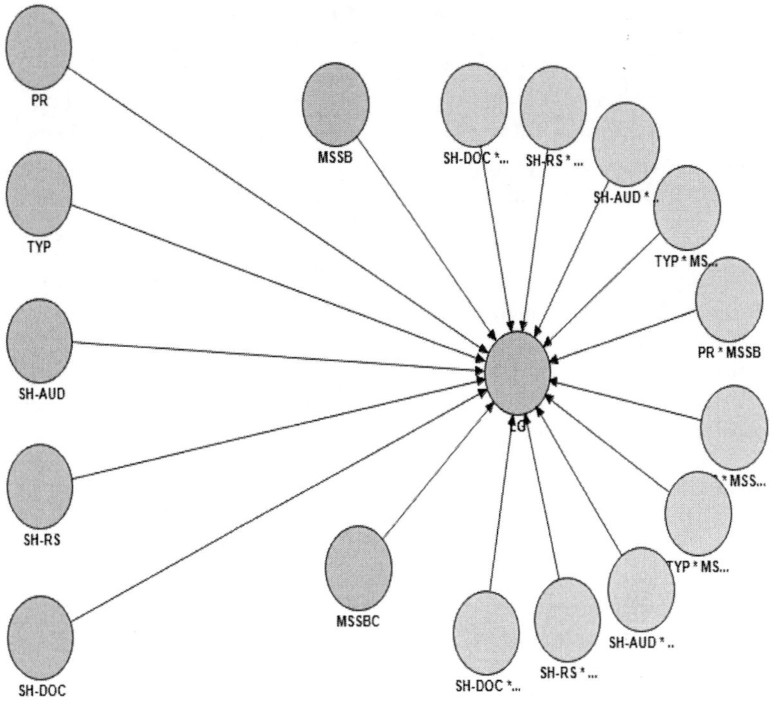


Figure.1: Structural Model

## Hypotheses Testing

Hypotheses H1, H2, H3, H4, and H5, which were assumed to result in either a positive or negative relationship between determinants (pricing, type of structure, *Shariah* auditing, *Shariah* risk and *Shariah* documentation) and *Sukuk* legitimacy, were tested simultaneously through the bootstrapping procedure. The path coefficient range should be greater than 0.1 to be considered acceptable (Tabachnick & Fidell 2007). After computing the path estimates from the initial set, three were revealed as significant and two as not significant. The results from this test are presented next.

Table 5.7 summarizes the results of the hypothesis testing. It shows that there were three determinants that have a positive relationship with *Sukuk* legitimacy, (pricing 0.340, type of structure 0.103, *Shariah* auditing 0.466) but two other determinants are found to have a negative relationship with *Sukuk* legitimacy (*Shariah* risk -0.179, and *Shariah* documentation -0.039).

The result showed that pricing has a significant impact on *Sukuk* legitimacy, where it is at $P < 0.01$, $t = 5.187$. It shows that the more *Shariah*-compliant the pricing, the higher the legitimacy of *Sukuk*. Therefore, H1 has been supported. With regard to the type of structure, the result showed that there is a positive relationship with *Sukuk* legitimacy $P < 0.05$, $t = 1.614$. This result indicates that the more compliant the structure is with *Shariah,* (i.e. asset backed), the higher the legitimacy of *Sukuk*. Thus, H2 is supported as well.

For *Shariah* auditing, the result showed that it has a significant effect on the legitimacy of *Sukuk* where $P < 0.001$, $t = 4.645$. This proves that *Sukuk* that is subjected to *Shariah* auditing has higher legitimacy. Therefore, H3 is also supported. The result showed that *Shariah* risk has a negative (i.e. inverse) relationship with *Sukuk* legitimacy where $P < 0.05$, $t = -1.957$. This means that when the *Shariah* risk is low, the legitimacy is higher, and vice versa. Therefore, H4 is supported.

It is notable that the results also showed that *Shariah* documentation has a negative relationship with *Sukuk* legitimacy where it was $P < 0.05$, $t = -0.591$. This result indicates that the amount of *Shariah* documentation has a negative impact on *Sukuk* legitimacy. This could be attributed to the fact that there is lack of documentation details provided in the *Shariah* pronouncement. Therefore, H5 is not supported. Overall, these results supported the assertion that the majority of determinants do impact the legitimacy of *Sukuk*.

**Table 6: Path Coefficient (Without Moderator)**

| **Hypotheses** | **Path** | **Path Co-efficient** | **Standard Error** | **t-value** | **Results** |
|---|---|---|---|---|---|
| **H1** | PR -> LG | 0.340 | 0.065 | ***5.187 | Supported |
| **H2** | TYP -> LG | 0.103 | 0.064 | *1.614 | Supported |
| **H3** | SHAUD -> LG | 0.466 | 0.100 | ***4.645 | Supported |
| **H4** | SHR -> LG | -0.179 | 0.091 | *1.957 | Supported |
| **H5** | SHD -> LG | -0.039 | 0.066 | 0.591 | Not supported |

Note: Significance levels: ***$p < 0.001$ ($t > 3.33$), **$p < 0.01$ ($t > 2.33$), *$p < 0.05$ ($t > 1.605$) (based in one-tailed test)

The next Figure, 5.2, shows the direct effects of the predictor variables on criterion variables which were tested using the bootstrapping procedure. Figure 5.2 shows the significant paths (at the minimum level of 0.1) for the model. As can be seen, of the initial five constructs, four appear to have significant effect on legitimacy, with pricing construct having the strongest influence.

Table 5.8 presents the results of the five hypotheses (i.e. H1, H2, H3, H4, and H5) where only four variables are supported, and one did not support it.

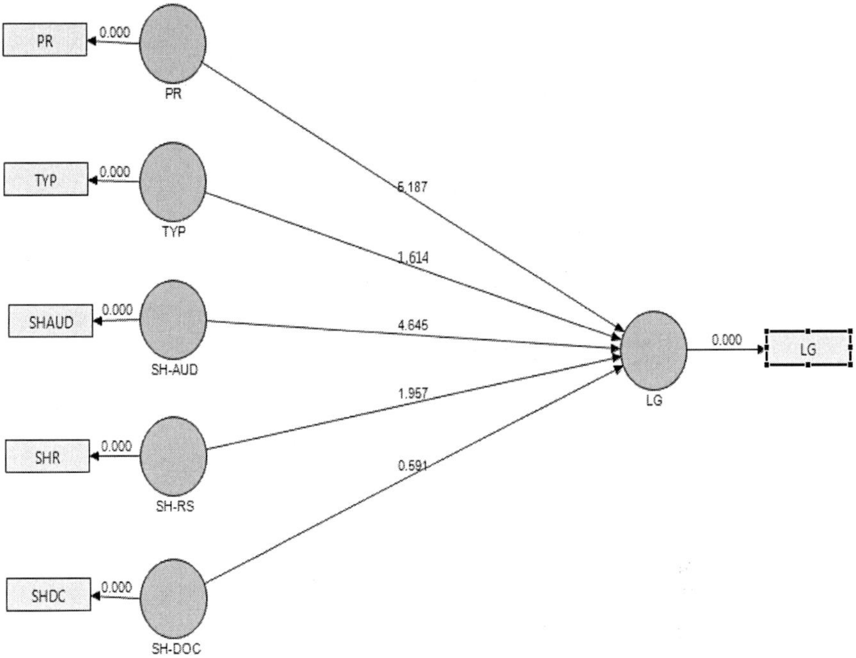


Figure 2: Statistical Significant Path Coefficients

## The Moderating Effect

A moderator is a qualitative or quantitative variable that affects the direction and or the strength of the relationship between a predictor variable and a criterion variable (Baron & Kenny 1986). To test the moderating effect, the influence of the predictor variable on the criterion variable, the direct effect of the moderating variable on the criterion variable and the influence of the interaction variable on the criterion variable are tested (Henseler & Chin 2010). Figure 5.3 shows that the moderator hypotheses are supported if the interaction path is significant (path c), independent of the magnitude of the path coefficients 'a' and 'b' (Baron & Kenny 1986).

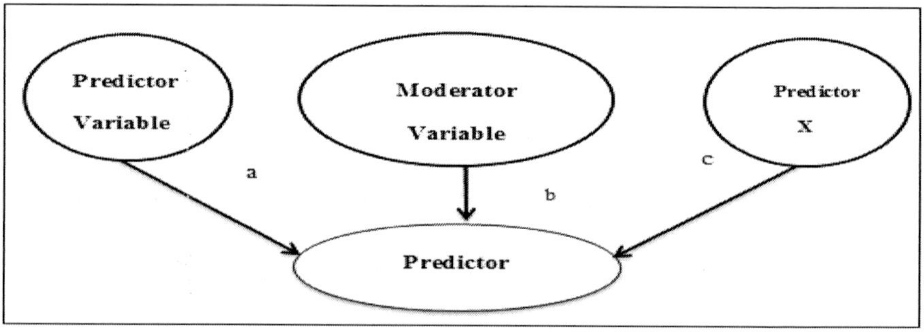


Figure.3: Moderator Model

In presenting the moderation analysis in this study, the PLS product indicator approach (Chin 2010) was applied to detect the moderating effect of two dimensions; SSBM and SSBC, on the relationship between determinants and *Sukuk* legitimacy.

## SSBM as a Moderator between Determinants and Legitimacy

Firstly, the moderating effect of SSBM is tested. In testing the possibility of such effect, determinants (predictor) and SSBM (moderator) were multiplied to create an interaction construct (determinants x SSBM) to *Sukuk* legitimacy. The estimated standardized path coefficient for the interaction (path c) is 2.175 ($t = 1.1205$) which is significant at $p < 0.05$ with a $R^2$ of 0.772; this is slightly higher than the $R^2$ of the main effect model which is 0.710 (refer to Appendix D). The effect size of the interaction is calculated as follows:

$$f^2 = \frac{R^2 \text{ model with moderator} - R^2 \text{ model without moderator}}{1 - R^2 \text{ model with moderator}}$$

$$\frac{0.772 - 0.710}{1 - 0.772}$$

$$= 0.271$$

The result shows that the size of the moderator is small ($f^2 = 0.271$) (Cohen 1988). However, Chin (2010) stated that small $f^2$ does not imply that the moderating effect is insignificant, because "even small interaction effects can be meaningful under extreme moderating conditions, if the resulting beta changes are meaningful, then it is important to take these conditions into account". Therefore, the study accepts that SSB does moderate the relationship between determinants and legitimacy. Figure 5.4 illustrates the moderating effect for one of moderating variables.

The analysis is started by testing the moderating effect of SSBM on the relationship between determinants and *Sukuk* legitimacy, as shown in Table 5.9. An assessment on the path coefficients for interaction terms shows that SSBM moderates the relationship only between two determinants and *Sukuk* legitimacy, namely the pricing at $p < 0.01$, $t = 3.028$, and *Shariah* documentation at $p < 0.05$, $t = 1.650$. The introduction of the terms made significant increases in model value, and raises $R^2$ around 6%. As such, the study confirms that SSBM does moderate the relationship between determinants and *Sukuk* legitimacy. However, SSBM shows no moderating effect between the other three determinants (type of structure, *Shariah* auditing and *Shariah* risks) with *Sukuk* legitimacy. Therefore, this result indicated that hypotheses H7, H8, and H9 are not supported. The PLS output is shown in Appendix D.

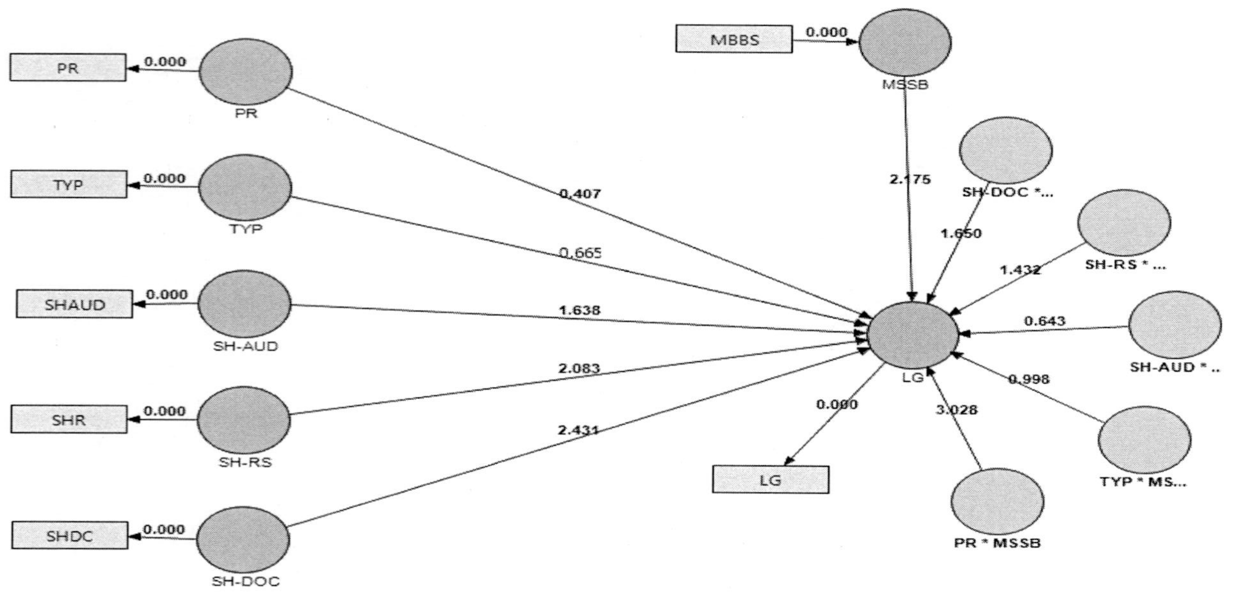


Figure 4: The Moderating Effect of SSBM

**Table 7: Moderating Effect of SSBM on The Relationship Between Determinants and *Sukuk* Legitimacy**

| Path | Path Coefficient | Standard Error | t-value | Results |
|---|---|---|---|---|
| **SSB -> LG** | -1.120 | 0.515 | *2.175 | Supported |
| **PR -> LG** | -0.042 | 0.103 | *0.407 | Not supported |
| **PR * SSB -> LG** | 0.473 | 0.156 | **3.028 | Supported |
| **TYP -> LG** | 0.087 | 0.131 | 0.665 | Not supported |
| **TYP * SSB -> LG** | 0.184 | 0.184 | 0.998 | Not supported |
| **SH-AUD -> LG** | 0.284 | 0.173 | *1.638 | Supported |
| **SH-AUD * SSB -> LG** | 0.179 | 0.279 | 0.643 | Not supported |
| **SH-RS -> LG** | -0.610 | 0.293 | *2.083 | Supported |
| **SH-RS * SSB -> LG** | 0.542 | 0.379 | 1.432 | Not supported |
| **SH-DOC -> LG** | -0.351 | 0.144 | 2.431 | Supported |
| **SH-DOC * SSB -> LG** | 0.550 | 0.333 | *1.650 | Supported |
| Note: Significance levels: ***p < 0.001, **p < 0. 01, *p < 0.05 | | | | |

To confirm this result, a graphical impact of this moderation effect was tested. Figure 5.5 illustrates the plotted graph used for analyzing the moderating effect of SSBM on the relationship between pricing and *Sukuk* legitimacy. The plotted graph demonstrates that when the level of pricing is high, the tendency for SSBM moderating effect to *Sukuk* legitimacy is higher. This shows that in *Sukuk* that have high SSBM involvement, pricing has a continuous positive impact on legitimacy. On the other hand, *Sukuk* that have low SSBM involvement show a weak relationship between pricing and *Sukuk* legitimacy. Thus, it can be inferred that *Sukuk* which have a high level of SSBM involvement have a higher and a positive relationship between pricing and legitimacy. Here, we can observe that strong *Sukuk* legitimacy results when SSBM involvement is stronger. Thus, hypothesis H6 is supported.

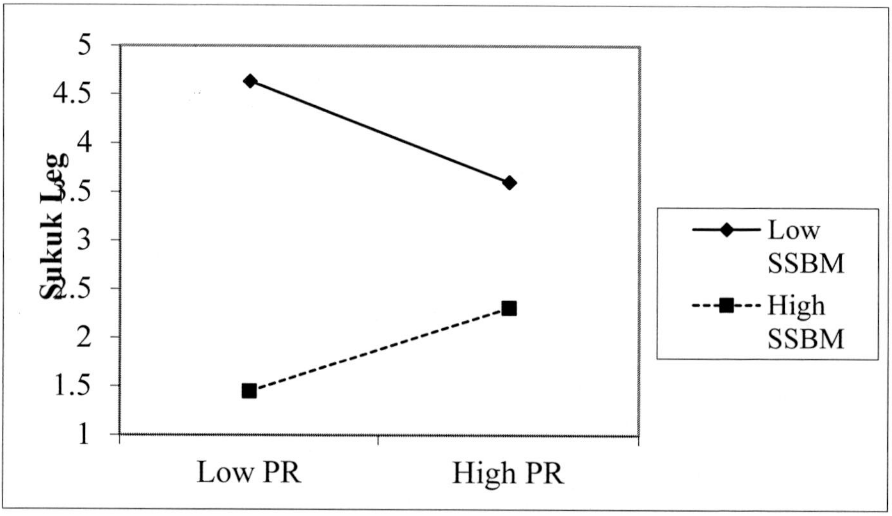


Figure 5: Moderating Effect of SSBM on the Pricing-*Sukuk* Legitimacy Relationship

The graph portrayed in Figure 5.6 further illustrates the moderating effect of SSBM on the relationship between *Shariah* documentation and *Sukuk* legitimacy. It can be observed from the figure, that *Sukuk* that have low SSBM involvement show a weak relationship between *Shariah* documentation and *Sukuk* legitimacy. In contrast, in *Sukuk* which have a high level of SSBM involvement, a positive impact is seen between *Shariah* documentation and *Sukuk* legitimacy level. The graph shows that the stronger the SSBM involvement, the stronger the relationship between *Shariah* documentation and *Sukuk* legitimacy. Therefore, hypothesis H10 is supported.

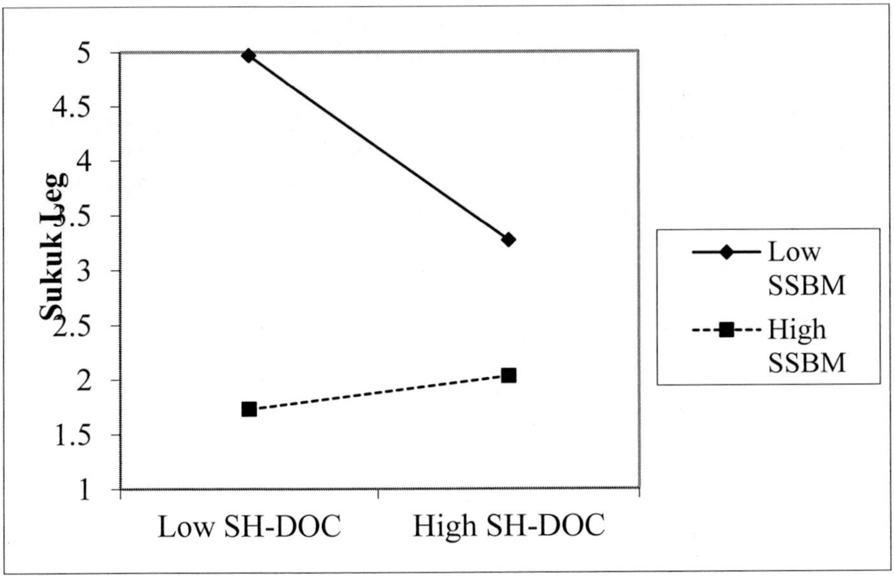


Figure 6: Moderating Effect of SSBM on the *Shariah* Documentation-*Sukuk* Legitimacy Relationship

## SSBC as a Moderator Between Determinants and Legitimacy

Next, the moderating effect of SSBC is tested. In testing the possibility of this effect, determinants (the predictor) and SSBC (the moderator) were multiplied to create an interaction construct (determinants x SSBC) to *Sukuk* legitimacy. The values of path coefficients reflect the degree of association between each of these variables (Cohen 1988). The Pearson correlation ranges between -1.00 and +1.00 in size, where 0 represents no relationship between variables, and a value of -1.00 or +1.00 indicates perfect correlation (Tabachnick & Fidell 2007). In interpreting the path coefficients for this study, path values of ± 0.5 and above reflect strong correlations between two variables. The effect size of the interaction is calculated as follows:

$$f^2 = \frac{R^2 \text{ model with moderator} - R^2 \text{ model without moderator}}{1 - R^2 \text{ model with moderator}}$$

$$\frac{0.782 - 0.710}{1 - 0.782}$$

$$= 0.330$$

The result shows that the size of the moderator effect is medium effect ($f^2 = 0.330$) (Cohen 1988). However, Chin (2010) states that medium $f^2$ does not imply that the moderating effect is insignificant, because "even small interaction effects can be meaningful under extreme moderating conditions, if the resulting beta changes are meaningful, then it is important to take these conditions into account". Therefore, the study accepts that SSBC does moderate the relationship between determinants and legitimacy. Figure 5.7 illustrates the example, to test the moderating effect for one of the moderating variables.

The analysis starts by testing the moderating effect of SSBC on the relationship between determinants and *Sukuk* legitimacy, as shown in Table 5.10. An assessment of the path coefficients for interaction terms shows that SSBC moderates the relationship only between two determinants and *Sukuk* legitimacy, namely the pricing at $p < 0.01$, $t = 2.703$, and *Shariah* risk at $p < 0.01$, $t = 2.439$. The introduction of the terms made significant increases in model value, and raises $R^2$ around 7%. As such, the study confirms that SSBC does moderate the relationship between determinants and *Sukuk* legitimacy. However, SSBC shows no moderating effect between the other three elements (type of structure, *Shariah* auditing, and *Shariah* documentation) with *Sukuk* legitimacy. Therefore, this result indicated that hypotheses H6 and H12 are not supported. The PLS output is shown in Appendix D.

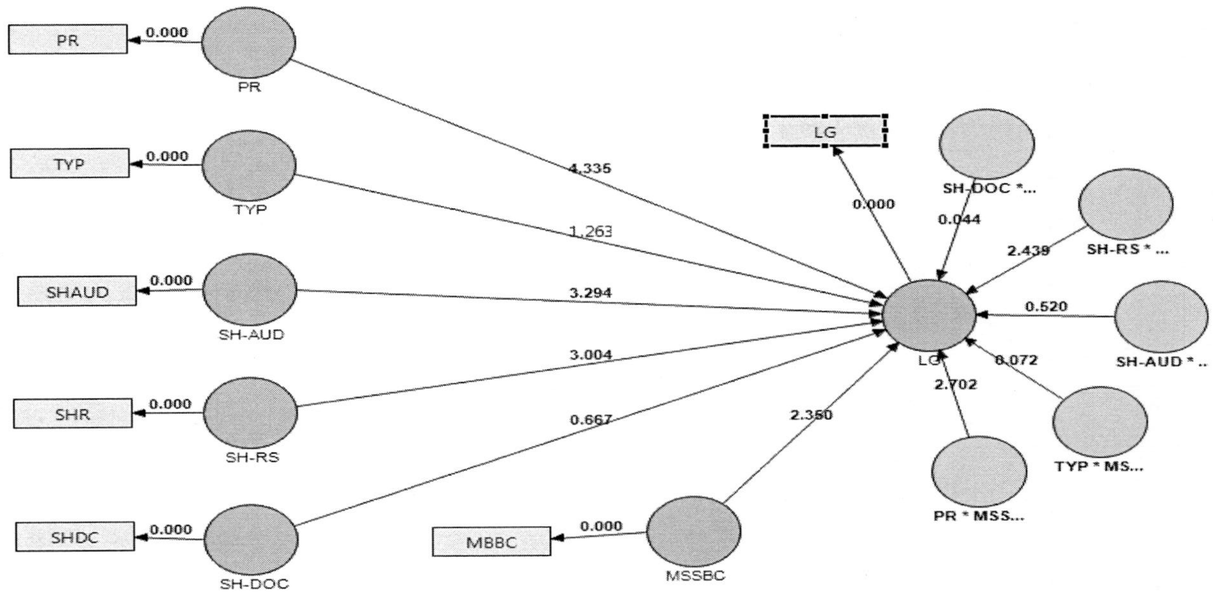


Figure.7: The Moderating Effect of SSBC

**Table 8: The Moderating Effect of SSBC Between Determinants and *Sukuk* Legitimacy**

| Path | Path Coefficient | Standard Error | t-value | Results |
|---|---|---|---|---|
| SSBC -> LG | 0.227 | 0.097 | 2.350 | Supported |
| PR -> LG | 0.269 | 0.062 | ***4.335 | Supported |
| PR * SSBC -> LG | 0.183 | 0.068 | ***2.703 | Supported |
| TYP -> LG | 0.137 | 0.109 | 1.263 | Not supported |
| TYP * SSBC -> LG | 0.010 | 0.142 | 0.072 | Not supported |
| SH-AUD -> LG | 0.362 | 0.110 | *3.294 | Supported |
| SH-AUD * SSBC -> LG | 0.040 | 0.077 | 0.520 | Not supported |
| SH-RS -> LG | -0.388 | 0.129 | *3.004 | Supported |
| SH-RS * SSBC -> LG | 0.243 | 0.100 | **2.439 | Supported |
| SH-DOC -> LG | -0.063 | 0.094 | 0.667 | Not supported |
| SH-DOC * SSBC -> LG | 0.006 | 0.146 | 0.044 | Not supported |
| Note: Significance levels: ***p < 0.001, **p < 0. 01, *p < 0.05 | | | | |

To confirm this result, a graphical impact of this moderation effect was tested. Figure 5.8 illustrated the plotted graph used for analyzing the moderating effect of SSBC on the relationship between pricing and *Sukuk* legitimacy. The plotted graph demonstrated that when the level of pricing is high, the tendency is that both pricing level and *Sukuk* legitimacy are higher when SSBC is moderating. This shows that in *Sukuk* that have a high level of SSBC involvement, pricing has a continuous positive impact on *Sukuk* legitimacy. On the other hand, *Sukuk* that have low SSBC involvement show a weak relationship between pricing and *Sukuk* legitimacy. Thus, it can be inferred that *Sukuk* which have a high level of SSBC involvement have a higher, positive relationship between pricing and *Sukuk* legitimacy. Here, we can observe that strong *Sukuk* legitimacy results when SSBC involvement is stronger. Thus, hypothesis H11 is supported.

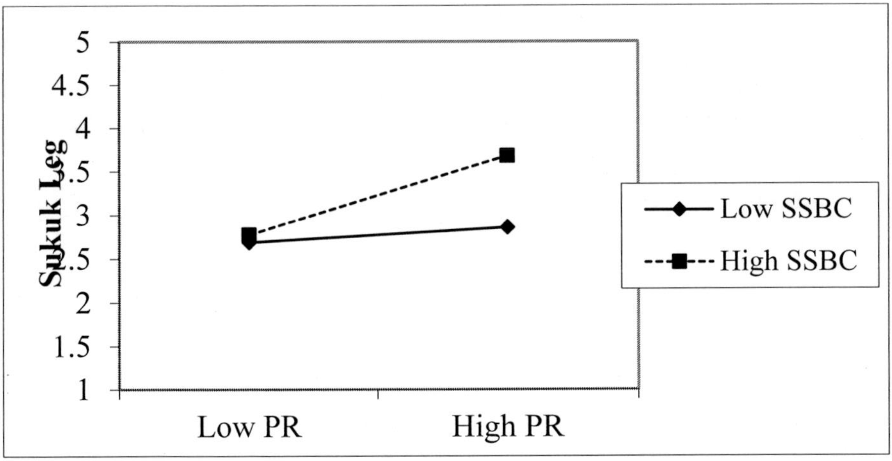


Figure 8: The Moderating Effect of SSBC on the Pricing-*Sukuk* Legitimacy Relationship

The graph portrayed in Figure 5.9 further illustrates the moderating effect of SSBC on the relationship between *Shariah* risk and *Sukuk* legitimacy. It can be observed from the figure that *Sukuk* that have low SSBC involvement show a weak relationship between *Shariah* risk and *Sukuk* legitimacy. In contrast, in *Sukuk* with a high level of SSBC involvement, a positive impact is seen between *Shariah* risk and *Sukuk* legitimacy level. The graph shows that, the stronger the SSBC involvement, the stronger the relationship between *Shariah* risk and *Sukuk* legitimacy. Therefore, Hypothesis H14 is supported.

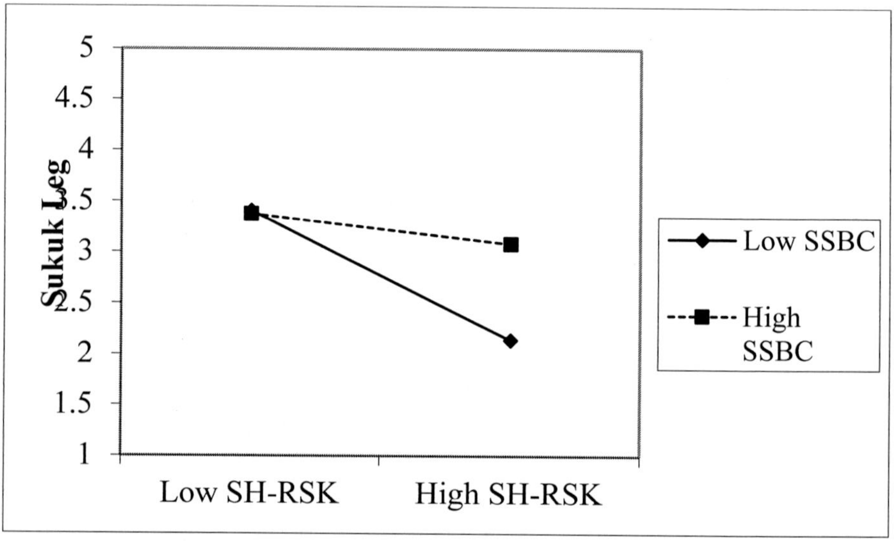


Figure 9: The Moderating Effect of SSBC on the *Shariah* risks-*Sukuk* Legitimacy Relationship

# CHAPTER 8

# RESEARCH FINDINGS (BASED ON QUALITATIVE DATA)

## Introduction

A mixed-mode interview method was adopted in interviewing participants. A checklist of questions was used to ensure that topics central to the question were covered in the interviews (DiCicco-Bloom & Crabtree 2006). The aim of semi-structured interviews was to obtain perspectives of opinion, reflections, and comments, from those who have special knowledge, expertise, and information, and who hail from specialized allied professions involved with the Islamic finance industry. Semi-structured interviewing is more adaptable than other research methods, such as the structured interview or survey, although the questions asked to deeply understand each issue arose during the interview process (Louise Barriball & While 1994). The use of open-ended questions allowed respondents to express their views on issues not necessarily anticipated by the interviewer, and provided the opportunity to cover factors deemed important by the respondents. Interviews were conducted in English and Arabic, where applicable.

Thematic analysis was used to discuss the issues under study. This study was conducted with mixed-mode interviews with members of the SSB, using several different semi-structured questions, covering various aspects of *Sukuk* legitimacy including pricing, type of structure, *Shariah* auditing, *Shariah* compliant risk, and *Shariah* documentation for *Sukuk* in IFIs. In addition, this study conducted a survey with two Muftis (Muslim legal experts) to widen the perspectives of the feedback on the above issues, to capture the depth of their experience. The researcher developed a sustainable professional relationship with the respondents, to enhance the quality of the questions, and consequently the analysis, and to allow for follow-up questions and clarifications where needed. The interviews started with pre-set questions which paved the way for a detailed discourse on the subject matter. The interviews comprised four phases. During the first phase, interviewees were asked to express their opinions on the legitimacy of *Sukuk* in IFIs. In phase two, the interviewees were asked to determine the factors (determinants) that have a high influence on *Sukuk* legitimacy. The third phase was inquiring about the relationship between determinants and legitimacy of *Sukuk*. The last phase was directed towards understanding the moderating effect of an SSB.

A total of 17 interviewees were approached via all mediums (face-to-face: five people, telephone: one person, and email: 11 people). Only three respondents from face-to-face, three from email, and one via telephone successfully completed the interview. The rest either refused to be interviewed, or failed to return the email questionnaire sent. The respondents who successfully completed the interview were able to explain their views in detail, and to discuss issues which might have been sensitive, on a confidential basis. The next section presents the detailed findings from the interviews. Table 5.12 shows the summary of the direct effect of the determinants on legitimacy, and Table 5.13 shows the moderating effect of the SSB on determinants, and its relationship to legitimacy.

**Table 1: Direct Relationship**

| No | PR | TYP | Sh-Aud | Sh-RK | Rh-DC | SSB |
|---|---|---|---|---|---|---|
| 1 | × | ✓ | ✓ | ✓ | ✓ | ✓ |
| 2 | ✓ | ✓ | ✓ | ✓ | ✓ | ✓ |
| 3 | × | × | ✓ | ✓ | ✓ | ✓ |
| 4 | ✓ | × | ✓ | ✓ | ✓ | ✓ |
| 5 | × | × | ✓ | ✓ | ✓ | ✓ |
| 6 | ✓ | ✓ | ✓ | ✓ | ✓ | ✓ |
| 7 | ✓ | ✓ | ✓ | ✓ | ✓ | ✓ |

**Table 2: Effect of SSB on Determinants**

| No | PR | TYP | Sh-Aud | Sh-RK | Sh Doc |
|---|---|---|---|---|---|
| 1 | × | × | ✓ | ✓ | ✓ |
| 2 | ✓ | ✓ | ✓ | ✓ | ✓ |
| 3 | ✓ | ✓ | ✓ | ✓ | ✓ |
| 4 | ✓ | ✓ | ✓ | ✓ | ✓ |
| 5 | ✓ | ✓ | ✓ | ✓ | ✓ |
| 6 | × | × | ✓ | ✓ | ✓ |
| 7 | ✓ | ✓ | ✓ | ✓ | ✓ |

## Measurement and Extent of Legitimacy of *Sukuk*

As pointed out in Chapter One, relatively little systematic effort has been dedicated to developing a valid measure of *Sukuk* legitimacy. However, there has been interest among researchers towards *Sukuk* legitimacy techniques (Usmani 2002, Kantakji & O'haj 2010, Hidayat 2013). In addition, there has been a lack of empirical studies investigating the legitimacy of *Sukuk*, especially in Malaysia. Therefore, this study sought to be the first to develop and validate measures of *Sukuk* legitimacy among Malaysian Islamic *Sukuk*, and then investigate the level of legitimacy of the *Sukuk* themselves.

The findings in this study showed that *Sukuk* legitimacy is contributed to by five determinants: pricing, type of structure, *Shariah* risk, *Shariah* auditing, and documentation. Therefore, this output fulfilled the research gap of previous studies regarding the measuring of legitimacy by using disclosure information, rather than *Sukuk* structure.

One of the key purposes of applying the interview approach in the current study was to investigate the extent of *Sukuk* legitimacy. The second issue posted by both methods (semi-structured interviews and emailing interviews) was aimed at evaluating the legitimacy of *Sukuk* based on the measurements that were used in *Shariah* reports. Seven *Shariah* Board members were asked to evaluate *Sukuk* legitimacy in their *Shariah* pronouncements, according to the content that constructs a *Shariah* report (structure, documentation, and approval). In addition, interviewees were required to provide explanation and justification about the legitimacy of *Sukuk*.

The demand for *Shariah*-compliant financial instruments is a major feature of the Malaysian market, and a key driver of the growth of the Islamic finance industry. This factor has convinced most issuers of *Sukuk* to comply with *Shariah* instead of conventional guidelines. The consensus amongst the seven interviewees interviewed was that *Sukuk* legitimacy will continue to rapidly increase the demand from customers. One of the interviewers was noted as saying "[…] companies should promote legitimacy of Sukuk for a better risk-return profile for their institutional and individual investors". Therefore, the launching of the secondary *Sukuk* market has substantially enhanced the prospects of *Sukuk* becoming a pivotal investment asset class, particularly for Muslim investors. Through the result of the semi-structured interviews, all *Shariah* Board members claimed that the *Sukuk* legitimacy is high, while two *Shariah* Board members agreed that the use of conventional benchmarks would affect the legitimacy of *Sukuk* negatively. The *Shariah*

Board members confirmed that the main concern of *Sukuk* is the usage of conventional pricing benchmarks like LIBOR. The findings of semi-structured interviews are run with the output of a quantitative study with regards to the legitimacy of *Sukuk*, and the factors which affect legitimacy. To recall, the quantitative findings showed that *Sukuk* legitimacy was generally high.

Furthermore, all seven SSB members have ranked four *Sukuk* determinants, namely type of structure, *Shariah* auditing, *Shariah* risk, and *Shariah* documentation, higher than pricing. Risk and price are the major drivers for any investment instrument. However, an illiquid *Sukuk* market, because of the lack of an active secondary market, could distort the pricing of future *Sukuk* issues, thus putting a dampener on future issuance. Seven out of the thirteen interviewees expressed concern over the effect of the global credit market crisis on *Sukuk* pricing, which they claimed could further distort pricing, and could threaten the ability of issuers to raise funding via *Sukuk*. One SSB respondent, Abdul Ghani said "[...] The problems would be in terms of the ability to properly price the Sukuk" The quantitative results concerning the extent of *Sukuk* legitimacy were supported and validated by the qualitative output. Most of the members of SSBs in the Islamic finance sector had confirmed the quantitative results regarding the extent of *Sukuk* legitimacy. In that, these qualitative findings were consistent with, and confirmed, the descriptive findings of the survey results outlined earlier in this chapter. The result showed that one *Sukuk* determinant factor (pricing) was ranked at the bottom of the list. In this regard, the SSB members provided some reasons behind the comparatively low extent of the effect of pricing on legitimacy. Firstly, the interviewee quoted that pricing is generally not a problem, if it is mentioned clearly in the contracts on the type of benchmarking used. Secondly, they said that the current pricing benchmark (i.e., LIBOR) is a weak measurement, hence IFI should move away from it to enhance *Sukuk* legitimacy.

## The Relationship between Determinants and *Sukuk* Legitimacy

Based on the interviews conducted, the determinants, and *Sukuk* legitimacy, with regard to the issues raised by SSB members, are discussed under a common theme.

## Pricing Benchmark

The pricing benchmark is one factor which effects the legitimacy of *Sukuk* (Wilson 2008, Usmani 2009, Herwany & Febrian 2010, Ahmed et al. 2014, Aloui et al. 2015). The pricing benchmark needs to be developed by SSBs, and has significant effect on pricing when making decisions on the pricing benchmark. The majority of previous studies have established that the method of distancing pricing from conventional benchmarks is a major challenge in the Islamic capital market (ICM), as pricing has an effect on the *Shariah*-compliance of Islamic financial instruments (Wilson 2008, Usmani 2009, Nanaeva 2010, Herwany & Febrian 2010, Ahmed et al. 2014, Aloui et al. 2015).

One of the interviewees believed, and strongly claimed, that there was no direct relationship between pricing and *Sukuk* legitimacy. On this point, he illustrated "[...] not necessarily. However, it could be an issue for some investors who consider use of a non-Shariah compliant interest-based index". This advances the argument that the usage of interest rates as a benchmark is not a desirable practice. Another respondent also indicate that *Sukuk* dealing with conventional benchmarks would be undesirable (Kantakji interview 2014).

*Sukuk* pricing based on any technical benchmark should be free from interest rates, non-real economic activities, and non-*halal* activities, such as indices of financial derivatives instruments. According to *Shariah* Board members at the World Bank, Hossein Askari, in an interview in 2014 said, "pricing *Sukuk* according to conventional benchmarks will not affect the legitimacy of *Sukuk*, because there is no alternative Islamic benchmark".

Another prominent member of the SSB had strong reservations about the lack of liquidity in the secondary market, which the interviewee stressed further distorted *Sukuk* pricing. In this case, the collaboration between the issuers, the SSB, and other stakeholders, is becoming a necessity to come up with solutions for developing an Islamic benchmark, rather than a conventional benchmark. This has become a major obstacle for financial institutions to source for solutions that comply with *Shariah*.

Three out of seven respondents reiterated the importance of the Islamic pricing benchmark, where the price is determined by the dynamics of cashflow for the project, or pricing benchmarks that can be obtained by creating a common pool, like lending in asset-backed tools such as *Musharakah*, *Ijarah*, and so forth. This shows a clear correlation between

*Sukuk* pricing and legitimacy, which could adversely affect future *Sukuk* issuance. However these risks would be incorporated and reflected in the pricing of *Sukuk* originations. The interviewees agreed that the SSB should play a stronger role in enhancing *Sukuk* legitimacy, by enforcing an Islamic pricing benchmark, to make *Sukuk* attractive and competitive against conventional bonds.

## Type of Structure

Based on the literature, the types of *Sukuk* structures differ significantly between the asset-backed and asset-based *Sukuk*, both from a *Shariah* and a market standpoint, with the ability to influence the level of positivity of the legitimacy of the *Sukuk* (Haneef 2009, Howladar 2009, Khnifer 2010b, Hidayat 2013, Alia et al. 2013, Shabana 2013, Abdulmalik 2013, Azmat et al. 2014a).

The interviewees agreed that the type of structure and the underlying assets are necessary for *Sukuk* legitimacy, especially in the case of potential default. Six out of seven interviewees agreed that *Sukuk* should be classified as asset-backed *Sukuk*, with tradable rights and obligations to the underlying assets. Nonetheless, two out of seven interviewees preferred the issuing to be in an asset-based *Sukuk*, due to the lack of developed legal infrastructure in the case of default. One interviewee mentioned "[...] Sukuk need assets to be securitized in a Shariah-compliant method. Most Sukuk are asset-based, and other Sukuk holders are discovering that they might not enjoy any more creditworthiness privileges than conventional counterparts in the event of default". Therefore, there is a need for greater *Sukuk* risk evaluation on *Sukuk* dissolution in the event of default. Three out of seven of the interviewees expressed their concern whether *Sukuk* are more secure than conventional bonds, as they are asset-backed with tangible assets. For example one of them said: "[…] In some jurisdictions, it is not easy to structure asset-backed, and therefore the issuer goes with asset-based, which is acceptable to the investors". One interviewee mentioned that if the type of *Sukuk* structure is categorized into two types (asset-backed and asset-based), this will further influence legitimacy, because asset-backed *Sukuk* is more compliant with *Shariah*. Nonetheless, there was consensus that the development of real asset-backed *Sukuk* should be in parallel with the development of the regulatory framework in IFIs. Thus, the focus on the asset-backed securities will lead to increasing legitimacy of *Sukuk* and the reduction of *Shariah* risks. Importantly, the interviews found that asset-backed *Sukuk* have a greater impact on the enhancement of *Sukuk* legitimacy, and have been shown to comply more with the rules of *Shariah* to increase the legitimacy of *Sukuk* in comparison to asset-based *Sukuk*.

## *Shariah* Auditing

*Shariah* auditing is one of the essential and unique components of both Board dynamics and overall quality of corporate governance mechanisms, overseeing an IFI's business conduct to ensure that all operations are totally compatible with the conditions and terms of the principles of *Shariah* (Casper 2012). This determinant is one of the useful mechanisms in alleviating one of the problems of *Sukuk* which are non-*Shariah* compliant (Rahman 2008). All the interviewees agreed that *Shariah* auditing is considered as a vital contribution to the legitimacy of *Sukuk*. The interviewees indicated that this determinant has played a very critical role in determining the *Shariah* structure for *Sukuk*, maintaining them, and consequently, enhancing their legitimacy. This is consistent with the previous studies done by Malik (2010), Lahsasna (2010), Kaseb (2010), Ahmed et al. (2013), and Nabil (2013). There is more compliance with the rules of *Shariah* whenever the *Shariah* auditing increases level of legitimacy of *Sukuk* through the induction of *Shariah* auditing, to ensure that *Sukuk* has more legitimacy.

## *Shariah* Risk

A *Shariah* risk is a crucial issue impacting the legitimacy (compliance) of *Sukuk*, and may influence the investors to support the instrument (Jadwa 2009, Ahmed et al. 2014). To the question of 'how important an effect the *Shariah* has on the legitimacy of *Sukuk*', six of seven interviewees commented that it is very important, only if there were a true legal sale of underlying *Sukuk* assets. However, one out of the seven interviewees thought that it is relatively necessary, and two out of the seven also thought that it is not important, as the majority of *Sukuk* issuances are unguaranteed. Therefore, the rising *Shariah* risks of the *Sukuk* structure caused fear among *Sukuk* holders and investors due to the financial recession. Six interviewees felt that they would only take the *Shariah* risk of the underlying assets if there was a true legal sale of the underlying assets, and all other risks were covered including the jurisdiction of enforceability. It is also critical to include the risk in pricing the *Sukuk*. All the interviewees were interested in more risk assessment, as it is becoming an important aspect when analyzing *Shariah* risk in the underlying assets, due to the fact that the limited transparency in the documentations is causing a critical lack of understanding of some of the *Sukuk* tools. Therefore, reducing the *Shariah* risks for *Sukuk* is an important element, whereby increasing the *Shariah*-compliance structure through the promotion of the role of *Shariah* advisors ought to enhance *Sukuk* legitimacy (Nanaeva 2010, Shafii et al. 2010, Casper 2012, Lahsasna 2014, Ahmed et al. 2014, Ginena 2014, Mizushima & Mizushima 2014, Abdullah et al. 2014).

## *Shariah* Documentation

*Shariah* documentation is the key for *Sukuk* investors, because it discloses all material information that an investor needs to inform their decision as to whether to invest in the *Sukuk* or not (Ali 2011). It is through an increased level of disclosure of *Shariah* documentation in these reports that important elements emerge, with the resulting decrease in the level of problems of non-compliance with *Shariah*, and enhancement in legitimacy of the Islamic financial instruments (Ahmed et al. 2013, Lahsasna, 2014). Therefore, IFIs can make use of improved levels of disclosure in the *Shariah* Board reports, and this disclosure is an important Islamic financial tool (Maali et al. 2006, Haniffa & Hudaib 2007). Thus, through the mechanism of the SAC, compatible *Shariah* matters can be determined to ensure legitimacy of the documentation of the *Sukuk* issue.

Some interviewees commented on the high level of transparency in the disclosure of *Sukuk* documentation in *Shariah* pronouncements. They said, "the disclosure of *Sukuk* documentation is mainly focused on the originator's balance sheet, business and risk profile". As a result, more SSB members are increasingly demanding greater transparency and extensive due diligence when it comes to the securitization of assets. Two interviewees reiterated apprehension about the different legal structures as they are linked to the evolution of different *Shariah* interpretations from different scholars. The need for a *Shariah* framework and standardized legal tools is vital to boost confidence in *Sukuk* legitimacy. Thus, it is proposed that *Shariah* principles and interpretations should be incorporated into *Sukuk* agreements, in order to add significant value for the credibility of *Sukuk* legitimacy. These interviewees agreed that a uniform, harmonized, *Shariah* framework for *Sukuk* would be difficult to reach among members of SSBs as they come from different schools of *Shariah*. At the same time, three interviewees thought that diversity of opinion is a valuable concept, as it enriches ideas for more evolution. Interviewees concurred on the importance of the legitimacy of *Sukuk* for IFIs finance in the ICM. The recent financial crisis, they stressed, has demonstrated a shift away from bank lending and to more long-term financing instruments, such as *Sukuk*, for using Islamic instruments and diversification purposes. Nonetheless, in recent years, *Sukuk* has expanded considerably as more major institutional entities are interested in engaging in longer duration Islamic financing tools to meet their long-term expansion, which is compatible with *Shariah* principles. Generally, the result of the interviews was consistent with, and validated, the quantitative findings presented, which found that four determinants had positive and significant impact on *Sukuk* legitimacy, and one negative impact.

In summary, most of the interviewees (five out of seven) agreed that three factors, namely, *Shariah* auditing, *Shariah* risk and *Shariah* documentations, were considered as vital contributors to the legitimacy of *Sukuk*. The interviewees indicated that these determinant factors have played a very critical role in determining the *Shariah* structures for *Sukuk* and maintaining them, and consequently, enhancing the legitimacy of *Sukuk*.

## The Moderating Effect of the *Shariah* Supervisory Board on the Relationship between Determinants and *Sukuk* Legitimacy

The last phase of the interview aimed to confirm the quantitative results in connection with the moderating effect of SSBs on the direct relationship between determinants and *Sukuk* legitimacy. In this part of the interview, the seven SSB members were asked to give their opinions to support the quantitative findings. The interviewees provided mixed results with regard to the effect of the two dimensions of SSB, namely SSBM and SSBC.

The first role for the SSB starts before the issuance of *Sukuk*, which is building *Sukuk* characteristics, because *Sukuk* are very complicated, and usually have many forms and dimensions. In this regard, some respondents are involved very deeply in structuring, while others just review the structure and then approve it or disapprove it with reasoning given. One respondent clearly mentioned that structuring is not their job: "[...] we do not do the *Sukuk* structure; this is not our jobs. We simply audit and review the structure of *Sukuk*, so the *Sukuk* structure is done by the capital markets department of the institution, so our role is reviewing and approving, or disapproving, not the structuring".

Most of the SSB members (five out of seven) confirmed that a higher number of SSB members during the issuing of *Sukuk* actions, "would lead to superior performance for *Sukuk* legitimacy". One of the interviewees pointed out that "[…] the role of the SSB members is to look at the documents to ensure that they reflect what the structure wants, and then make sure that the terms and conditions used in the structure meet *Shariah* requirements". The justification is that an increase in the number of SSB members will lead to higher monitoring and verification of all processes, structures and documentations of *Sukuk*, to ensure they comply with *Shariah* rules. Moreover, two SSB members have asserted that a decrease in the number of SSB members, if an Islamic financial institution did not generate and actually use the external committees to increase legitimacy and update strategy, could negatively affect *Sukuk* legitimacy. One of interviewees pointed out that "[…] if the Supervisory Board is credible (or totally incredible at the other extreme), the credibility of board members will determine the fallout […]". Thus, it becomes more important for *Sukuk* to increase the members of SSB so that the *Sukuk* does not lose its legitimacy with the international capital market, and so the SSB can review further reports and information, such as financial reports, transactions and policies. With regard to the numbers of SSB members, one of the interviewees noted "[…] It may not affect price and ratings, but it may affect other things". This indicates that the members of SSBs have an effect on *Shariah* auditing, *Shariah* risks and documentation, but do not affect *Sukuk* pricing or type of structure. Another interviewee mentioned that the *Shariah* committees affect pricing, when they adhere to conditions and terms. Further enquiries showed that a majority of the interviewees indicated that members and committees of SSBs have an influence on the relationship between *Shariah* auditing, *Shariah* risk, *Shariah* documentation, and *Sukuk* legitimacy.

In general, the SSB members confirmed that the main roles for the legitimacy of *Sukuk* in Islamic financial institutions, such as *Shariah* auditing, *fatwas*, supervision, and *Sukuk* structure, are the work of SSBs. Six SSB members indicated that, under this *Sukuk* legitimacy situation, together with the *Shariah* supervisory board in IFIs, determinants provided very important information to modify the strategy and to update *Sukuk* structures to achieve better legitimacy. Further inquiries showed that six out of seven interviewees had confirmed the impact of SSBs on the relationship between determinants and the legitimacy of *Sukuk*. They illustrated that SSB members played an important role in increasing, and enhancing, overall *Sukuk* legitimacy.

These qualitative results concerning the moderating effect of SSBs were consistent with the results obtained from the quantitative study conducted in the first phase of the current study. These results from the mixed-mode interviews, as well as the quantitative study results, did provide strong evidence for the moderating effect of SSBs on the relationship between determinants and *Sukuk* legitimacy.

## Summary

This chapter provided an explanation regarding the analysis performed, and the results of the findings have been explained. Based on the results, the conclusion of the hypotheses testing has also been discussed, whereby out of 15 hypotheses tested, 8 were supported. Finally, this chapter presents the results of a qualitative approach which was generated from the interview. The next chapter reviews and discusses the results, and their implications, as well as limitations and conclusions.

# CHAPTER 9

# DISCUSSION

The current chapter discusses the results and findings of the study, which were presented in Chapter Five. This chapter is divided into five parts. Firstly, it begins with the recapitulations and the findings of the study. Secondly, it discusses the direct relationships and the moderating effects of the explanatory variables. Thirdly, it explains the theoretical, methodological and practical implications of the study findings. The fourth part discusses the limitations of the study. Finally, the fifth part presents a number of suggestions and recommendations for future research.

The present study attempts to investigate the relationship between the determinants (pricing, type of structure, *Shariah* auditing, *Shariah* risk, and *Shariah* documentation) and *Sukuk* legitimacy in IFI's under the exempt regime in Bursa Malaysia. In addition, this study also investigates the moderating role of the SSB between determinants and legitimacy of *Sukuk*. To summarize the findings of the quantitative results, the representation of *Sukuk* legitimacy is seen in the *Shariah* compliance disclosure, as it positively and significantly affects some of the determinants, such as pricing, type of structure and *Shariah* auditing. However, both *Shariah* risk and *Shariah* documentation negatively impact *Sukuk* legitimacy. Moreover, the results also revealed that the SSBM moderates the relationship between pricing and *Shariah* documentation with *Sukuk* legitimacy. This means that the existence of SSBM positively and significantly impacts some of the determinants' relationships with *Sukuk* legitimacy (high level of *Shariah* compliance). Thus, the legitimacy is positively and significantly affected by pricing and *Shariah* documentation, which consequently leads to the indication that pricing and *Shariah* documentation positively enhances the level of *Sukuk* legitimacy.

In addition, the results also revealed that the SSBC plays a moderating role between pricing and *Shariah* risks with *Sukuk* legitimacy. This implies that the existence of the SSBC causes determinants such as pricing to have a strongly positive and significant impact on legitimacy (high level of *Shariah* compliance). Moreover, the existence of the SSBC causes *Shariah* risks to have a negative and significant impact on legitimacy. This indicates that the legitimacy is positively and significantly affected by pricing, but a significantly negative affect is seen on *Shariah* risks, which consequently leads to the indication that pricing and *Shariah* risks positively and negatively enhance level of *Sukuk* legitimacy.

Finally, the current study has partially applied a qualitative method, with the intention of validating the quantitative results, the results from semi-structured interviews, and the email interviewing method, which was designed based on the quantitative results. This method provided better-quality confirmation and validation of the results which were obtained via the questionnaire survey in the first phase of the current study. Moreover, the results by qualitative study have added some new insights that clarified the reasons behind the relationship between determinants and *Sukuk* legitimacy, as well as the impact of the SSB on the direct relationship between determinants and *Sukuk* legitimacy.

## Discussions

Based on the results shown in the previous section, the current section further discusses the findings of the study. The discussion will be based on a theoretical perspective, empirical evidence, and what has been done in previous studies that are related to the current study. An explanation and justification is provided for both the predicted and unpredicted findings of the hypotheses.

It is worth mentioning that, to the best of the researcher's knowledge, no prior work has been done in developed or developing economies, including Malaysia, to ascertain *Sukuk* legitimacy with a given set of determinants and a moderator. There is no past research which has attempted to empirically investigate the relationship between determinants and *Sukuk* legitimacy, with SSBs as moderators. This study is, therefore, an attempt in that direction, an effort to determine the legitimacy of *Sukuk*, and to determine the relationship between determinants and *Sukuk* legitimacy. Additionally, it is important to determine the role of the SSB as a moderator on the relationship between determinants and *Sukuk* legitimacy in IFI.

## Evaluation on the Legitimacy of *Sukuk*

For the legitimacy of *Sukuk*, the findings showed an R-square value of 71%. This result indicates that the independent variables are interpreted as representing 71% of the legitimacy level of *Sukuk*, and the remaining 29% is represented by other factors related to the legitimacy of *Sukuk*, which are not included in the scope of this study. The current study divided legitimacy into three levels; low, medium, and high, which represent the legitimacy disclosure in *Shariah* pronouncement that has been approved by the SSB. The results showed that the average value of *Sukuk* legitimacy by all *Sukuk* selected is 0.62. The minimum level of legitimacy for *Sukuk* is 0.33, and the maximum level of legitimacy for *Sukuk* is 0.89. The importance of these findings is that the combination of the determinants and the SSB leads to greater monitoring, and therefore, more compliance with *Shariah* tenets and rules, which all lead to higher disclosure levels of *Sukuk* legitimacy. Furthermore, these results show that the existence of the SSB as a moderator enables the legitimacy level to be higher, as more legitimacy disclosure information is provided in the *Shariah* reports. The level of *Sukuk* legitimacy disclosure moderated by the SSB reflects high conformance to the Islamic *Sukuk* guidelines in Malaysia. Given that the SC guidelines set out minimum disclosure requirements, the disclosure by 27 *Sukuk*, at best, achieves only that. It merely meets the minimum disclosure to fulfil the mandatory requirement, and is considered very brief for *Shariah* reports. The limited information may not facilitate the operators to achieve the purpose of organizational transparency and *Sukuk*-holder engagement or dialogue (Hess 2007).

Legitimacy disclosure on *Sukuk* in IFIs seems to develop in much the same manner as other disclosure practices, that is, a tendency to comply with rules rather than with principles. Drawing insights from institutional theory, conformance due to regulatory pressures, such as the SC guidelines demonstrates coercive isomorphism. IFIs are complying to meet minimum regulation requirements in fear of having their eligibility to offer *Sukuk* disapproved by SC. Since there is high legitimacy in the *Sukuk* moderated by the SSB, the *Sukuk* operator's conformance is seen as following the norms, or normative isomorphism.

To enhance *Sukuk* disclosure on *Shariah* compliance in the *Shariah* reports, the role of the SSB members needs to be strengthened. As *Shariah* governance mechanisms, both the SC reports and the SSB members can be utilized to enhance the identity of Islamic *Sukuk* and fulfill the religious obligations. The finding highlights the need for increased transparency through adequate and relevant disclosure of *Shariah* compliance information in the *Shariah* report of *Sukuk*. It also raises the concern that the advisory role entrusted to SSB members and committees might not be adequate for them to effectively ensure that compliance with *Shariah* principles is adhered to at all times, as expected by SC.

While the distinctive and confidence features of *Sukuk* operations draw heavily on *Shariah* compliance, reported by the SSB through the *Shariah* pronouncement, there is a lack of legitimacy information to facilitate investors and other external *Sukuk*-holders to make well-informed decisions, and to enable them to ascertain whether *Sukuk* is indeed a *Shariah*-compliant security. Therefore, investors and *Sukuk*-holders consider the legitimacy disclosure in *Sukuk* operations as an important issue, because it emphasizes purity of the income earned and expenditure incurred, while non-compliance has a negative impact on the revenue of *Sukuk*, as revenue earned from illegal disclosure of *Shariah* compliance is to only be considered for charity, as mentioned by Lahsasna (2014).

In general, the disclosure in the *Sukuk Shariah* report contains a sentence which was intended to confirm legitimacy. The term "*Shariah* pronouncement" used by the SSB befits the content of the report, as it contains only a statement to inform conformance. Although the disclosure is brief, it still reflects a high compliance with, and almost a reproduction of, the report, as set out in the SC guidelines on *Shariah* statements for *Sukuk* operators. In this respect, the disclosure of information tends to be driven by regulations or rules, rather than principles. As such, the disclosure on legitimacy in the *Shariah* report by the SSB tends to be mandatory, rather than voluntary. However, *Sukuk* in a low level of legitimacy do not conform to the exact wording and format, as stated in the SC guidelines. Although the *Shariah* report was not verbatim, the SSB has not violated the SC requirements because the report has provided reasonable assurance that the IFI has not violated *Shariah* rules and principles.

## The Impact of Determinants on *Sukuk* Legitimacy

In the current study, the first objective was to investigate the direct relationship between determinants (pricing, type of structure, *Shariah* risks, *Shariah* auditing and *Shariah* documentation) and *Sukuk* legitimacy. *Sukuk* listed in Bursa Malaysia under the exempt regime was examined in this study. The study also used a disclosure index as the proxy for *Sukuk* legitimacy. *Sukuk* legitimacy is claimed as one of the essential components, or proxies, of *Shariah* compliance in previous literatures (See Wilson 2004, Dawood 2008, Zulkhibri 2015).

While some studies have investigated the legitimacy and *Shariah* compliance as an important indicator to represent *Sukuk* structure in its relationship with determinants, to the best knowledge of the researcher, there is no previous study that has investigated determinants and *Sukuk* legitimacy by using disclosure as a proxy for *Sukuk* legitimacy.

The first determinant tested in this study was pricing. Numerous studies have identified pricing as one of the most important factors that impact the legitimacy of *Sukuk* (Wilson 2008, Usmani 2009, Herwany & Febrian 2010, Ahmed et al. 2014, Aloui et al. 2015). The pricing benchmark plays an important role in enhancing legitimacy of *Sukuk*. However, *Shariah* scholars and Muslim economists have criticized the use of the interest rate as a readily available indicator of profitability (Usmani 2002, Al-Bashir 2008). Scholars and researchers for more than ten years have focused on the important role and the effect of the pricing on *Sukuk* legitimacy and an alternative to the interest rate, which is *Shariah* compliant (Wilson 2008, Jadwa 2009, Usmani 2009, Nanaeva 2010, Herwany & Febrian 2010, Ahmed et al. 2014, Aloui et al. 2015).

The results of the path coefficient analysis presented in Table 5.7 shows a significant positive relationship between pricing and *Sukuk* legitimacy ($\beta = 0.344$, $p < 0.01$). This is consistent with the hypothesis proposed in the current study, which implies that *Sukuk* which use an Islamic pricing benchmark have a higher legitimacy as compared to those using a conventional benchmark. In other words, the result indicates that there is a significant positive relationship between pricing and *Sukuk* legitimacy. This result reveals that the pricing benchmark used is a strong determinant which enables the *Sukuk* structure to reach a higher level of legitimacy. The positive association that the current study observed between pricing and *Sukuk* legitimacy is consistent with the study of Ahmed et al. (2015), which found that *Sukuk* that use a *Shariah* pricing benchmark generally have a high level of legitimacy. Likewise, this result is consistent with Nanaeva (2010) and Aloui et al, (2015), who claim that the Islamic pricing benchmark is preferred to have high effect on *Shariah*-compliant *Sukuk*. This finding demonstrates that the *Shariah* pricing benchmark may be used as a tool of pressure which the SSB can use to follow higher *Shariah* compliant levels and consequently enhance *Sukuk* legitimacy. A study into the Malaysian context done by Hayat and Kraeussl (2011) showed evidence of a positive relationship between the Islamic pricing benchmark and Islamic equity funds (IEFs). Another study, by Ahmed et al. (2015), tested the relationship between the pricing and legitimacy of *Sukuk*. The study also found a strong positive relationship between pricing and legitimacy. This finding is supported by Usmani (2009), who argued that using the interest rates as a benchmark is not in accordance with *Shariah* requirements, a claim that is echoed by Islamic scholars. Thus, it was recommended that corporate *Sukuk* ought to be benchmarked against the financial institutions' performance indicators instead.

The interview results showed that most of the members of the SSB believed that Islamic pricing benchmark utilization would lead to better legitimacy of *Sukuk* structure. For instance, one SSB member said, "pricing *Sukuk* according to conventional benchmarks will not affect the legitimacy of *Sukuk*, because there is no alternative Islamic benchmark". Another member echoed a similar sentiment, by saying some Muslims may not care about the interest rate as long as the products are called '*Sukuk*', which are deemed to be *Shariah* compliant. Whereas, another respondent said that the interest rate only matters to those who thinks they are not *Shariah*-compliant.

However, the findings of the current study showed that pricing was positively and significantly related to the legitimacy of *Sukuk*. The positive findings might be due to several reasons. Firstly, IFIs resort to using the Islamic benchmark for *Sukuk* pricing in order to make *Sukuk* attractive, particularly for Muslim investors, and competitive against conventional bonds. Secondly, *Shariah* scholars believe that the current pricing benchmark (i.e., LIBOR) is a weak measurement benchmark applied to *Sukuk,* hence, IFIs should move away from it to enhance *Sukuk* legitimacy. When the pricing is in compliance with *Shariah* principles, it increases the legitimacy of *Sukuk*. The legitimacy can be validated by auditing the determinants to ensure that *Sukuk* is compliant with *Shariah* principles. Eventually, this reveals that the more Islamic the pricing benchmark, the higher the legitimacy of the *Sukuk* structure. Thus it can be concluded, that the reasonable justification for getting this result for the first hypothesis, is that there is an increased awareness of using the Islamic pricing benchmark to increase the level of *Sukuk* legitimacy, therefore acting as a guide to eventually enhance the legitimacy.

The second determinant tested in this study was the type of structure. The result shows that there is significant relationship between the type of structure (asset-based and asset-backed *Sukuk)* and legitimacy ($t = 0.109$, $P < 0.01$). The results showed that asset-backed *Sukuk* have differed from asset-based *Sukuk* with regard to *Shariah* compliance, where the asset-backed *Sukuk* have a greater impact with regard to legitimacy than asset-based *Sukuk*. This finding is in line with the objective of the study. This implies that asset-backed *Sukuk* are more in line with the *Shariah* and provide more protection to the *Sukuk* holders in the event of a default. This result is consistent with some of the previous studies (Haneef 2009, Howladar 2009, Khnifer 2010b, Hidayat 2013, Alia et al. 2013, Shabana 2013, Abdulmalik 2013, Azmat et al. 2014b) which investigated the relationship between the type of structure and *Sukuk* legitimacy. For instance, Hidayat (2013) investigated the relationship between asset-backed and asset-based *Sukuk* structures with *Shariah* compliance, and found that there was a positive relationship between the type of structures and *Shariah*-compliant *Sukuk*. Similarly, Shabana (2013) found a different relation between type of structure (asset-backed and asset-based *Sukuk*) and true ownership. Also Alia et al. (2013) reported that *Shariah* mortgage-backed securities have provided a higher rate of return on investment to the investors. Furthermore, another study by Abdulmalik (2013) affirmed that asset-backed *Sukuk* are more in alignment with the principles of *Shariah*, and thus allow increased levels of protection to the holders of *Sukuk* in the event of default. Howladar (2009) asserted that, in asset-based *Sukuk*, the frameworks satisfy the pattern of an agreement with too much sophistication, which eventually points to an Islamic equivalent of unsafe traditional bonds. In the same tone, Haneef (2009) mentioned that asset-backed *Sukuk* are more efficient when offered than asset-based ones. Accordingly, as confirmed by a study done in the Malaysian context, by Ahmed et al. (2015), the type of structure is an important element that has impact on *Sukuk*. The study found that asset-backed *Sukuk* have more impact on *Sukuk* legitimacy enhancement, and have been shown to be more compliant with the *Shariah* rules in increasing the legitimacy of *Sukuk*, compared to an asset-based *Sukuk*. Overall, the result of the direct relationship between type of structure and *Sukuk* legitimacy shows that type of structure is an important mechanism to enhance the level of legitimacy. This result is consistent with the objective of the present study, to show that there is a positive relationship between the type of structure and *Sukuk* legitimacy. That is to say that the type of structure is an important factor of determinants to improve the level of *Sukuk* legitimacy.

The third determinant used in the current study is *Shariah* auditing. The importance of *Shariah* auditing is in ensuring that all transactions are compatible with *Shariah* principles and to distinguish between conventional and Islamic *Sukuk*. This determinant is one of the useful mechanisms in alleviating non-*Shariah* compliant *Sukuk* problems (Rahman 2008). It is the only way of certifying that *Sukuk* transactions and procedures actually comply with *Shariah* tenets. Therefore, in the emerging Islamic financial industry, *Shariah* auditing has to be considered a significant factor (Lahsasna 2010). The role of *Shariah* auditing is so important in the business world because of its concern for justice, honesty, and goodwill, and its endeavour to prevent uncertainties and fraud. The current study tested this determinant and the results showed that the relationship between *Shariah* auditing and *Sukuk* legitimacy is significant ($t = 0.461$, $p > 0.01$). Hence, this result does confirm the objective of the current study that there is a positive relationship between *Shariah* auditing and legitimacy of *Sukuk*. This is consistent with the hypothesis proposed in the current study, which implies that *Sukuk* that are subjected to *Shariah* auditing have higher level of legitimacy, and vice versa. The results of the current study supported this relationship. The results showed that if *Sukuk* in financial institutions have many reports, this implies that the SSB has done adequate *Shariah* auditing, while an inadequate number of *Shariah* auditing reports implies a lack of SSB involvement in conducting or reporting audit findings. This result is consistent with an empirical study done by Ahmed et al. (2015) through a sample of Malaysian *Sukuk* listed on Bursa Malaysia. According to the study, *Shariah* auditing has a significant relationship with *Sukuk* legitimacy. Likewise, this result is also consistent with Kaseb (2010), who suggested that the regulators ought to conduct *Shariah* reviews and update the current *Sukuk* guidelines so that there is more clarity and a more comprehensive guidance on structure of *Sukuk*. This is also supported by ISRA (2013) who reasoned that neglecting to properly scrutinize any documentation might lead to non-*Shariah* compliance, and, to some extent, might have adverse legal implications on *Sukuk* issuance. Other viewpoints in previous studies demonstrated that providing continuous *Shariah* supervision and due diligence to review transactions and procedures can lead to a better outcome than routine audits. The *Sukuk* are found to be more in compliance with the rules of *Shariah* whenever *Shariah* auditing is present, therefore increasing the level of *Sukuk* legitimacy. This result is consistent with the objective of the present study, that there is a positive relationship between *Shariah* auditing and *Sukuk* legitimacy, in that *Shariah* audits and *Sukuk* legitimacy are found to be positively related, since *Shariah* auditing is obligated by *Shariah* provision practices.

The fourth determinant tested was *Shariah* risk, to identify its relationship with *Sukuk* legitimacy. The results related to this variable showed that there is a negative and significant relationship between *Shariah* risk and *Sukuk* legitimacy. These results demonstrate that the fewer *Shariah* risks in the Malaysian *Sukuk*, the more the legitimacy. These results are in line with what has been proposed in the current study (there is a negative relationship with *Sukuk* legitimacy), showing a negative and significant direction (t = -0.181, p < .0.05). This indicates that *Sukuk* legitimacy is significantly influenced by *Shariah* risk. Such a finding is consistent with some studies in the literature (Nanaeva 2010, Shafii et al. 2010, Casper 2012, Lahsasna 2014, Ahmed et al. 2014, Ginena 2014, Mizushima & Mizushima 2014, Abdullah et al. 2014), which investigated the relationship between *Shariah* risk and *Sukuk* legitimacy. For instance, Casper (2012), and Lahsasna (2014), stated that increasing *Shariah* risks in Islamic finance securities will have an effect on IFI's credibility which can lead to a reduction in the confidence of shareholders and investors, who realize that the institution is not living up to its commitments. Similarly, an empirical study done by Nanaeva (2010) investigated the *Shariah* risk on non-*Shariah* compliant *Sukuk*, and found that *Sukuk* with higher risks require more control and monitoring. Institutional theory shows that regulatory pressures are needed on the *Shariah* Boards to control and monitor the operations of IFIs, due to their non-*Shariah* compliant risks (Aziah Abu Kasim 2012, Ahmed, et al. 2014). The result of the current study is also consistent with literature on determinants. These literatures propose that the number of members in the SSB promotes legitimacy effectiveness. That is, *Shariah* risk could be reduced through the SSB's confirmation that there is a validation of *Sukuk* operations to fulfil the demand of *Shariah* compliance, thus assuring *Sukuk* holders. Therefore, the association of *Shariah* supervisors with *Sukuk* monitoring and governance will ensure investors' confidence remains high. In the same tone, a study by Ahmed et al (2015) found that there is a significant effect of *Shariah* risks on *Sukuk* legitimacy. Thus, it can be concluded that the reasonable justification for getting this result for the fourth hypothesis is that a lesser *Shariah* risk can eventually lead to enhancing *Sukuk* legitimacy. It shows that if *Sukuk* have no *Shariah* risks, they have higher legitimacy. Results have shown a negative relationship between *Shariah* risks and *Sukuk* legitimacy, indicating a significant effect of *Shariah* risks on increasing or decreasing the *Sukuk* legitimacy. Thus, *Sukuk* with low *Shariah* risks have a higher legitimacy.

For the *Shariah* documentation, the findings show that there is a negative relationship between *Shariah* documentation and *Sukuk* legitimacy. This result indicates that the amount of *Shariah* documentation has a negative impact on *Sukuk* legitimacy. These results are not in line with what has been proposed in the objective of the current study (there is a positive relationship with *Sukuk* legitimacy), which shows a negative and significant direction (t = -0.040, P < 0.05). This could be attributed to the fact that there is a lack of documentation details provided in the *Shariah* pronouncement. Furthermore, Maali et al. (2006) stated that mistakes and negligence of disclosure in reports will lead to backfiring. This result is not in line with what has been set in the objectives of the current study. The study cannot deduct a significant relationship between *Shariah* documentation and *Sukuk* legitimacy. However, the study found the existence of a significant relationship between *Shariah* documentations and *Sukuk* legitimacy when a moderating variable was considered. The study will further discuss the moderating role of the SSB on the relationship between *Shariah* documentation and *Sukuk* legitimacy in the coming sections.

## The Moderating Effects of *Shariah* Supervisory Boards on the Relationship between Determinants and *Sukuk* Legitimacy

Apart from the direct examination of the relationship between determinants and *Sukuk* legitimacy, the study investigated the role of the moderating effect of SSB (SSBM and SSBC) on the relationship between determinants and *Sukuk* legitimacy. There are five hypotheses developed for SSBM and five for SSBC. As a result, several interesting findings have come to light and will be discussed in the next subsection.

### The Moderating Effects of *Shariah* Supervisory Board Membership (SSBM) on the Relationship between Determinants and *Sukuk* Legitimacy

The first section discusses the moderating effect of the first dimension of the SSB, the *Shariah* Supervisory Board Membership (SSBM). In accordance with what the study has proposed, the statistical results show that there is a significant relationship between determinants and *Sukuk* legitimacy when SSBM exists. The results show that the $R^2$ in the main direction (without a moderator) relationship is 0.71 percent, and $R^2$ with a moderator was 0.77 percent. This shows that there is an increase in model value and $R^2$ around 6%, which means that the independent variables (determinants) account for 77.2% of the change in dependent variable (*Sukuk* legitimacy). This implies that when SSBM exists in a moderating role, it will have significant effect on determinants and *Sukuk* legitimacy. This finding is supported by Akhtaruddin et al. (2009) and Chaganti et al, (1985) who mentioned that the SSBM board size can affect controlling, monitoring, and the level of disclosure. A greater number of members in an SSB would provide more effective monitoring and more consistency with the rules and principles of *Shariah*. According to Chen and Jaggi (2000), a larger size of board may decrease the possibility of information asymmetry.

In addition, a higher number of members of the board may also reduce uncertainty and the lack of information (Birnbaum 1984). The pattern of results revealed that the moderator analysis supported the hypotheses that SSBM played a significant role in moderating the relationship between determinants and *Sukuk* legitimacy. In summary, the study confirms that SSBM does moderate the relationship between determinants and *Sukuk* legitimacy.

This study discovered that SSBM moderates the relationship between two components of determinants (pricing and *Shariah* documentation) with *Sukuk* legitimacy. First, the study found that the positive relationship between the pricing benchmark and *Sukuk* legitimacy is stronger when SSBM exists. In line with what the study has proposed, the statistical results show that there is a positive and significant relationship between pricing and *Sukuk* legitimacy when SSBM exists ($t = 3.028$, $p < 0.05$). This reveals that the relationship between pricing and *Sukuk* legitimacy is stronger when there is a moderating effect represented by SSBM. Hence, this reveals that SSBM is an important moderator variable to strengthen the positive relationship between pricing and *Sukuk* legitimacy. This finding supports the objective of the study (that the positive relationship between pricing and *Sukuk* legitimacy is stronger when SSBM exist) as shown in Figure 5.5. It is observed that when the SSBM number is larger, the pricing benchmark used was found to be more *Shariah* compliant, thus continuously influencing the level of *Sukuk* legitimacy as recommended by SC and AAOIFI. Therefore, this study found that pricing compliance to *Shariah* is enhanced with close monitoring by SSBM, thus contributing towards the increased legitimacy of the *Sukuk*. That is to say, *Sukuk* which have *Shariah* compliant pricing and greater SSBM involvement are more prone to have an increase in the legitimacy of *Sukuk*.

Secondly, the current study examined the moderating effect of SSBM on the relationship between *Shariah* documentation and *Sukuk* legitimacy. The study revealed that there is a positive relationship between the *Shariah* documentation and *Sukuk* legitimacy when SSBM exists ($t = 1.650$, $p < 0.05$). This shows that when SSBM moderates, the amount of *Shariah* documentation is higher, and thus has a positive impact on *Sukuk* legitimacy (which is identical to the proposed hypothesis). In general, increasing disclosure in *Shariah* documentation in the *Shariah* reports is an important element that enhances level of legitimacy in *Sukuk*. This conforms to the indebtedness theory where the role of the SSB is to dutifully observe *Shariah* rules in Islamic financial operations. The result showed that SSBM has been significant in having a moderating effect on the relationship between *Shariah* documentation and *Sukuk* legitimacy. The figures in Figure 5.6 reveal that when the SSBM number is higher, the amount of *Shariah* documentation or disclosure is also higher, thereby having a continuous positive impact on *Sukuk* legitimacy. In retrospect, the trend in *Shariah* documentation's impact on the level of *Sukuk* legitimacy is seen to be increasing for *Sukuk* with a higher involvement of SSBM. In summary, these results indicate that a positive relationship between *Shariah* documentation and *Sukuk* legitimacy is noted when SSBM involvement is higher. In the light of this finding, it becomes more important for *Sukuk* to improve the level of legitimacy by increasing the number of members of the SSB, so that the *Sukuk* does not lose its legitimacy with external power in Islamic capital markets. The graph shows that *Sukuk* that have more *Shariah* documentation have higher legitimacy when SSBM numbers are higher. The SSBM should ensure that all *Sukuk* issuers of the IFIs (management, shareholders, employees, suppliers, community, and depositors) have full confidence in reading *Shariah* reports about *Sukuk* structure (Farook et al. 2011, Haniffa and Hudaib 2007, Maali et al. 2006). Farook et al. (2011) mentioned that the existence of the SSB in IFIs will improve the monitoring and controlling of Islamic securities. Numerous studies have suggested that board size can affect monitoring, controlling, and the level of disclosure (Akhtaruddin et al. 2009, Chaganti, et al. 1985). Rahman and Bukair (2013) recommended having SSBM of between three and seven; three being the common size of SSBM in IFIs, which is compatible with AAOIFI standards. The more the number of SSB members, the more effective and holistic the monitoring to ensure consistency with the principles and rules of *Shariah*. Likewise, Birnbaum (1984) stated that a higher number of members of the Board implies that they would be willing to reduce the lack of information and uncertainty. The SSBs size is also predicted to affect its ability in conducting audits and reviews of all transactions and operations of *Sukuk*, to ensure their structures are in compliance with the rules of *Shariah*. In addition, SSB members' ability to audit *Sukuk* increases investors' confidence if more members are on the Board. In addition, the collective experience and knowledge of the SSB will increase with more members on board, consequently leading to greater legitimacy of *Sukuk*.

The results of the current study suggests that *Sukuk* that have higher SSBM involvement are characterized by an adequacy of SSBM, ensuring legitimacy and compliance, which may encourage IFIs to provide greater monitoring over their Islamic securities. SSBs must give more attention to their tasks and ensure all *Sukuk* documentations are verified, to validate their adherence to *Shariah* compliance. Any negligence or mistake might lead to difficulties in *Sukuk* issuance, due to non-compliance with *Shariah* requirements. The *Shariah* operation documents need to be reviewed and audited by the SSB providing the *fatwa* for *Sukuk* legitimacy, because those documents form the essence of *Sukuk* for *Shariah* compliance (Rahail 2011). This study has found that constant SSBM monitoring may enhance the amount of *Shariah* documentation and contribute towards increased compliance and legitimacy for *Sukuk*. That is to say, *Sukuk* which has active involvement from SSBM would have increased *Shariah* documentation, which ultimately increases the legitimacy of the *Sukuk*.

## The Moderating Effects of *Shariah* Supervisory Board Committees (SSBC) on the Relationship between Determinants and *Sukuk* Legitimacy

The moderating effect of the second dimension of the SSB, the *Shariah* Supervisory Board Committee (SSBC), is discussed in this section. As proposed by this study, the statistical results show that there is a significant relationship between determinants and *Sukuk* legitimacy, when the SSBC exists. This implies that when the SSBC exists in a moderating role, it will have a significant effect on determinants and *Sukuk* legitimacy. The pattern of results revealed that the moderator analysis supported the hypotheses that the SSBC played a significant role in moderating the relationship between determinants and *Sukuk* legitimacy. These results are discussed in detail below.

This study discovered the degree of the SSBC's role in moderating the relationship between two components of determinants (pricing and *Shariah* risk) with *Sukuk* legitimacy. This study found that a positive and stronger relationship between a pricing benchmark used with *Sukuk* legitimacy exists when an SSBC is present. In accordance with what the study has proposed, the statistical results show that there is a positive and significant relationship between pricing and *Sukuk* legitimacy when an SSBC exists. This reveals that, indeed, the relationship between pricing and *Sukuk* legitimacy is stronger when there is a moderating effect represented by an SSBC. As per the finding of this study, it can be ascertained that the SSBC is an important moderator variable to strengthen the positive relationship between pricing and *Sukuk* legitimacy. This finding supports the objective of the study (that the positive relationship between pricing and *Sukuk* legitimacy is stronger when an SSBC exists) as shown in Figure 5.7. Therefore, this study found that pricing compliance to *Shariah* is enhanced with constant monitoring by an SSBC, thus contributing towards increased legitimacy of the *Sukuk*. That is to say, *Sukuk* that have *Shariah*-compliant pricing and greater SSBC involvement are more prone to have an increase in legitimacy.

As for *Shariah* risk, results show that there is an inverse relationship between *Shariah* risk and Sukuk legitimacy when an SSBC exists in a moderating role. The study revealed that there is a negative relationship between *Shariah* risk and *Sukuk* legitimacy when an SSBC exists. This shows that, when an SSBC exists, *Shariah* risk have a negative impact on *Sukuk* legitimacy (which is the same as the proposed hypothesis).

Figure 5.9 shows that many *Sukuk* that are moderated by an SSBC have a negative *Shariah* risk, thus a continuous negative impact on *Sukuk* legitimacy. In retrospect, the trend of *Shariah* risk impact on the level of legitimacy is seen to be decreasing for *Sukuk* with a higher involvement of the SSBC. In summary, these results indicate that a negative relationship is noted between *Shariah* risk and *Sukuk* legitimacy when SSBC involvement is higher. Therefore, it is important for *Sukuk* legitimacy to be improved by increasing the number of *Shariah* committees, so that the *Sukuk* does not lose its legitimacy with external power in Islamic capital markets. Thus, the graph shows that for *Sukuk* with less *Shariah* risk, when the SSBC number is higher, the legitimacy is higher.

This result implies that *Sukuk* that are governed by a greater number of SSBCs are characterized by an adequacy of SSBC involvement, ensuring legitimacy and compliance that may encourage Islamic financial institutions to provide greater monitoring. The SSBC must give more attention to their tasks, and must audit all structures of *Sukuk* to identify *Shariah* risks. Thus, to increase the legitimacy of *Sukuk* and to reduce *Shariah* risks, the role of *Shariah* advisors should be enhanced. In conclusion, *Sukuk* that have less *Shariah* risk with a high number of SSBCs are more likely to increase the legitimacy of the *Sukuk*.

# CHAPTER 10

# CONCLUSION

The findings highlighted earlier lead to several implications. The discussion on these implications will be divided into three perspectives, namely theoretical, methodological, and practical.

## Theoretical and Methodological Implications

This study contributes to the knowledge by reconceptualising and developing measurements of *Sukuk* legitimacy and presenting a systematic framework that demonstrates the underlying indebtedness theory through which determinants are connected with legitimacy of *Sukuk* structure. Indebtedness theory refers to a theory that deals with the human existence and humans' relationship with Allah, the Creator. Creations have to submit to Allah and comply with *Shariah* rules as an act of obedience to Allah.

Previous studies in Islamic finance (Rosly 2007, Ahmed 2012, Ahmed et al. 2014), have focused on the first level of *Shariah* compliant theory, and paid less attention to the second level of the theory. The first level provided the underlying link between the *Shariah* compliant variables and Islamic financial instruments, but without examining their effects on legitimacy. Considered as the more modern and sophisticated framework, the second level of indebtedness theory suggests that the interaction, or fit, between the SSB and determinants ultimately affects *Sukuk* legitimacy.

The majority of previous *Sukuk* studies have applied either a quantitative or qualitative approach. The application of a mixed method approach in the current study provides a better insight on the Islamic finance context, and provides a less-explored methodological contribution in this area. It chooses to combine methods to avoid weaknesses arising from a single study approach, which is chosen for convenience in the Malaysian context, due to the ease of data availability and stringent guidelines. This can encourage more future researchers to apply a mixed-methods approach in addressing *Sukuk* structure research problems in the context of Islamic finance.

This study provides several theoretical implications. The first regards the *Sukuk* legitimacy (dependent variable). The current study takes into consideration two important things when choosing the disclosure index as measurement of legitimacy level (dependent variable). It chooses a new structure that consists of the *Shariah* board report, and uses an indexing procedure to measure and evaluate the disclosure level of *Sukuk* legitimacy information, which is adopted from SC and AAOIFI. In doing so, this study can be considered as a response to calls for new research into the area of Islamic financial instruments, because, as admitted by (Haniffa & Hudaib 2007, Maali et al. 2006) the index of legitimacy still needs more contributions to recover and overcome the lack in the disclosure index of legitimacy. Thus, the present study contributes globally to the legitimacy measurement by choosing the disclosure index to measure and evaluate *Sukuk* legitimacy in *Shariah* reports.

Secondly, regarding the disclosure index in IFIs, this study uniquely contributes to the literature that deals with determinants and legitimacy by introducing the disclosure index as a measurement to represent *Sukuk* legitimacy. Moreover, the present study has a methodological implication, by focusing not only on the importance of disclosure index measurement, but also on the way it's computed. Thus, the use of the disclosure index to measure the level of *Sukuk* legitimacy in the presence of determinants of legitimacy in IFIs is considered as a unique contribution to the existing literature. Therefore, methodologically, this study has contributed by introducing a new way of measuring the legitimacy.

Thirdly, this study is considered as the first study that uses the disclosure index as a measurement for legitimacy of *Sukuk* with determinants. Previous studies have only used social information to measure the disclosure index with *Shariah* compliant information in IFIs. However, no research was done by analysing the *Shariah* reports and Islamic financial instruments. In doing so, the current study is the first of its kind to provide new insights on the relationship between some selected determinants and the legitimacy of *Sukuk*. It therefore provides new indicators considered as an extension to prior researches in this discipline, which, to the best of the researcher's knowledge, has covered this area from Islamic finance perspectives.

Fourthly, this study utilized the SSB as a moderating variable, which is a powerful tool that can be used by IFIs to address the non-*Shariah* compliant problems, or those conflicting with *Shariah* tenets. The existence of the SSB influences the governance mechanisms in IFIs. It enhances and strengthens the role of the SSB towards ensuring that the Islamic financial operations are *Shariah* compliant, and in line with the interests of the *Sukuk*-holders and investors who invest after taking into consideration the *Shariah* risks reported. IFIs would tend to follow stringent guidelines set by the SSB in order to protect their financial products; therefore the SSB can influence IFIs to follow the instructions related to *Shariah* rules. In doing so, this will enhance the purity of the income earned by the *Sukuk*-holders, and promote legitimacy. On the other hand, the use of such an instrument in monitoring the activities of the SSB committees has not been given special attention before this study. In addition, SSB, being the most important reliable factor to interact with IFIs, is also seen interacting with variables in the current study. It further contributes to institutional consistency research by testing the normative isomorphism framework that assumes similarity among IFIs, including the *Shariah* pronouncements and the guidelines of professional bodies.

This study is the first that uses the SSB to moderate the relationship between determinants and *Sukuk* legitimacy. Moreover, this variable has not been used as a moderator variable in Islamic finance area, or other areas of management and accounting studies. Thus, this study fills a gap that exists in the literature of *Sukuk* with respect to what has been done in previous literatures. In so doing, the contribution of this study will add to the international and the Islamic finance literature, by enriching and expanding such literatures, and the knowledge of *Sukuk* and legitimacy.

In general, the current study uniquely enriches the literature by adding a new discussion that deals with *Sukuk* and their legitimacy area, especially through the two measurements that represent legitimacy of *Sukuk* (disclosure index) and through investigating SSB as a moderator variable in this relationship, which is unique, as compared to previous studies. Furthermore, the study is intended to increase public awareness of *Sukuk* legitimacy and the importance of *Shariah* compliance, not only in the form but also in substance. In addition, this study will provide more benefits for IFIs, in the sense that they should amend some of their regulatory frameworks to push the *Sukuk* market investors to move towards asset-backed structures. Finally, this study contributes to both academic and practitioner individuals. The findings may have some policy implications with regards to *Sukuk* legitimacy and governance policy (*Shariah* advisory council, IFI management).

## Practical Perspective

This study will be useful to financial institutions in taking into consideration the determinants that will enhance the legitimacy of *Sukuk*, since this study found that some determinants significantly affect the legitimacy of *Sukuk*. This study implies that when determinants are properly implemented with *Shariah* rules, *Sukuk* legitimacy will be improved. Thus, this improved legitimacy will enhance the structures of *Sukuk*, and consequently lead to an improved economy of the country in the long run.

SSBs should promote the importance of, and attention to, as well as increase the legitimacy of, Islamic *Sukuk*. This study implies that the SSB could be an important control instrument that can be used by IFIs to monitor their financial operations, as the study found that SSBs can significantly moderate the relationship between determinants and *Sukuk* legitimacy. The committees of SSBs in central banks must also look into the importance of increasing the legitimacy of *Sukuk* and applying it to IFIs. The importance of increasing attention to legitimacy will also act as a guideline for the financial institutions in their *Sukuk* operations. New IFIs or new *Sukuk* issuers in the market would be aware of the requirements and nature of *Sukuk* structure in conducting their operations, thus they would duly comply to ensure that the legitimacy of their *Sukuk* does not conflict with the *Shariah*, nor affect the *Sukuk* holder's religious orientation.

This study gives a clear picture, and a better understanding, of determinants for Muslim investors to achieve the ultimate goal of maximizing the *halal* profit and compliance with *Shariah*. This would happen in light of being alert to *Shariah* risks which dominate SSB members' minds, and it could become an instrument to encourage them to enhance legitimacy. The current study may help standard makers in central banks in general, and Malaysia in particular, to set wise and deliberate policies related to *Shariah* risks, and to promote SSB members' commitment toward aggressively monitoring *Sukuk* issuers by applying *Shariah* compliant criteria. Ultimately, such a procedure will enhance *Sukuk* governance mechanisms' practices and legitimacy to be *Shariah* compliant.

## Limitations of the Study

This study is not without limitations, and these limitations must be taken into consideration when explaining its results. The limitations of the current study could be discussed from a few perspectives. Firstly, one of the limitations of this study is that it is dependent on *Shariah* pronouncements (*Shariah* reports) to examine the legitimacy. Other studies may choose to review different types of report which include legitimacy. Secondly, the current study selected a disclosure index to measure the legitimacy. Thus, there's a possibility that measuring the *Sukuk* legitimacy by using a questionnaire might lead to enriching this study and its framework. Thirdly, it has been confirmed that bootstrapping analysis can explain the effect of predictor variables on the creation variable, even though the advantage of such methods, the nature and design of the current study, and the small sample size, inhibited the use of more powerful statistical approaches, such as Structural Equation Modelling (SEM), which would require a larger sample size. Fourthly, the sample size of this study is the *Sukuk* issuance listed on the Bursa Malaysia under the exempt regime. Hence, future studies may choose to apply the research in other countries in the Middle East, such as the UAE, Saudi Arabia, or Qatar. Fifthly, the current study has designed a mixed method, and employed a mainly quantitative approach, as the main research methodology with partially qualitative data used to validate the quantitative results. In addition, funding and time constraints prohibited the researcher from using a larger sample for interviews. Finally, the study was limited only to a few variables that have a relationship with *Sukuk* legitimacy. There might be some other factors contributing to *Sukuk* legitimacy which could be investigated in other studies.

## Recommendations for Future Research

The present study introduced invaluable insights into the determinants and their relationship with *Sukuk* legitimacy, in the context of Malaysia. This study offered new knowledge relating to determinants, practices, and *Sukuk* legitimacy discipline in IFIs in Malaysia. Nevertheless, although the results of this study presented a new measurement represented by moderating variables, there is a need for more research to confirm these results in other contexts. Thus, for future research there is a need to examine whether the same results can be achieved by examining these variables in different countries that have different Islamic accounting standards. It is recommended that future studies are undertaken with IFIs in other countries to compare the findings. Nonetheless, although the results of this study presented a reasonable structure for *Sukuk* legitimacy, there is need for more research in order to confirm these results in other contexts. Besides this, future scholars may delve into the findings of this study in more detail, and explore the salience of *Shariah* committees and other *Sukuk* issuers by examining to what extent their influence can guide *Sukuk* to comply with *Shariah* rules.

In addition, future researchers may probe into the findings of the current study in detail and explore other key results by investigating a few suggestions: Firstly, future research should investigate the framework of the study for more than one year. In doing that, they should use time series or panel data, which might get new results to enrich the framework drawn by the current study. Secondly, researchers are also recommended to investigate other determinants, such as special purpose vehicle (SPV) investors, and *Shariah* internal audits to examine their relationship with the *Sukuk* legitimacy, in order to enrich the framework of the current study and assess the results. Furthermore, it is recommended for future studies to apply qualitative methods, such as case studies specifically on each of the independent variables and moderators to better understand *Sukuk* legitimacy in IFIs. Finally, this study focused on the role of the SSB as a moderating variable. It is suggested that a field experiment study be conducted with internal *Shariah* auditing as a moderating variable on the relationship between determinants and *Sukuk* legitimacy.

## Conclusions

This study has made a unique contribution to the body of literature concerning the influence of determinants (pricing, type of structure, *Shariah* auditing, *Shariah* risks and *Shariah* documentation) on *Sukuk* legitimacy by using the population of *Sukuk* listed under the exempt regime in Bursa Malaysia for the period of 2005-2015. Furthermore, it seeks to examine the effect of the SSB as a moderator of the relationship between determinants and *Sukuk* legitimacy. The results of this study have found that the level of legitimacy of *Sukuk* in Islamic financial institutions in Malaysia is generally high. The findings confirmed that there is a positive relationship between four components of *Sukuk* determinants on *Sukuk* legitimacy, namely pricing, type of structure, *Shariah* auditing, and *Shariah* documentation, whereas the other component (*Shariah* risks) has a negative relationship with *Sukuk* legitimacy.

The current results also indicated that the two dimensions of the SSB (SSBM and SSBC) have partial moderating effects on the relationship between five determinants (pricing, type of structure, *Shariah* auditing, *Shariah* compliant risks and *Shariah* documentation) with the legitimacy of *Sukuk*. The results revealed that SSBM was found to have a partial moderating effect on the relationship between two determinants (pricing and *Shariah* documentation), with legitimacy of *Sukuk.* On the other hand, the SSBC is seen to have a moderating effect on the relationship between two determinants (pricing and *Shariah* risk) with *Sukuk* legitimacy. Overall, it can be concluded that *Sukuk* with the higher determinants complying with *Shariah*, will lead to a higher legitimacy, when the involvement of the SSB is higher. The finding of the study also provided valuable knowledge and information to IFIs regarding the impact of determinants on the legitimacy of *Sukuk*.

This study tested a research model that conceptualized the influence of determinants on *Sukuk* legitimacy. The research model was found to be sound, and able to explain the variation in *Sukuk* legitimacy indicators under study. The research found that the selected determinants, which could be used as subjects of reference in determining the existence of legitimacy in *Sukuk,* influence legitimacy. This is significant for at least three parties, i.e. investors, IFIs, and the relevant authority bodies, to strategize on increasing the legitimacy of *Sukuk* by controlling the selected determinants, thereby producing IFI securities that are in compliance with *Shariah* principles and tenets.

# REFERENCES


AAIOIFI (2008) Accounting, Auditing & Governance Standards (for Islamic Financial Institutions), (2008), Shariah Standards. Manamah.

AAIOIFI (Accounting and Auditing Organization for Islamic Financial Institutions) (1999), Governance Standard for Islamic Financial Institutions No. 1 - Shari'a Supervisory Board: Appointment, Composition and Report.

AAIOIFI (Accounting and Auditing Organization for Islamic Financial Institutions) (2012) Shari'ah Standard No. 17 on Investment Sukuk, AAOIFI.

AAOIFI Accounting and Auditing Organization for Islamic Financial Institutions (Bahrain) – AAOIFI Standard 17(20 – as quoted Securities Commission Malaysia, Islamic, 2008).

AAOIFI, 2007. Accounting, Auditing and Governance Stabdards. Manama: AAOIFI.

AAOIFI. (2010). Accounting, Auditing and Governance Standards for Islamic Financial Institutions. Manama, Bahrain: Accounting and Auditing Organization for Islamic Financial Institutions.

Ab Majid, H., Shahimi, S., & Bangaan, M. H. S. (2010). Sukuk defaults and its implication: A case study of Malaysian capital market. In 8th International Conference on Islamic Economics and Finance.

Abdal-Haqq, I. (2006). Understanding Islamic Law: From Classical to Contemporary. AB McCloud (Ed.), 4.

Abdelaal, M. A. (2012). Taqlid v. Ijtihad: The Rise of Taqlid as the Secondary Judicial Approach in Islamic Jurisprudence. J. Juris, 14, 151.

Abdel-Khaleq, A. H., & Richardson, C. F. (2006). New horizons for Islamic securities: Emerging trends in Sukuk offerings. Chi. J. Int'l L., 7, 409.

Abdulmalik, A. (2013) A critical look at Asset based and Asset back Sukuk defaults. INCEIFThe Global Institute for Islamic Finance http://www.academia.edu/6943153/A_critical_look_at_Asset_based_a nd_Asset_back_Sukuk_defaults

Abdul Rahim (2008). ISRA Islamic Finance Seminar shariah audit for Islamic Finance services: the needs and challenges 1.

Abdul Rahman, A., Md. Hashim, M.F.A., & Abu Bakar, F. (2010). Corporate Social Reporting: A Preliminary Study of Bank Islam

Malaysia Berhad (BIMB). Issues in Social and Environmental Accounting, 4(1), 18-39.

Abdullah, A. A., Yazid, A. S., Abdullah, A., & Kamarudin, M. S. (2014). Risk in Funding Infrastructure Projects through Sukuk or Islamic Bonds. International Review of Management and Business Research, 3(2), 915.

Abdullah, A. K. (2011). Overcoming the Weaknesses in Sukuk: Toward Risk-Sharing Instruments in Islamic Finance. Islam and Civilisational Renewal (ICR), 2(4).

Abdullah, A. K., 2012. Asset Backed Vs Asset-Based Sukuk, Kuala Lumpur: International Institute of Advanced Islamic Studies (IAIS) Malaysia.

Abu Alkhiel A. (2012): Ethical Banking and Finance: A Theoretical and Empirical Framework for the Cross Country and Inter-bank Analysis of Efficiency, Productivity, and Financial Performance. University of Hohenheim-Germany.

Adam, N. J., & Thomas, A. (2004a). Islamic fixed income securities: Sukuk.Islamic Asset Management–Forming the Future for Shari'a-Compliant Investment Strategies'', Euromoney Books, 75.

Adam, N. J., & Thomas, A. (2004b). Islamic Bonds: Your guide to issuing, structuring and investing in Sukuk. Euromoney Books.

Afshar, T. (2013). Compare and contrast Sukuk (Islamic Bonds) with conventional bonds, are they compatible? Journal of Global Business Management, 9(1), 44-52. Chicago.

Aggarwal, R; K and T. Yousef (2000). Islamic Bank and Investment Financing. Journal of Money, Credit and Banking, 32(1): pp. 93–120.

Ahmad Sanusi Hussin, 2010 Financial Sector Talent Enrichment Programme, Islamic Banking Handbook, Institut Bank-Bank Malaysia (35880-P) Wisma IBI, 5 Ja;an Semantan Damansara Heights, 50490 Kuala Lumpur.

Ahmad, A. U. & Hassan, M. K. (2006). The time value of money concept in Islamic finance. American Journal of Islamic Social Sciences, 23(1), 66.

Ahmad, M., & MKhatun, M. (2013). The Compliance with Shariah Governance System of AAOIFI: A Study on Islamic Banks Bangladesh. Journal of Islamic Economics, Banking and Finance, 9(3), 177-191.

Ahmed, E. R., & Yahya, S. B. (2013). The Relationship between Bank Orientation and Shubuhat: A Study On Islamic Banks In Malaysia. Economics, Management, and Financial Markets, (2), 95-109.

Ahmed, E. R., Alabdullah, T. T. Y., Islam, M. A., & Asmar, M. (2014) "Sukuk Legitimacy: A New Measurement Based on Content Analysis"

16th Malaysian Finance Association Conference in Sasana Kijang Central Bank of Malaysia, Kuala Lumpur, June 4-6, 2014.

Ahmed, E. R., Islam, A., & Ku Ariffin, K. H. (2015). An Empirical Analysis on Legitimacy of Sukuk: An Insight of Malaysian Sukuk. Asian Social Science, 11(13), 84–97. http://doi.org/10.5539/ass.v11n13p84.

Ahmed, E. R., Islam, M. A., & Alabdullah, T. T. Y. (2014). Islamic Sukuk: Pricing Mechanism and Rating. Journal of Asian Scientific Research, 4(11), 640-648.

Ahmed, E. R., Islam, M. A., & Al-Harthy, F. N. (2013). The Relationship between Shareholders and Shubuhat: A Study on the Islamic Banks in Malaysia. Journal of Asian Scientific Research, 3(6), 538-548.

Ahmed, e. R., Islam, m. A., ariffin, b., halim, k., & moniruzzaman, m. (2013). Journal of Self-Governance & Management Economics, 1(4).

Ahmed, H. (2011a), ''Shari'ah governance regimes for Islamic finance: types and appraisal'', Journal of Institute of International Economics, Vol. 44 No. 4, pp. 393-411.

Ahmed, H. (2011b). Product Development in Islamic Banks. Edinburgh University Press.

Ahmed, K. (2011). Sukuk: Definition, Structure and Accounting Issues.

Aida Othman, (2012) Auditing Islamic Finance, Internal Audit Conference.

AIMS, (2011). Sukuk (Islamic bonds) Academy for International Modern Studies, UK. http://www.kantakji.com/fiqh/files/markets/f237.pdf.

Akhtaruddin, M., Hossain, M., Hossain, M., & Yao, L. (2009). Corporate Governance and Voluntary Disclosure in Corporate Annual Reports of Malaysian listed firms. Journal of Applied Management Accounting Research, 7(1), 1-20.

Aksoy, S. (2005). Making regulations and drawing up legislation in Islamic countries under conditions of uncertainty, with special reference to embryonic stem cell research. Journal of Medical Ethics, 31(7), 399-403.

Alam, K.F. (1998), "Islam, ethics and accounting practices", Accounting, Commerce & Finance:The Islamic Perspective Journal, Vol. 2 No. 2, pp. 67-85.

Alam, N., Hassan, M. K., & Haque, M. A. (2013). Are Islamic bonds different from conventional bonds? International evidence from capital market tests. Borsa Istanbul Review, 13(3), 22-29.

Alam, S. M. (2011). Islamic Finance: an Alternative to the Conventional Financial System. Korea Review of International Studies, 37-59.

Al-Amine, M. A. (2008). Sukuk market: innovations and challenges. ISLAMIC CAPITAL MARKETS, 33.

Al-Amine, M., & Al-Bashir, M. (2001). The Islamic bonds market: possibilities and challenges. International Journal of Islamic Financial Services, 3(1), 1-18.

Al-Bashir, M.A. (2008), "Sukuk market: innovations and challenges", Islamic Economic Studies, Vol. 15 No.2. January 2008.

Al-Bastawaisi, I.A., 2006. Ahkam Wadiah al-Sukuk Fi Fiqh Islami Wa al-Qanun Wad`i. Iskandariah: Dar al-Jama`ah al-Jadidah lil Nasyar.

Al-Buolayan, A. (2006). Rapid Surge in Sukuk market. Arab news www.arabnews.com.

Al Elsheikh, A. A. A., & Tanega, J. (2011). Sukuk structure and its regulatory environment in the Kingdom of Saudi Arabia. Law and Financial Markets Review, 5(3), 183-200.

Alia, R., Ismailb, S., & Bakric, M. H. (2013). The Use of Residential Mortgage-Backed Securities for Better Financial Performance: A Comparative Analysis Between Conventional and Shariah.

Ali, R. (2011). An overview of the Sukuk market. Sukuk and Islamic Capital Markets: A Practical Guide, 7-20.

Ali Saeed, 2012 3rd Quarter 2012 Islamic Capitals Market Quarterly Bulletin, Capital Market Development Authority, and Volume: 5 - October 1, 2012.

Al Istithmar, D. (2006). Sukuk-An Introduction to the Underlying Principles and Structure. Retrieved on October, 24, 2013.

Al-Jumuah, AM, (2000). Mu`jam al-Mustalahat al-Iqtisadiah wa al-Islamiyyah. Riyadh: Maktabah al-Abikan.

AL-Maghlouth, A. K. (2009). Sukuk; an inside study of its background, structures, challenges &Cases.

Al-Mahmoud, A.L. (2007). Towards a Systematic Model of a Policy for Shari'a Supervisory Board and their Commitment Letter, Paper Presented at AAOIFI 6th Annual Conference of SSB (in Arabic), 1-36.

Alnasser, S., & Muhammed, J. (2012). Introduction to corporate governance from Islamic perspective. Humanomics, 28(3), 220-231.

Aloui, C., Hammoudeh, S., & Hamida, H. B. (2015). Price discovery and regime shift behavior in the relationship between sharia stocks and Sukuk: A two-state Markov switching analysis. Pacific-Basin Finance Journal, 34, 121-135.

Al-Saati, A. B. (2003). The permissible Gharar (risk) in classical Islamic jurisprudence. Islamic Economics, 16(2), 3-19.

Alsaeed, K. & Sulaiman (2012) "Sukuk Issuance in Saudi Arabia: Recent Trends and Positive Expectations" Durham theses, Durham University.

Al-Salem, F. H. (2009). Islamic financial product innovation. International Journal of Islamic and Middle Eastern Finance and Management, 2(3), 187-200.

Archer, S. & Haron, A. (2007), ‘‘Operational risk exposures of Islamic banks’’, in Archer, S. and Abdel.

Ariff, M., Iqbal, M., & Mohamad, S. (Eds.). (2012). The Islamic debt market for Sukuk securities: The theory and practice of profit sharing investment. Edward Elgar Publishing.

Arshad, N. C., & Ismail, A. G. (2010). Shariah parameters for Musharakah Contract: A comment. International Journal of Business and Social Science, 1(1), 145-162.

Ayub, M. (2005, November). Securitization, Sukuk and fund management potential to be realized by Islamic Financial Institutions. In Sixth International Conference on Islamic Economics, Banking and Finance.

Ayub, M., 2007. Understanding Islamic Finance. Chichester: John Wiley & Sons.

Aziah Abu Kasim, N. (2012). Disclosure of Shariah compliance by Malaysian takaful companies. Journal of Islamic Accounting and Business Research, 3(1), 20-38.

Aziz, Z. A. (2008). Enhancing Interlinkages and Opportunities: The Role of Islamic Finance. NBR ANALYSIS, 18(4), 5.

Aziz, A., Pahlavi, R., & Gintzburger, A. S. (2009). Equity-Based, Asset-Based and Asset-Backed Transactional Structures in Shari’a-Compliant Financing: Reflections on the Current Financial Crisis. Economic Papers: A journal of applied economics and policy, 28(3), 270-278.

Azmat, S., Skully, M., & Brown, K. (2014b). Issuer's choice of Islamic bond type. Pacific-Basin Finance Journal, 28, 122-135.

Azmat, S., Skully, M., & Brown, K. (2014a). The Shariah compliance challenge in Islamic bond markets. Pacific-Basin Finance Journal, 28, 47-57.

Ba¨ lz, K. (2008), ‘‘Shari’ah risk? How Islamic finance has transformed Islamic contract law’’, Occasional Publications 9, Islamic Legal Studies Program, Harvard Law School, Cambridge, MA.

Babbie, E. (1995). The Practice of Social Research, 7th edn. Toronto: Wadsworth Publishing Company.

Babu Das Augustine, 2015 Global Sukuk issuance to gain momentum in 2015. Published: 13:29 March 15, 2015 Gulf News.

Bacha, O. I. (1999). Derivative instruments and Islamic finance: Some thoughts for reconsideration.

Bank Negara Malaysia (2010). Shariah Governance Framework for Islamic Financial Institutions. Available online at http://www.bnm.gov.my/ (accessed on 1st December 2014).

Ba¨lz, K. (2008), ''Shari'ah risk? How Islamic finance has transformed Islamic contract law'', Occasional.

Barriball, K. L., & While, A. (1994). Collecting data using a semi-structured interview: a discussion paper. Journal of Advanced Nursing, 19(2), 328-35. Retrieved from http://www.ncbi.nlm.nih.gov/pubmed/8188965.

Baron, R. M., & Kenny, D. A. (1986). The moderator–mediator variable distinction in social psychological research: Conceptual, strategic, and statistical considerations. Journal of personality and social psychology, 51(6), 1173.

Baydoun, N. & R. Willett. (1997) Islam and accounting: Ethical issues in the presentation of financial information. Accounting, commerce & Finance: The Islamic Perspective. Vol.1, No.1 [June]: 1-25.

Baydoun, N., & Willett, R. (2000). Islamic Corporate Reports. Abacus, 36(1), 71-90.

Bellalah, M., & Ellouz, S. (2004). Islamic Finance, Interest Rates And Islamic Banking A Survey of The Literature. Finance India, 18, 533-546.

Benjelayel, K. (2011). The Scope of Application of Islamic Contract Law to Securities Transactions Vis a Via Conventional Transactions. Available at SSRN.

Bertillo, D., Julius, B., Salando, D., Bertillo, J., Nieva, D., & Ortega, F. (2013). Global Impact of Islamic Financial Systems in the Arab World. Josefina Bertillo and Nieva, Dr. Florabel Ortega, Global Impact of Islamic Financial Systems in the Arab World (June 30, 2013).

Besar, M. H. A., Abd Sukor, M. E., Abdul Muthalib, N., & Gunawa, A. Y. (2009). The practice of Shariah review as undertaken by Islamic banking sector in Malaysia. International Review of Business Research Papers, 5(1), 294-306.

Billah, M. M. (2009) Takaful Feature: Shariah Supervisory Boards http://applied-islamicfinance.com/pdf/mediaviews/Roleof ShariahBoard.pdf.

Bin Ibrahim, M., & Wong, A. (2006). The corporate bond market in Malaysia. Bank for International Settlements Press & Communications CH-4002 Basel, Switzerland E-mail: publications@ bis. or g Fax: + 41 61 280 9100 and+ 41 61 280 8100, 26(22.0), 114.

Birnbaum, P. (1984). The choice of strategic alternatives under increasing regulation in high technology industries. Academy of Management Journal, 27(3), 489-510.

Black, B. S., Jang, H. & Kim, W. (2003). Does corporate governance affect firms' market value? Evidence from Korea. Working Paper No. 237, Stanford Law School, John M. Olin Program Law and Economics, July, 1 – 70.

Blalock, A.B. & Blalock Jr., H.M. (1982). Introduction to social research. Englewood Cliffs, N.J.: Prentice-Hall.

Bley, J., & Kuehn, K. (2004). Conventional versus Islamic finance: student knowledge and perception in the United Arab Emirates. International Journal of Islamic Financial Services, 5(4), 17-30.

BNM & SC., 2009 Malaysian Debt Securities and Sukuk Market -A Guide for Issuers and Investors. Bond Market Department and PDS Issues Department, Securities Commission Malaysia.

BNM, 2007 Shariah resolutions in Islamic Finance. Bank Negara Malaysia, 2007.

BNM, 2010 shariah resolutions in Islamic finance - Bank Negara Malaysia, second edition Second Edition Published 2010 www.bnm.gov.my.

BNM, 2013 Guidelines on Takaful Operational Framework, Islamic Banking.

BNM. 2007. Resolution Sharia in Islamic Finance, Glossary. Kuala Lumpur, Malaysia. Eisenhardt, K. M. 1989. "Building Theories from Case Study Research", Academy of Management Review, vol. 14, no.4, pp 532 – 550.

Braudel, F. (1995). The Mediterranean and the Mediterranean world in the age of Philip II (Vol. 2). Univ of California Press.

Brewer, J., & Hunter, A. (1989). Multimethod research: A synthesis of styles. Newbury Park, CA: Sage.

Bryman, A. (2006). Integrating quantitative and qualitative research: how is it done?. Qualitative research, 6(1), 97-113.

Cakir, S., & Raei, F. (2007). Sukuk vs. Eurobonds: Is there a difference in value-at-risk?. International Monetary Fund.

Carmassi, J., & Herring, R. J. (2013). Living wills and cross-border resolution of systemically important banks. Journal of Financial Economic Policy, 5(4), 361-387.

Casper, M. (2012). Sharia Boards and Sharia Compliance in the Context of European Corporate Governance. Available at SSRN 2179412.

Central Bank of Malaysia (2007) Financial Stability and Payment Systems Report, 2007, pp: 56-57. Website: http://www.bnm.gov.my/files/publication/fsps/bm/2007/cp02_rencana_01.pdf.

Chaganti, R.S., Mahajan, V., & Sharma, S. (1985). Corporate Board Size, Composition and Corporate Failures in Retailing Industry. Journal of Management Studies, 22(4), 400-417.

Chapra, M. U. & Ahmed, H. (2002). Corporate governance in Islamic Financial Institutions.Occasional Paper No. 6, Islamic Research and Training Institute, IslamicDevelopment Bank, Kingdom of Saudi Arabia.

Chen, C.J.P., & Jaggi, B. (2000). Association between independent non-executive directors, family control and financial disclosures in Hong Kong. Journal of Accounting and Public Policy, 19(4-5), 285-310.

Chen, H., Lindeke, R. R., & Wyrick, D. A. (2010). Lean automated manufacturing: avoiding the pitfalls to embrace the opportunities. Assembly Automation, 30(2), 117-123. Chicago.

Chik, M. N. B. (2012). Sukuk: Shariah guidelines for Islamic bonds. In Islamic Banking Operations and Regulatory Framework Workshop, Colombo.

Chin, W. W. (1998). The partial least squares approach to structural equation modeling. Modern methods for business research, 295(2), 295-336.

Chin, W. W. (2010). How to write up and report PLS analyses, in Handbook of Partial Least Squares: Concepts.

Choudhury, M. A. (Ed.). (1997). Money in Islam: a study in Islamic political economy (Vol. 3). Psychology Press.

Churchill, G. (1987) Marketing research Fort Worth (1987).

CIMB, 2012. Sukuk and capital market, Islamic finance news. http://www.islamicfinancenews.com/2012_supplement/2012capitalmarket/CapitalMarket2012.pdf.

Cohen, J. (1988). Statistical power analysis for the behavioral sciences. Mahwah, NJ: Lawrence Erlbaum Associates.

Cohen, L., Manion, L. and Morrison, (2000). Research Methods in Education (5th ed.). London: Routledge Falmer.

Collis, J., & Hussey, R. (2009). Business research: A practical guide for undergraduate and postgraduate students.

Cooper, D. R., Schindler, P. S., & Sun, J. (1998). Business research methods: Irwin/McGraw-Hill Burr Ridge, IL.

Creswell, J. W., & Garrett, A. L. (2008). The" movement" of mixed methods research and the role of educators. South African Journal of Education, 28(3), 321-333.

Creswell, J. W., Plano Clark, V. L., Gutmann, M. L., & Hanson, W. E. (2003). Advanced mixed methods research designs. Handbook of mixed methods in social and behavioral research, 209-240.

Cupchik, G. (2001, February). Constructivist realism: an ontology that encompasses positivist and constructivist approaches to the social sciences. In Forum Qualitative Sozialforschung/Forum: Qualitative Social Research (Vol. 2, No. 1).

Curasi, C.F. (2001). A critical exploration of face-to-face interviewing vs. computer-mediated interviewing. International Journal of Market Research, 43(4), 361–375.

Dawood, M. (2008), "Ensuring the quality of Shariah advice", paper presented at MEFX, Dubai Financial Center, Dubai,1-3 June.

Déjean, F., & Oxibar, B. (2003). An Alternative Approach to Evaluate Corporate Social Performance. In Trabajo presentado en el Congreso de la European Accounting Associa tion.

DeLorenzo, (2010). Shari`ah Supervisionin ModernIslamic Finance.

DeLorenzo, Y. and McMillen, M. (2007), ''Law and Islamic finance: an interactive analysis'', in Archer, S. and Abdel Karim, R. (Eds), Islamic Finance: The Regulatory Challenge, John Wiley & Sons, Singapore, pp. 132-197.

deMarrais, K. (2004). Qualitative interview studies. In K. deMarrais & S. D. Lapan (Eds.), Foundations for research: Methods of inquiry in education and the social sciences (pp. 51–68). Mahwah, New Jersey: Lawrence Erlbaum Associates.

Denscombe, M. (2003). The good research guide. Maidenhead: Open University Press.

Denzin, Norman K. & Lincoln, Yvonna S. 2003, The Landscape of Qualitative Research, Sage, London.

Derigs, U., & Marzban, S. (2009). New strategies and a new paradigm for Shariah-compliant portfolio optimization. Journal of Banking & Finance, 33(6), 1166-1176.

De Vroede, P. (1981). De cheque: de post cheque ende reis cheque. Kluwer Rechtswetenschappen.

DiCicco-Bloom, B., & Crabtree, B. F. (2006). The qualitative research interview. Medical Education, 40, 314-321.

Di Mauro, F., Caristi, P., Couderc, S., Di Maria, A., Ho, L., & Kaur Grewal, B. & Zaheer, S. (2013). *Islamic finance in Europe*.

DiMaggio, P.J. and Powell, W. (1991), "The iron cage revisited: institutional isomorphism and collective rationality in organisational fields", in Powell, W.W. and DiMaggio, P.J. (Eds), The New Institutionalism in Organizational Analysis, University of Chicago Press, Chicago, IL, pp. 63-82.

Dow Jones (2013). Guide to the Dow Jones Sukuk Index, S&P Dow Jones Indices LLC, a subsidiary of The McGraw-Hill Companies, Inc.

Drever, E. (1995). Using Semi-Structured Interviews in Small-Scale Research. A Teacher's Guide.

Driscoll, D. L., Appiah-Yeboah, A., Salib, P., & Rupert, D. J. (2007). Merging qualitative and quantitative data in mixed methods research: How to and why not. Ecological and Environmental Anthropology (University of Georgia), 18.

Dusuki, A. W. (2009a). Shariah issues on asset-based Sukuk. Manama, Bahrain: Accounting and Auditing Organisation for Islamic Financial Institution.

Dusuki, A. W. (2009b). Challenges of realizing Maqasid al-Shariah (Objectives of Shariah) in Islamic capital market: Special focus on equity-based Sukuk. ISRA Research Paper, (6o. 5/2009).

Dusuki, A. W. (2010a). Do equity-based Sukuk structures in Islamic capital markets manifest the objectives of Shariah? &quest. Journal of Financial Services Marketing, 15(3), 203-214.

Dusuki, A. W. (2010b). Critical Appraisal of Shariah Issues on Ownership in Asset-Based Sukuk as Implemented in the Islamic Debt Market, ISRA Research Paper (No. 8/2010).

Ebrahim, M. S., & Khan, T. (2002). On the pricing of an Islamic convertible mortgage for infrastructure project financing. International Journal of Theoretical and Applied Finance, 5(07), 701-728.

El Ariff, M., Iqbal, M., & Mohamad, S. (Eds.). (2012). The Islamic debt market for Sukuk securities: The theory and practice of profit sharing investment. Edward Elgar Publishing. Qorchi, M. (2005). Islamic finance gears up. Finance and Development, 42(4), 46.

Elasrag, H. (2011). Principals of the Islamic finance: A focus on project finance. Available at SSRN 1806305.

El-Gamal, M. A. (2005). Islamic bank corporate governance and regulation: a call for mutualization. Rice University.

El-Gamal, M. A. (2007). 20 Mutualization of Islamic banks. Handbook of Islamic Banking, 310.

El-Hawary, D., & Grais, W. (2003). Regulating Islamic financial institutions: the nature of the regulated (Vol. 3227). World Bank Publications.

El Shazly, M. R., & Tripathy, P. (2013). Sukuk Structures, Profiles and Risks.

El-Quqa, O. M., Hasan, F., Rout, B., & Joubaili, A. (2008). Sukuks – a new dawn of Islamic finance era. Global Investment House. Retrieved from http://www.gulfbase.com/ ScheduleReports/Sukuk-170108.pdf.

Engku Ali, E.R.A. (2005). Islamic Debt Securities/Bonds. Paper presented in Workshop on Islamic Bonds, Sukuk and Securitization, 6-7 September 2005.

Fairchild, A. J., & MacKinnon, D. P. (2009). A general model for testing mediation and moderation effects. Prevention Science, 10(2), 87-99.

Faiz. W (2011). Challenges and opportunities Islamic financial institutions are facing in the western countries, Master Thesis Aarhus School of Business, University of Aarhus.

Farook, S., Hassan, K., & Lanis, R. (2011). Determinants of corporate social responsibility disclosure: The case of Islamic banks. Journal of Islamic Accounting and Business Research, 2(2), 114 – 141.

Farooq, M. O. (2006). The Doctrine of Ijma: Is there a consensus?

Farooq, M. O. (2007). Partnership, equity-financing and Islamic finance: whither profit-loss sharing? Review of Islamic Economics (Special Issue), 11, 67-88.

Ferry, J. (2010). Scuppered by Sukuk. Risk, 23, 90-92.

Feuerverger, A., Stigler, S. M., Fuchs, C., Bentley, D. L., Bird, S. M., Höfling, H., ... & Kadane, J. B. (2008). Statistical Analysis of an Archeological Find [with Discussion]. The Annals of Applied Statistics, 3-112.

Fitri, M. R. (2007) pricing of Murabahah and Ijarah Product in malaysia: A critical analysis from shariah perspective, Master Thesis.

Fisher Jr, W. P., & Stenner, A. J. (2011). Integrating qualitative and quantitative research approaches via the phenomenological method. International Journal of Multiple Research Approaches, 5(1), 89-103.

Fornell, C. & Cha, J. (1994). Partial least squares. In R.P. Bagozzi (Ed.). Advanced methods in marketing research. Cambridge: Blackwell, 52-78.

Fornell, C., Larcker, D.F. (1981). Evaluating structural equation models with unobservable variables and measurement error. Journal of Marketing Research 18 (1), 39-50.

Frazier, P. A., Tix, A. P., & Barron, K. E. (2004). Testing moderator and mediator effects in counseling psychology research. Journal of counseling psychology, 51(1), 115.

Gambling, T.E., & Karim, R.A.A. (1991). Business and Accounting Ethics in Islam (1st Ed.). Mansell Publishing Limited, London.

Gay, L. R., & Airasian, P. (2003). Education research. Competencies for Analysis and Applications, New Jersey.

Gheeraert, L. (2014). Does Islamic finance spur banking sector development? Journal of Economic Behavior and Organization, 103(March 2012), S4–S20. http://doi.org/10.1016/j.jebo.2014.02.013.

Ginena, K. (2014). Shariah risk and corporate governance of Islamic banks. Corporate Governance, 14(1), 86-103.

Godlewski, C. J., Turk Ariss, R., & Weill, L. (2011). Do markets perceive Sukuk and conventional bonds as different financing instruments?

Godlewski, C. J., Turk, R., & Weill, L. (2014). Do the Type of Sukuk and Choice of Shari'a Scholar Matter? International Monetary Fund–Middle East Center for Economics and Finance. WP/14/147.

Golcer, 2013 "Islamic Finance Bulletin "Gulf One Lancaster Centre For Economic Research, ums.lancs.ac.uk/research/centres/golcer.

Goodhue, D., Lewis, W., & Thompson, R. (2006, January). PLS, small sample size, and statistical power in MIS research. In System Sciences, 2006. HICSS'06. Proceedings of the 39th Annual Hawaii International Conference on (Vol. 8, pp. 202b-202b). IEEE.

Goodwin, J. (2003). The Glory That Was Baghdad. The Wilson Quarterly, 24-28.

Governor of Central Bank of Malaysia, (2007). "The Global Islamic Financial Services Industry", May 14, website http://www.bis.org/review/r070515b.pdf (accessed on 6th February 2011).

Grais, W., & Pellegrini, M. (2006). Corporate governance in institutions offering Islamic financial services: issues and options (Vol. 4052). World Bank Publications.

Grassa, R. (2013). Shariah supervisory system in Islamic financial institutions: New issues and challenges: A comparative analysis between Southeast Asia models and GCC models. Humanomics, 29(4), 333-348.

Grassa, R. (2015a). Shariah supervisory systems in Islamic finance institutions across the OIC member countries: An investigation of regulatory frameworks. Journal of Financial Regulation and Compliance, 23(2), 135-160.

Grassa, R. (2015b). Corporate governance and credit rating in Islamic banks: Does Shariah governance matters? Journal of Management & Governance, 1-32.

Gray, R., Kouhy, R., & Lavers, S. (1995a). Corporate social and environmental reporting: a review of the literature and a longitudinal study of UK disclosure. Accounting, Auditing and Accountability Journal, 8(2), 47-77.

Gray, R., Kouhy, R., & Lavers, S. (1995b). Methodology themes construction research database of social and environmental reporting by UK companies. Accounting, Auditing and Accountability Journal, 8(2), 78-101.

Green, S. B., Salkind, N. J., & Akey, T. M. (1997). Using SPSS for windowsPrentice Hall. Upper Saddle River (NJ).

Greenberg, M. S. (1980). A theory of indebtedness. In Social exchange (pp. 3-26). Springer US.

Gujarati, D. N. (2003). Basic Econometrics Fourth Edition McGraw Hill Gujarati, DN, (2003). Basic Econometrics.

Guthrie, J., Cuganesan, S., & Ward, L. (2008, March). Industry specific social and environmental reporting: The Australian Food and Beverage Industry. InAccounting Forum (Vol. 32, No. 1, pp. 1-15). Elsevier.

Guthrie, J.E., & Parker, L.D. (1989). Corporate Social Reporting: A Rebuttal of Legitimacy Theory. Accounting and Business Research, 19(76), 343-352.

Hackston, D., & Milne, M. J. (1996). Some determinants of social and environmental disclosures in New Zealand companies. Accounting, Auditing & Accountability Journal, 9(1), 77-108.

Hafizi & Shahida, 2011 "Sukuk Defaults and Its Implication: A Case Study of Malaysian Capital Market" 8Th International Conference on Islamic Economics and Finance. Center for Islamic Economics and Finance, Qatar Faculty of Islamic Studies, Qatar Foundation.

Hair, J. F., Anderson, R. E., Tatham, R. L., & Black, W. C. (1998). Multivariate analysis. Englewood: Prentice Hall International.

Haji Besar, Sukor, Abdul Muthalib & Gunawa (2009). The Practice of Shariah Review as Undertaken by Islamic Banking Sector in Malaysia, International Review of Business Research Papers Vol.5 No. 1 January 2009 Pp. 294-306.

Hakim, S., & Rashidian, M. (2004, March). Risk and return of Islamic stock market indexes. In International Seminar of Non-Bank Financial Institutions: Islamic Alternatives, Kuala Lumpur, Malaysia.

Hamid, N. A. (2000). Guide to the Malaysian Bond Market. Rating Agency Malaysia.

Hamid, S., Craig, R., & Clarke, F. (1993). Religion: a confounding cultural element in the international harmonization of accounting? Abacus, 29(2), 131-148.

Hamza, H. (2013). Sharia governance in Islamic banks: effectiveness and supervision model.

Hamza, Qais H. (2006) Islamic Sukuk securities as financing instruments: An examination of bond pricing in the conventional and Islamic setting and a survey of literature on alternative benchmarks to the interest-based system. Masters thesis, Durham University.

Haneef, R. (2009). From "Asset-Backed" to "Asset-Light" Structures: The Intricate History of Sukuk. ISRA International Journal of Islamic Finance, 1(1).

Hanif, M. (2010). Differences and similarities in Islamic and conventional banking. International Journal of Business and Social Sciences, 2(2).

Hanifa, M. H., Masih, M., & Bacha, O. (2014). Testing Sukuk And Conventional Bond Offers Based On Corporate Financing Theories Using Partial Adjustment Models: Evidence From Malaysian Listed Firms.

Haniffa, R., & Hudaib, M. (2007). Exploring the ethical identity of Islamic banks via communication in annual reports. Journal of Business Ethics, 76(1), 97-116.

Hair, J. F., Black, W. C., Babin, B. J., & Anderson, R. E. (2010). Multivariate data analysis (7th ed.). Englewood Cliffs: Prentice Hall.

Haral, T. A. (2010). Regional Head North, Senior Vice President, Arif Habib Investments Ltd. Pakistan. [Telephonic, 23 April 2010].

Harasani, H. (2013). Role of Ijtihad in Progressing Islamic Law in Modern Times, The. US-China L. Rev., 10, 361.

Haron, A., & Hock, J. L. H. (2007). Inherent risk: credit and market risks. Islamic finance: The regulatory challenge, 2.

Haron, H. (2012). Malaysian Rating Corporation Berhad: Rating Approach To Sukuk: A MARC Perspective, 1–14.

Haron, R., & Ibrahim, K. (2012). The Impact of Sukuk on Corporate Financing: Malaysia Evidence. Journal of Islamic Finance, 1(1).

Hasan, A. (2007). Islamic structured products: Issues and Challenges and Finance, 189.

Hasan, A., & Sabirzyanov, R. (2015) Optimal Shari'ah Governance Model in Islamic Finance Regulation. International Journal of Education and Research Vol. 3 No. 4 April 2015.

Hasan, M., & Dridi, J. (2011). The effects of the global crisis on Islamic and conventional banks: A comparative study. Journal of International Commerce, Economics and Policy, 2(02), 163-200.

Hasan, M., Dridi, J. (2010). The Effects of the Global Crisis on Islamic and Conventional Banks: A Comparative Study. IMF Working Paper # WP/10/201.

Hasan, Z. (2010a). Islamic Finance: Structure-objective mismatch and its consequences.

Hasan, Z. (2012), Shari'ah Governance in Islamic Banks, Edinburgh University Press, Edinburgh.

Hasan, Z., & bin Hasan, Z. (2012). Shari'ah Governance in Islamic banks. Edinburgh University Press.

Hashmi, Nasir. (2010). Financer controller, Pregna Group Dubai. [Telephonic, 5].

Hassan Scott (2009). Corporate Governance in takaful, ICMIF.

Hassan, A., & Shahid, M. A. (2010). Management and Development of the Awqaf Assets. In Seventh International Conference-The Tawhidi Epistemology: Zakat and Waqf Economy. UKM.

Hassan, K., & Mahlknecht, M. (2011). Islamic capital markets: products and strategies (Vol. 609). John Wiley & Sons.

Hayat, R. (2006). An empirical assessment of Islamic equity fund returns. Failaka website, 1-69.

Hayat, R., & Kraeussl, R. (2011). Risk and return characteristics of Islamic equity funds. Emerging Markets Review, 12(2), 189-203.

Heck, G. W. (2006). Charlemagne, Muhammad, and the Arab roots of capitalism. Walter de Gruyter.

Heeler, R.M. and M.L. Ray (1972). "Measure Validation in Marketing." Journal of Marketing Research, 9(Nov.), 361-370.

Henderson, A.R. (2005). The bootstrap: A technique for data-driven statistics. Using computer-intensive analyses to explore experimental data. Clinica Chimica Acta, 359:1-26.

Henseler, J., Chin, W.W. (2010). A comparison of approaches for the analysis of interaction effects between latent variables using partial least squares path modeling, Structural Equation Modeling 17 (1), 82e109.

Herwany, A., & Febrian, E. (2010). A Value at Risk Analysis on the Performance of Sukuk and Conventional Bonds: The Case of ASEAN Markets. Available at SSRN 1659799.

Hess, D. (2007), “Social reporting and new governance regulation: the prospects of achieving corporate governance accountability through transparency”, Business Ethics Quarterly, Vol. 17 No. 3, pp. 453-76.

Hidayat, S. E. (2013). A Comparative Analysis between Asset Based and Asset Backed Sukuk: Which One is More Shariah Compliant. International SAMANM Journal of Finance and Accounting, 1(2). http://dx.doi.org/10.1596/978-0-8213-7141-1.

Hitchcock, G., & Hughes, D. (1995). Research and the teacher: A qualitative introduction to school-based research (2nd ed.). London: Routledge.

Holmbeck, G. N. (1997). Toward terminological, conceptual, and statistical clarity in the study of mediators and moderators: examples from the child-clinical and pediatric psychology literatures. Journal of consulting and clinical psychology, 65(4), 599.

Howe, K. R. (1988). Against the quantitative-qualitative incompatibility thesis or dogmas die hard. Educational researcher, 17(8), 10-16.

Howladar, K. (2009). The Future of Sukuk: Substance over Form? Understanding Islamic securitisation, Asset-Backed and AAOIFI principles. Moody's Investors Service, 1-13.

Hughes, S.B. & Anderson, A. (1995). Corporate Environmental Performance and Environmental Disclosure: Are They Related? Paper presented at the American Accounting Association Annual Conference, Orlando, Florida, United States.

Ibn Manzur (n.d.). Lisan Arab. Cairo: Dar al-Ma`arif, pp: 24.

Ibrahim, M. F., Eng, O. S., & Parsa, A. (2009). International articles: Shariah property investment in Asia. Journal of Real Estate Literature, 17(2), 231-248.

IDB and IFSB (2007) Islamic Development Bank (IDB) and Islamic Financial Services Board (IFSB) (2007), Islamic Financial.

IDB. (2000). Resolutions and Recommendations of the Council of the Islamic Fiqh Academy (Islamic Development Bank). (1985-2000).

Idris, U. M. (2008). Evaluation of Research Developments on the Islamic Securities (Sukuk).

IFIS, 2010 “Global Sukuk Market”, [H2-2010Report].

IFSB (2005), Guiding Principles of Risk Management for Institutions (Other than Insurance Institutions) Offering Only Islamic Financial Services, IFSB, Kuala Lumpur.

IFSB Islamic Financial Services Board (Malaysia) (2009) – IFSB Standard 7 – Capital Adequacy requirements for Sukuk, securitizations and real estate investment, para 1.1 (version January 2009.

Ingram, R. W., & Frazier, K. B. (1980). Environmental performance and corporate disclosure. Journal of accounting research, 614-622.

International Association of Islamic Banks (IAIB) (2001). Directory of Islamic banks and Institutions, IAIB, Jedah. International harmonization of accounting?”, Abacus, Vol. 29 No. 2, pp. 131-48.

Iqbal, Z. (1997). Islamic financial systems. Finance and Development, 34, 42-45.

Iqbal, Z., & Mirakhor, A. (2011). An introduction to Islamic finance: theory and practice (Vol. 687). John Wiley & Sons.

Islamic Development Bank (IDB) and Islamic Financial Services Board (IFSB) (2007), Islamic Financial Services Industry Development: Ten-year Framework and Strategies, IFSB, Kuala Lumpur.

Islamic Financial Services Board (2005), Guiding Principles of Risk Management for Institutions (Other Than Insurance Institutions) Offering Only Islamic Financial Services, IFSB, Kuala Lumpur.

Islamic Financial Services Board (2006), Guiding Principles on Corporate Governance for Institutions Offering Only Islamic Financial Services, IFSB, Kuala Lumpur.

Islamic Financial Services Board (2007a), Guidance on Key Elements in the Supervisory Review Process of Institutions Offering Islamic Financial Services, IFSB, Kuala Lumpur.

Islamic Financial Services Board (2007b), Disclosures to Promote Transparency and Market Discipline for Institutions Offering Islamic Financial Services, IFSB, Kuala Lumpur.

Islamic Financial Services Board (2009), Guiding Principles on Sharı'ah Governance for Institutions Offering Islamic Financial Services, IFSB, Kuala Lumpur.

Ismail, A. G. (2009). "Sukuk Structure: An International Comparison" Research Center for Islamic Economics and Finance, Universiti Kebangsaan Malaysia.

Ismail, S., Ali, R., Serguieva, A., & Gregoriou, A. (2008, March). Asset backed securities as attractive financing and investment: The Malaysian experience. In Proceedings of the Eight International Business Research Conference Dubai (pp. 1-9).

ISRA (2013). The Role OF Shariah Advisors in Sukuk issuance. http://www.ifikr.isra.my/documents/10180/16168/ISRA%20Bloomberg%20Bulletin%20November%202013%20-%20Fatwa%20in%20Islamic%20Finance.pdf.

Izhar, H. (2010). Identifying operational risk exposures in Islamic banking. Kyoto Bulletin of Islamic Area Studies, 3(2), 17-53.

Jadwa Investment (2009). The Saudi Sukuk Market KFH, 2012. Islamic financial research, http://kfhresearch.com/uploads/reports/samples/a83549cedbdffaf7868eb8a90c0f03e60934cabd.pdf.

Jaffer, S. (Ed.). (2004). Islamic asset management: forming the future for Shari'a-compliant investment strategies. Euromoney Books.

Jamal, A. (2002) Commentaries on Imam Nawawi's Forty Hadith. Publications 9, Islamic Legal Studies Program, Harvard Law School, Cambridge, MA.

Jamilah A. J, & Abdul Rahman, Z. (2012). Sukuk investment: Comparison of the profits obtained by using Ijarah and Musharakah Mutanaqisah principles with long-term tenure. Qualitative Research in Financial Markets, 4(2/3), 206-227.

Janin, H., & Kahlmeyer, A. (2007). Islamic Law: The Sharia from Muhammad's Time to the Present. McFarland.

Jobst, A. (2010). Risk Management of Islamic finance instruments. QFINANCE//http://www.qfinance.com/contentFiles/QF01/94fqn4jz/10/0/ risk-management-of-islamic-finance-instruments.

Jobst, A., Kunzel, P., Mills, P., & Sy, A. (2008). Islamic bond issuance: what sovereign debt managers need to know. International Journal of Islamic and Middle Eastern Finance and Management, 1(4), 330-344.

Johnson, R. B., & Onwuegbuzie, A. J. (2004). Mixed methods research: A research paradigm whose time has come. Educational researcher, 33(7), 14-26.

Junaid Haider & Muhammad Azhar (2010). Islamic Capital Market Sukuk and its Risk Management in the Current Scenario, Umea School of Business & Economics, Umea University, Sweden.

Junaid. H & Muhammad. A (2010). Sukuk and its Risk Management in the Current Scenario. Umea School of Business & Economics, Umea University, Sweden.

Kahf, M. (1997). The Use of Assets Ijara Bonds for Bridging the Budget Gap. Islamic Economic Studies, 4(2), 82.

Kamali (2009). Maqasid al Shariah made simple. The International Institute of Islamic Thought IIIT (2009).

Kamaluddin, N., Manan, A., Khadijah, S., Sufian, F., & Htay, S. (2012, October). Shari'ah principles of Sukuk structure in Malaysia Islamic capital market. In Terengganu International Business and Economic Conference III 2012. Faculty Of Business Management, Uitm Terengganu.

Kamil, K. H., Abdullah, M., Shahimi, S., & Ismail, A. G. (2010). The subprime mortgages crisis and Islamic securitization. International Journal of Islamic and Middle Eastern Finance and Management, 3(4), 386-401.

Kamso, N. (2013). Investing in Islamic Funds: A Practitioner's Perspective (Vol. 874). John Wiley & Sons.

Kantakji. S. (2012) Mathematics of Fiqh Al-Muamalat, Dar abilfida, Hamah, Syira. ISBN 9789933912901. http://islamicec.ir/uploads/MFM_ver_1_118616.pdf

Kantakji. S. (2003) Islamic Financial Transactions Performance Measurement Criterion A Substitute for LIBOR Rate.

Kantakji. S & O'haj, B. (2010) performance Benchmark for Islamic Financial Transactions.

Karchmer, R.A. (2001). The journey ahead: Thirteen teachers report how the Internet influences literacy and literacy instruction in their K–12 classrooms. Reading Research Quarterly, 36(4), 442–466.

Karim, R.A.A. (1990). Standard setting for the financial reporting religious business organizations: The case of Islamic banks. Accounting and Business Research, 20(80), pp. 299-305.

Karim, R.A.A. (2001). The Nature and Rationale of a Conceptual Framework for Financial Reporting by Islamic Banks, Accounting and Business Research, 25(100), 285-300.

Kaseb, B. A. (2010) Harmonization between The Shariah Guidelines and The Practices in Malaysian Sukuk Market International Islamic University Malaysia, Kulliyah of Economics and Management Sciences.

Kasim, N. A. (2012). Disclosure of Shariah compliance by Malaysian takaful companies. Journal of Islamic Accounting and Business Research, 3(1), 20-38.

Kasim, N., Ibrahim, M., Hameed, S., & Sulaiman, M. (2009). Shariah auditing in Islamic financial institutions: exploring the gap between the" desirable" and the" actual". Global Economy & finance journal, 2(2), 127-137.

Kettell, B. (2010). Frequently asked questions in Islamic finance. John Wiley & Sons.

KFH (2014). Islamic Finance Outlook 2014. KFH Research Ltd.

Khan, G. (1993). Arabic legal and administrative documents in the Cambridge Genizah collections (Vol. 10). CUP Archive.

Khan, M. A. (2004). Islamic economics and finance: a glossary. Routledge.

Khan, M. A. (2013). What is wrong with Islamic economics? Analysing the present state and future agenda. Edward Elgar Publishing.

Khan, M. F. (2007). 18 Islamic methods for government borrowing and monetary management. Handbook of Islamic Banking, 285.

Khan, M. M., & Bhatti, M. I. (2008). Development in Islamic banking: a financial risk-allocation approach. Journal of Risk Finance, The, 9(1), 40-51.

Khan, T. & Ahmed, H. (2001). Risk Management: An Analysis of Issues in Islamic Financial Industry, Islamic Development Bank, and Jeddah.

Khnifer, M. (2010a). Constructing Sukuk. Islamic Banking & Finance, 8(1), 27.

Khnifer, M. (2010b). Stand and Default. Islamic Business & Finance, October edition.

Kokab, Faizan Ullah. (2010). Chief Financial Officer, Lynchpin Financial Centre.

Krichene, N. (2012). Islamic Capital Markets: Theory and Practice. John Wiley & Sons.

Krippendorff, K. (2004). Reliability in content analysis. Human Communication Research, 30(3), 411-433.

Kuen, Y. L. (2007). Essential Elements for Effective Supervision of Takaful Operators, Financial Regulators Forum on Islamic Finance.

Lahsasna, (2010). Shariah aspects in business and finance. INCEIF: Kuala Lumpur.

Lahsasna, A. (2014). Shari'ah Non-compliance Risk Management and Legal Documentations in Islamic Finance. John Wiley & Sons.

Lahsasna, A., & Idris, U. (2008). Examination of the AAOIFI pronouncement on Sukuk issuance and its implication on the future Sukuk structure in the Islamic Capital Market. In 6 th Interntional Islamic Finance Conference 2008 Peer Reviewed Paper.

Lahsasna, A., & Lin, L. S. (2012). Issues in Islamic capital markets: Islamic bond/Sukuk. In 3rd International conference on Business and Economic Research. Proceeding (pp. 12-13).

Lahsasna, A., Ibrahim, S, H., & Othman, D, S., (2014) Shariah Audit: Evidence & Methodology in Islamic Finance. BNP Paribas – INCEIF Centre for Islamic Wealth Management (CIWM).

Laldin, A 2013, 'Shari'ah Non-compliance Risk' in Banks' in Islamic Finance The New Regulatory Challenge, 2nd edition, John Wiley and Sons Singapore Private Limited, pp.237-257.

Laldin, M. A. (2008). The Role of Shari'ah Advisors in the Development of Islamic Securities. Fundamentals and Practices in Islamic Finance, ISRA Series in contemporary Islamic finance. Kuala Lumpur.

Lane, K. (2006) Sukuk broadens global following, Wall Street Journal,19th November 19.

Leedy, P. D., & Ormrod, J. E. (2001). Practical research: Planning and design: Pearson Merrill Prentice Hall.

Lewis, M. K. (2001). Islam and Accounting. Accounting Forum, 25(2), 103-127.

Lin, A. C., & Loftis, K. (2005). Mixing qualitative and quantitative methods in political science: a primer. In APSA Annual Conference. Washington, DC.

Lindlof, T. R., & Taylor, B.C. (2002). Qualitative communication research methods (2nd ed.). Thousand Oaks, CA: Sage.

Lipka, M., & Hackett, C. (2015). Why Muslims Are the World's Fastest-Growing Religious Group. Retrieved from FactTank: The News In Numbers: http://www. pewresearch. org/fact-tank/2015/04/23/why-muslims-are-the-worlds-fastest-growing-religious-group.).

LMC (2008). The guide to Sukuk market, Liquidity Management Centre, Bahrain.www.Imcbahrain.com.

Lohmöller JB (1989) Latent variable path modeling with partial least squares. Physica, Heidelberg.

Louise Barriball, K., & While, A. (1994). Collecting Data using a semi-structured interview: a discussion paper. Journal of advanced nursing, 19(2), 328-335.

Lu, C. S., Lai, K. & Cheng, T. E. (2007). Application of structural equation modeling to evaluate the intention of shippers to use Internet services in liner shipping. European Journal of Operational Research, 180(2), 845-867.

Lynn, P. (2012) Longitudinal Survey Methods for the Household Finances and Consumption Survey. Institute for Social and Economic Research, University of Essex.

Maali, B., Casson, P. and Napier, C. (2006), "Social reporting by Islamic banks", Abacus, Vol. 42 No. 2, pp. 266-89.

Machmudi, Y. (2008). Islamising Indonesia: the rise of Jemaah Tarbiyah and the prosperous justice party (PKS). ANU E Press.

Madey, D. L. (1982). Some benefits of integrating qualitative and quantitative methods in program evaluation, with illustrations. Educational Evaluation and Policy Analysis, 223-236.

Maiyaki, A. A. (2013). Principles of Islamic Capital Market. International Journal of Academic Research in Accounting, Finance and Management Sciences, 3(4), 278-283.

Makiyan, S. N. (2008). Risk management and challenges in Islamic Banks.Journal of Islamic Economics, Banking and Finance, 4(3), 45-54.

Malaysia Securities Commission – Guidelines on the Offering of Islamic Securities 2004 – Para 1.05(a) – as quoted Securities Commission Malaysia, Islamic Capital Market – Vol 5 – The Islamic Securities (Sukuk) Market (Lexis Nexis, 2009), p 9.9 In Sukuk = Islamic bond.

Malaysia, B. N. (2010). Shariah governance framework for Islamic financial institutions. Bank Negara Malaysia, Kuala Lumpur.

Malaysian Accounting Standards Board Discussion Paper i-2 Sukuk Comments received by 16 March 2012.

Malaysian Debt Securities and Sukuk Market, 2009. "A Guide for Issuer and Investor", a joint Publication by Central Bank of Malaysia and Securities Commission Malaysia, pp: 29-34.

Malik, M. R. (2010). Shariah Supervisory Board in Islamic Finance. International Center for Education in Islamic Finance, INCEIF.

Malkawi, B. H. (2014). A Bright Future: Towards an Enhanced Shariah Supervision in Islamic Finance.

Manaf, I.A. (2007). 'Islamic bonds (Islamic Bond): Its introduction and application'. Available at http://www.sebi.ac.id/(accessed 7 January 2011).

MARC. (2010a). Rating Approach to Sukuk: A Marc Perspective. Malaysian Rating Corporation Berhad http://www.marc.com.my/home/userfiles/file/Methodologies/Rating%20Approach%20to%20Sukuk%20%20A%20MARC%20Perspective.pdf.

MARC. (2010b). Rating Symbols and Definitions. Kuala Lumpur. Malaysian Rating Corporation Berhad. Retrieved 10 September 2010.

Marlowe-Noren, J. (2002). "Investment grade Shari'ah (Islamic) compliant financial product." U.S. Patent Application 10/270,225.

MASB, Malaysia accounting standards board 2004, financial reporting standards i-1: presentation of financial statements of Islamic Financial Institutions.

Masudi (2005). Islamic way of life (English, Trans. Second edition ed Vol. 1). New Delhi: Himilaya publishers.

Mat, I., & Ismail, Y. (2008). A Review of Fiqh al-Mua'malat Subjects in Economics and Related Programs at International Islamic University Malaysia and University of Brunei Darussalam.

Maxcy, S. J. (2003). Pragmatic threads in mixed methods research in the social sciences: The search for multiple modes of inquiry and the end of the philosophy of formalism. In A.Tashakkori & C. Teddlie (Eds.), Handbook of mixed methods in social and behavioral research (pp. 51–89). Thousand Oaks, CA: Sage.

McDaniel, C. and Gates, R. (2001), Marketing Research Essentials, 3rd ed., South-Western College Publishing, Cincinatti, OH.

McMillen, M. J. T. (2008). Asset securitization Sukuk and Islamic capital markets: Structural issues in these formative years. Wisconsin International Law Journal, 25, 703 772.

Mehmet, A. (2007). Conceptualisation of the second best solution in overcoming the social failure of Islamic finance: Examining the overpowering of homoislamicus by homoeconomicus. IIUM Journal of Economics and Management 2007, 15, 1- 17.

Mehmood, Zahid. (2010). Chief Executive, Accounts House 'Chartered Certified Accountants and 'Tops London Limited, England. [Telephonic, 27 April 2010].

Meho, L. I. (2006). E-mail interviewing in qualitative research: A methodological discussion. Journal of the American society for information science and technology, 57(10), 1284-1295.

Meho, L.I., & Tibbo, H.R. (2003). Modeling the information-seeking behavior of social scientists: Ellis's study revisited. Journal of the American Society for Information Science and Technology, 54(6), 570–587.

Merriam, S. B. (2001). Qualitative research and case study applications in education (2nd ed.). San Francisco: Jossey-Bass Publishers.

Metawa, S. A., & Almossawi, M. (1998). Banking behavior of Islamic bank customers: perspectives and implications. International Journal of Bank Marketing, 16(7), 299-313.

Meyer, J.W. and Rowan, B. (1977), "Institutionalized organizations: formal structures as myth and ceremony", American Journal of Sociology, Vol. 83, pp. 340-63.

MIFC, 2013 Sukuk growing relevance in infrastructure development. http://www.mifc.com/index.php?ch=28&pg=72&ac=53&bb=uploadpdf.

Miller, N. D., Challoner, J., & Atta, A. (2007). UK Welcomes the Sukuk. International Financial Law Review, 26(5), 24 – 25.

Milne, M. J., & Adler, R. W. (1999). Exploring the reliability of social and environmental disclosures content analysis. Accounting, Auditing & Accountability Journal, 12(2), 237-256.

Mirakhor, A. (2006). Islamic finance and globalization: A Convergence? Journal of Islamic Economics, Banking and Finance (JIEBF), 13, 11 – 72.

Mirakhor, A. (1996). Cost of capital and investment in a non-interest economy. Islamic Economic Studies, 4(1), 35-46.

Mirakhor, A., & Zaidi, I. (2007). Profit-and-loss sharing contracts in Islamic finance. In M.K. Hassan & M.K. Lewis, Handbook of Islamic Banking, 49.

Mitchell, M. C., Rafi, M. I., Severe, S., & Kappen, J. a. (2014). Conventional vs. islamic finance: The impact of ramadan upon sharia-compliant markets. Organizations & Markets In Emerging Economies, 5(1), 105–125. Retrieved from http://www.om.ef.vu.lt/cms/cache/RePEc_files/article_59.pdf.

Mizushima, T., & Mizushima, T. (2014). Corporate Governance and Shariah Governance at Islamic Financial Institutions: Assessing from Current Practice in Malaysia. 麗沢学際ジャーナル, 22(1), 59-84.

Moaddel, M. (2005). Islamic modernism, nationalism, and fundamentalism: episode and discourse. University of Chicago Press.

Modansky (2011). Asset-Based Financing Basics, journal of accountancy. http://www.journalofaccountancy.com/issues/2011/aug/20113992.

Mohamad, S., & Razif, N. F. M. (2013) Shariah-Compliant Securities, Sukuk and Islamic Reits in Malaysia, Islamic Economics, Banking and Finance: Concepts and Critical Issues.

Mohd Yusof, R., Kassim, S. H., Shabri A. Majid, M., & Hamid, Z. (2011). Determining the viability of rental price to benchmark Islamic home

financing products: Evidence from Malaysia. Benchmarking: An International Journal, 18(1), 69-85.
Mokhtar, S. (2009). A synthesis of shariah issues and market challenges in the application of wa'd in equity-based Sukuk. ISRA International Journal of Islamic Finance, 1(139-145).
Monecke A, Leisch F (2012). SemPLS: Structural equation modeling using partial least squares. J Stat Softw (forthcoming).
Moody's, (2014) An Outlook of the Global Sovereign Sukuk Market, Dar Al Sharia Legal and Financial Consultancy.
Mounira, B. A., & Anas, E. (2008). Managing Risks and Liquidity in an interest free banking Framework: The case of the Islamic banks. International Journal of Business and Management, 3(9), P80.Chicago.
Mseddi, S., & Naifar, N. (2013). Rating methodology and evaluating the issuer of Sukuk. International Journal of Management Science and Engineering Management, 8(4), 262-275.
Muhamed, n. A., & radzi, r. M (2011). Implication of Sukuk structuring: the comparison on the structure of asset based and asset backed ijarah Sukuk.
Muhamad, R. (2011), ''Market segmentation and the shari'ah compliancy process in Islamic banking institutions'', International Shari'ah Research Academy for Islamic Finance Research Paper No. 21.
Muhamad Sori, Z., Mohamad, S., & Shah, M. E. (2015). Shariah Committee Independence: An Insider's View. INCEIF Quarterly Research Bulletin, 6.
Muhammad, N. M. N., & Mokhtar, M. (2008, February). Islamic equity mutual fund performance in Malaysia: Risk and return analysis. In The Midwest Finance Association (MFA) Conference.
Munawar A, 2013 Islamic Banking Newsletter Published by the Institute of Islamic Banking Vol. 1, No. 3, 2013.
Murray, C.D. (2004). An interpretive phenomenological analysis of the embodiment of artificial limbs. Disability and Rehabilitation, 26(16), 963–973.
Murray, C.D., & Harrison, B. (2004). The meaning and experience of being a stroke survivor: An interpretive phenomenological analysis. Disability and Rehabilitation, 26(13), 808–816.
Musa, H., & Obadi, S. M. (2009). Islamic Financial Systems. Studia Universitatis" Vasile Goldiş" Arad-Seria Ştiinţe Economice, (1-1), 124-130.
Muwazir, M.R., Muhamad, R., & Noordin, K. (2006). Corporate Social Responsibility Disclosure: A Tawhidic Approach. Journal Syariah, 14(1), 125-142.

Nabil. S, 2013 The Non- Financial Factors Influencing The Performance of Islamic Insurance In Kenya: A Case Study of Takaful Insurance of Africa, European Journal of Business and Management Vol.5, No.13, 2013.

Naifar, N., & Mseddi, S. (2013). Sukuk spreads determinants and pricing model methodology. Afro-Asian Journal of Finance and Accounting, 3(3), 241-257.

Nanaeva, Z. K. (2010). How risky Sukuk are: comparative analysis of risks associated with Sukuk and conventional bonds.

Naser, K., Jamal, A., & Al-Khatib, K. (1999). Islamic banking: a study of customer satisfaction and preferences in Jordan. International journal of bank marketing, 17(3), 135-151.

Nathan Garas, S. (2012). The conflicts of interest inside the Shari'a supervisory board. International Journal of Islamic and Middle Eastern Finance and Management, 5(2), 88-105.

Nathie, M. A. (2008). Embracing Islamic investment in Australia using the Malaysian model: challenges and opportunities. The Challenges and Opportunities of Islam in the West: The Case of Australia, on March, 3-5.

Nathif, A. and Abdulkader, T. (2004) Islamic Bonds: Your Guide to Issuing, Structuring and Investing in Sukuk. London: Euromoney Books, 200.

Nazar K, 2011 Regulatory and Financial Implications of Sukuk's Legal Challenges for Sustainable Sukuk Development in Islamic Capital Market1, Center for Islamic Economics and Finance, Qatar Faculty of Islamic Studies, Qatar Foundation.

Nazar, J. K. (2015). Regulatory and financial implications of Sukuk's legal challenges for sustainable Sukuk development in Islamic capital market. Ethics, Governance and Regulation in Islamic Finance, 135.

Nazim Ali, 2008 Islamic Finance and Economics as Reflected in Research and Publications. Review of Islamic Economics, Vol. 12, No.1, 2008.

Newbold, P. (2003). Spurious rejections by cointegration tests induced by structural breaks. Applied Economics, 35(9), 1117-1121.

Nisar, S. (2007). Islamic Bonds (Sukuk): its introduction and application. Electronic Article at: www. financeinislam. com.

Nomani, M. Z. M. (2013). Journal of Humanity & Islam. Journal of Humanity & Islam, 3(2), 71-79.

Obaidullah. M, (2005) Islamic financial Service, Islamic Economics Research Centre.

Omar, (2009) Roles & Responsibilites of Shariah Advisors in Islamic Banking Institutions.

Omar, A., Abduh, M., & Sukmana, R. (2013). Fundamentals of Islamic Money and Capital Markets. John Wiley & Sons.

Omar, Azmi, M., Noor, A. M., & Meera, A. K. M. (2010). "An Islamic Pricing Benchmark", ISRA Research Paper No. 17/2010.

Ongena, S., Smith, D. C., & Michalsen, D. (2003). Firms and their distressed banks: lessons from the Norwegian banking crisis. Journal of Financial Economics, 67(1), 81-112.

Onwuegbuzie, A. J., & Johnson, R. B. (2004, April). Validity issues in mixed methods research. Paper presented at the annual meeting of the American Educational Research Association, San Diego, CA.

Onwuegbuzie, A. J., & Johnson, R. B. (2006). The validity issue in mixed research. Research in the Schools, 13(1), 48-63.

Onwuegbuzie, A. J., & Leech, N. L. (2004). On becoming a pragmatic researcher: The importance of combining quantitative and qualitative research methodologies. Manuscript submitted for publication.

Oppenheim, A. N. (1998). Questionnaire design, interviewing and attitude measurement: Pinter Pub Ltd.

Oppenheim, A. N. (1998). Questionnaire design, interviewing and attitude measurement: Pinter Pub Ltd.

Palmon, O., Smith, B.A. and Sopranzetti, B.J. (2004), “Clustering in real estate prices.

Patton, M. Q. (1990). Qualitative evaluation and research methods (2nd ed.). Newbury Park, CA: Sage.

Pearl, D. (1979). A Textbook on Muslim Law (Vol. 27). London: Croom Helm.

Peillex, J., & Ureche-Rangau, L. (2013). Is There A Place for A Shariah-Compliant Index on the Paris Stock Market? International Journal of Business, 18, 2.

Perceptions of Accounting Academicians, Audit Practitioners and Shariah Scholars. Paper presented at the IIUM Accounting Conference, Gombak.

Qureshi, A. A. (2011). Analyzing the sharia'h compliant issues currently faced by Islamic Insurance. Journal of Contemporary Research in Business, 3(5).

Radelet, S., & Sachs, J. (1998). The onset of the East Asian financial crisis (No. w6680). National bureau of economic research.

Radzi, R. M., & Muhamed, N. A. (2012). An International Comparative Study on Shariah Governance Supervision of Sukuk Defaults. Journal of Islamic Economics, Banking and Finance, Vol. 8 No. 3, July - Sep 2012.

Ra'fatt, J., (2015) What is Missing in Pricing Sukuk Securities? European Academi Research Vol. III, Issue 2/ May 2015.

Rahail, 2011 Sukuk" and Islamic Capital Markets London: Globe Law and Business.

Rahman, A. A., & Bukair, A. A. (2013). The Influence of the Shariah Supervision Board On Corporate Social Responsibility Disclosure By Islamic Banks Of Gulf Co-Operation Council Countries. Asian Journal of Business and Accounting, 6(2).

Rahman, A. R. A. (2008). Shari'ah audit for Islamic financial services: the needs and challenges. In ISRA Islamic Finance Seminar (Vol. 11, pp. 1-14).

Rahman, J. M. (2014). The current perception and practice of "Shariah Auditing" in Bangladeshi Islamic Banks. Available at SSRN 2538568.

Rahman, M. P., Omar, M. A., & Kassim, S. H. (2013). An Application of GARCH Modeling on the Malaysian Sukuk Spreads. Journal of Islamic Finance, 2(2).

Rahman, S. (2015). Ethical Investment in Stock Screening and Zakat on Stocks. Journal of Islamic Finance, 4(1), 39-62.

Rauf, A. A., & Ibrahim, Y. (2014). Determinants of risk and return performance with special reference to GCC Sukuk market structure.

Rehman, J. (2007). The sharia, Islamic family laws and international human rights law: Examining the theory and practice of polygamy and talaq. International Journal of Law, Policy and the Family, 21(1), 108-127.

Riessman, C.K. (2004) Narrative analysis. In The Sage Encyclopaedia of Social Science Research Methods (Vols. 1–3). eds M.S. Lewis-Beck, A. Bryman & T.F. Liao, pp. 705–709. London: Sage Publications.

Rizvi, S. (2014). Relevance and scope of Islamic finance in recent era. Management Insight, 9(2).

Roe, M. J. (2006). Legal origins and modern stock markets.

Rohmatunnisa, D. (2008). Design of Ijarah Sukuk. Unpublished MA in Finance and Investment, University of Nottingham, Nottingham, UK.

Rosly, S, A. (2007) Why Shariah Compliance is fundamental in Islamic finance? Theory of Indebtedness Al-Mithaq. https://www.scribd.com/doc/5042197/Why-Shariah-Compliance.

Roy, D. A. (1991). Islamic banking. Middle Eastern Studies, 27(3), 427-456.

S&P Dow Jones, (2013) Indices: S&P Dow Jones Indices: Dow Jones Sukuk Index Methodology, S&P Dow Jones Indices LLC, a part of McGraw Hill Financial.

Sabli, N., & Noor, R. M. (2012). Tax Planning and Corporate Governance. In Journal International Conference On Business and Economic Research ISBN (pp. 978-967).

Sachedina, A. (2005). End-of-life: The Islamic view. The lancet, 366(9487), 774-779.

Sadiq, K., & Black, A. (2012). Embracing Sharia-Compliant Products through Regulatory Amendment to Achieve Party of Treatment. Sydney L. Rev., 34, 189.

Saeed, A. (2006). Islamic thought: An introduction. Routledge.

Saeed, A., & Salah, O. (2012). History of Sukuk: pragmatic and idealist approaches to structuring Sukuk. The Islamic Debt Market for Sukuk Securities: The Theory and Practice of Profit Sharing Investment, 42.

Saeed, A., & Salah, O. (2014). Development of Sukuk: Pragmatic and Idealist Approaches to Sukuk Structures. Journal of International Banking Law and Regulation, 29(1), 41-52.

Safari, M., Ariff, M., & Mohamad, S. (2014). Sukuk Securities: New Ways of Debt Contracting. John Wiley & Sons.

Saidi, N., Scacciavillani, F., & Prasad, A. (2009). Local Bond Markets as a Cornerstone of Development Strategy. Dubai International Finance Centre Discussion Note, (7).

Sairally, S. "Evaluating the 'Social Responsibility' of Islamic Finance: Learning from the Experiences of Socially Responsible Investment Funds." In Advances in Islamic Economics and Finance: Proceeding of the 6th International Conference on Islamic Economics and FinanceVol. 1, edited by Munawar Iqbal, Salman Syed Ali and Dadang Muljawan, 279-320. Jeddah: Islamic Research and Training Institute, IDB, 2007.

Salami, I., & Alkhadhari, A. (2010). Bonds and Loans in the Islamic Financial Law; and a Comparison with International Bond Issues.

Saleh Md. Arman (2013). Shariah Compliance Features Of Islamic Financial Institutions And Its Challenges, Arabian Journal of Business and Management Review (Oman chapter) Vol. 3, No.4; Nov. 2013.

Salman Shaikh, (2011) Microcredit using Equity Financing: an Alternate Approach to Micro financing in an Interest Free Economy.1st Intl. Conference on Islamic Banking – Riphah Intl. University. February, 2011.

Salman, S. (2013) A Critical Assessment of Asset-based versus asset backed Sukuk structures and legal resource in case of defaults. INCEIF, Global University of Islamic Finance Malaysia.

Salman, S. (2014) Issue(s) related to the pricing mechanism for the Islamic capital market products in particular Sukuk instrument.

Sang, S., Lee, L. D. & Lee, J. (2010) E-government: people, process, and policy, 4(2). Emerald Group Publishing Limited, Bingley, 138-157.

Saripudin, K. N., Mohamad, S., Razif, N. F. M., Abdullah, L. H., & Rahman, N. N. A. (2012). Case Study on Sukuk Musharakah Issued in Malaysia. Middle-East Journal of Scientific Research, 12(2), 168-175.

Saunders, M., Lewis, P., & Thornhill, A. (2007). Research methods for business students: Prentice Hall.

Saunders, M. L. (2003). P. and Thornhill. Research Methods for business students

SC. (2003). Guidelines on the Offering of Private Debt Securities, (April).

SCM, (2014) Internationalisation of Islamic Finance bridging economies. Securities Commission Malaysia Jan–June 2012 vol 7 no 1.

Scott, W.R. (2001), Institutions and Organizations, 2nd ed., Sage, Thousand Oaks, CA.

Securities Commission Malaysia, 2007 Resolutions of The Securities Commission Shariah Advisory Council, Securities Commission Persiaran Bukit Kiara Bukit Kiara, Kuala Lumpur.

Securities Commission Malaysia, (2009). The Role of Islamic Finance in Shaping the Future Global Financial and Capital Market LandScape. Malaysian ICM, 4(3), 1–20.

Securities Commission Malaysia, (2011) Guidelines on Sukuk - Securities Commission of Malaysia, Islamic securities guidelines (Sukuk guidelines) Revised: 12 July 2011.

Securities Commission Malaysia, Islamic Capital Market – Vol 5 – The Islamic Securities (Sukuk) Market (Lexis Nexis, 2009.

Securities Commission Malaysia. (2004). Annual Report. Kuala Lumpur: Securities Commission. Retrieved on April 20, 2011 from http://www.sc.co.my.

Securities Commission Malaysia. Islamic Securities Guidelines, (Sukuk Guidelines), revised July 2011. Retrieved July 4, 2012.

Securities Commission, (2008) guidelines on real estate Investment trusts. www.sc.com.my.

Sekaran, U. (2003). Research Methods For Business: A Skill Building Approach (Fourth ed.). New Jersey: John Wiley & Sons, Inc.

Sekaran, U., & Bougie, R. (2010). Research Method for Business, A Skill Building Approach. John Wiley & Sons Inc.

Selim, T.H. (2008). An Islamic capital asset pricing model. Humanomics, 24(2), pp. 122- 129.

Shabana M. Hasan, 2013 asset-backed and asset-based Sukuk: an introduction. Fatwa in Islamic finance, Researcher at International Shariah Research Academy (ISRA). Bloomberg.

Shafi, R. M., & Redzuan, M. A. (2010). Modelling Sukuk structures in Indonesia: economic development and the risk management. Universiti Teknologi, MARA Johor.

Shafii, Z., Salleh, S., & Shahwan, S. H. (2010). Management of Shariah non-compliance audit risk in the Islamic financial institutions via the development of Shariah compliance audit framework and Shariah audit programme. Kyoto Bulletin of Islamic Area Studies, 3(2), 3-16.

Shah, R. and Goldstein, S.M. (2006), "Use of structural equation modeling in operations management research: looking back and forward", Journal of Operations Management, Vol. 24 No. 2, pp. 148-169.

Shahul Hameed, Mulyany R. (2007). Shariah Audit for Islamic Financial Institutions (IFIs).

Shahul, (2009) Alternative disclosure & performance measures for Islamic banks.

Shaikh, S., & Saeed, S. (2010). Sukuk bond: The global Islamic financial instrument. MPRA Paper, 26700.

Shaikh, Salman (2010). "An Ideal Islamic Economic System: A Gone Case" MAPRA Munich Personal RePEc ArchiveOnline at http://mpra.ub.uni-muenchen.de/26701/ MPRA Paper No. 26701, posted 17. November 2010 06:28 UTC.

Shaikh, Salman (2010). "Proposal for a New Economic Framework Based on Islamic Principles". Karachi: Islamic Economics Project.

Sharma, P. N., & Kim, K. H. (2013). A comparison of PLS and ML bootstrapping techniques in SEM: A Monte Carlo study. In New perspectives in partial least squares and related methods (pp. 201-208). Springer New York.

Sharma, S., Durand, R. M., & Gur-Arie, O. (1981). Identification and analysis of moderator variables. Journal of marketing research, 291-300.ivariate statistics. Boston: Allyn & Bacon, 243-310.

Shaukat. M. (2010). Common Structures of Sukuk, Published In the Global Islamic Finance Magazine- United Kingdom, december 2010 issue-Also available at http://instituteofhalalinvesting.org/Articles/Mughees-Shaukat.htm.

Shehatah, H. (2008) Controls and efficiency criteria and the development of the functioning of Islamic banks.

Shehatah, H. (2009) Islamic Financial Analysis for the financial statements of companies.

Sheila, Mohamad, Soualhi & Zaharin (2013). Accounting, Auditing and Governance for Takaful Operations, John Wiley & sons.

Shubber, Kadom, et Eid Alzafiri. (2008). Cost of capital of Islamic banking institutions: an empirical study of a special case. International Journal of Islamic and Middle Eastern Finance and Management, 1, n° 1 (2008): 10 19.

Siddiqi, M. N. (2006, April). Shariah, economics and the progress of Islamic finance: The role of Shariah experts. In Concept Paper presented at Pre-Forum Workshop on Select Ethical and Methodological Issues in Shari'a-Compliant Finance., Cambridge, Massachusetts, USA.

Simmons & Simmons LLP (2010). An introduction to Islamic finance http://www.simmons-simmons.com/docs/an_introduction_to _islamic_finance.pdf.

Srairi, S. (2015). Corporate Governance Disclosure Practices and Performance of Islamic Banks in GCC Countries. Journal of Islamic Finance, 4(2).

Srivastava, D. K., & Surana, S. (2006). The Role of Religion in International Business: The Case of LIC's Entry into Islamic Insurance. Management Case Study Journal, The, 6(2), 67.

Standard & Poor's (2007), "Chief Drivers Behind Islamic Finance's Global Expansion", Commentary Repor.

Sulaiman, M. (2001). Testing a model of Islamic corporate financial reports: Some experimental Evidence.IIUM Journal of Economics and Management. Vol 9(2).

Sulaiman, M., & Willett, R. (2003). Using the Hofstede-Gray Framework to Argue Normatively for an Extension of Islamic Corporate Reports, Malaysian Accounting Review, 2(1), 81-104.

Sulaiman, M., Majid, N. A., & Ariffin, N. M. (2011). Corporate governance of Islamic financial institutions in Malaysia. In 8th International Conference on Islamic Economics and Finance (pp. 1-21). Chicago.

Sultan, S. A. (2007). A Mini Guide to Shariah Audit for Islamic Financial Institutions-A Primer. Kuala Lumpur, Malaysia: CERT Publications.

Tabachnick, B. G., & Fidell, L. S. (2007). Multivariate analysis of variance and covariance. Using mult Takaful Department BNM/RH/GL 004-22 Durham E-Theses Online: http://etheses.dur.ac.uk/3502/Capital Market – Vol 5 – The Islamic Securities (Sukuk) Market (Lexis Nexis, 2009), p 9.

Taher, N., & Al-Hajjar, B. (2013). Energy and Environment in Saudi Arabia: Concerns & Opportunities. Springer Science & Business Media.

Tahmoures, A. A. (2013). Compare and Contrast Sukuk (Islamic Bonds) with Conventional Bonds, Are they Compatible? Journal of Global Business Management, 9(1), 44–52.

Talahma, K. I. (2015). Islamic Bonds (Sukuk): Opportunities and Challenges. Asper Rev. Int'l Bus. & Trade L., 15, 391.

Tariq, A. A. (2004). Managing financial risks of Sukuk structures. Loughborough University, UK, September (mimeo).

Tariq, A.A. and Dar, H. (2007). "Risks of Sukuk Structures: Implications for Resource Mobilization", Thunderbird International Business Review, vol. 49, no.2, pp. 203– 223.

Tashakkori, A., & Teddlie, C. (1998). Mixed methodology: Combining qualitative and quantitative approaches. Applied Social Research Methods Series (Vol. 46). Thousand Oaks, CA: Sage.

Tashakkori, A. and Creswell, JW. (2007). Exploring the nature of research questions in mixed methods research. Journal of Mixed Methods Research, 1: 207-211.

Teddlie, C., & Tashakkori, A. (Eds.). (2009). Foundations of mixed methods research: Integrating quantitative and qualitative approaches in the social and behavioral sciences. Sage Publications Inc.

Thomas, A. S. (Ed.). (2006). Interest in Islamic economics: understanding riba. Psychology Press.

Udovitch, A. L. (1981). Bankers without banks: commerce, banking, and society in the Islamic world of the Middle Ages. Program in Near Eastern Studies, Princeton University.

Ul Haque, N., & Mirakhor, A. (1998). The design of instruments for government finance in an Islamic economy.

Urbach, N., & Ahlemann, F. (2010). Structural equation modeling in information systems research using partial least squares. Journal of Information Technology Theory and Application, 11(2), 5-40.

Usmani, M. (2008). Sukuk and their contemporary applications. South Africa: Mujlisul Ulama of South Africa, 1–15.

Usmani, M. T. (2007). Sukuk and their Contemporary Applications [(Translated from the original Arabic by Sheikh Yusuf Talal DeLorenzo)]. In AAOIFI Shariah Council meeting, Saudi Arabia.

Usmani, M. T., (2002) An Introduction to Islamic Finance. Maktaba Ma'arif Al Quran, Karachi, Pakistan.

Usmani, M. T., (2009) Post crisis reforms – some points to ponder, presented at the World Economic Forum.

Vallely, P. (2006). How Islamic inventors changed the world. The Independent, 11.

Van Greuning, H., & Iqbal, Z. (2008). Risk analysis for Islamic banks. World Bank Publications.

Van Wijnbergen, S., & Zaheer, S. (2013). Sukuk Defaults: On Distress Resolution in Islamic Finance, Tinbergen Institute Discussion Paper, No. 13-087/VI/ DSF57.

Vishwanath, S. R., & Azmi, S. (2009). An overview of Islamic Sukuk bonds. The Journal of Structured Finance, 14(4), 58-67. Chicago.

Visser, H. (2013). Islamic finance: Principles and practice. Edward Elgar Publishing.

Waines, D. (2003). An introduction to Islam. Cambridge University Press. Handbook for Islamic Banking. Cheltenham: Edward Elgar Publishing.

Wajdi, A and Abdullah, N. (2006). The Ideal of Islamic Banking: Chasing A Mirage? Retrieved January 16, 2009, from www.asyrafwajdi.com/download.php?f=0013(downloaded-fromasyrafwajdi.com).pdf.

Walden, W. D., & Schwartz, B. N. (1997). Environmental disclosures and public policy pressure. Journal of Accounting and Public Policy, 125–154.

Wass, V. J., & Wells, P. E. (1994). Principles and practice in business and management research: Dartmouth.

Watson, W. (1990). Types of pluralism. The Monist, 73(3), 350–367.

Wedderburn-Day, A. R. (2010). Sovereign Sukuk: Adaptation and Innovation.Law & Contemp. Probs., 73, 325.

Weiss, B. G. (1998). The spirit of Islamic law (Vol. 5). University of Georgia Press.

Weiss, B. G. (Ed.). (2002). Studies in Islamic legal theory (Vol. 15). Brill.

Williams, S. L. M. (1998). Voluntary environmental and social accounting disclosure practices in the Asia-Pacific region (Doctoral dissertation, Murdoch University).

Williams, S. M. (1999). Voluntary environmental and social accounting disclosure practices in the Asia-Pacific region: An international empirical test of political economy theory. The International Journal of Accounting, 34(2), 209-238.

Wilson, R. (2003). Regulatory challenges posed by Islamic capital market products and services. Centre for Middle Eastern and Islamic Studies, University of Durham, UK.

Wilson, R. (2004). Overview of the Sukuk market. Islamic Bonds: Your Guide to Issuing, Structuring and Investing in Sukuk, Euromoney Books, London, 6-7.

Wilson, R. (2006). Islamic Capital Markets: The Role of Sukuk.

Wilson, R. (2008). Innovation in the structuring of Islamic Sukuk securities. Humanomics, 24(3), 170-181. www.Imcbahrain.com.

Wilson, R. (2012). Legal, regulatory and governance issues in Islamic Finance. Edinburgh University Press.

Yahaya, M. Z., Samsudin, M. A., & Lalulddin, H. (2013). An Overview of the Principles of Jurisprudence Vis-A-Vis Legal Maxim. Asian Social Science,10(2), p157.

Yean, T. W. (2009). Sukuk: Issues and the way forward. International Legal News, 6(2), 1-20.

Young, S., Persichitte, K.A., & Tharp, D.D. (1998). Electronic mail interviews: Guidelines for conducting research. International Journal of Educational Telecommunications, 4(4), 291–299.

Zahan. M & Ron S. Kenett, (2012) hedging instruments in conventional and Islamic finance. Electronic Journal of Applied Statistical Analysis: Decision Support Systems and Services Evaluation EJASA: DSS (2012). Vol 3, Issue 1, 59 – 74.

Zaid, M, (2011a). The Effectiveness of Sukuk in Islamic Finance Market, Australian Journal of Basic and Applied Sciences, 5(12): 472-478, 2011, ISSN 1991-8178.

Zaid, M. (2011b): The Implementation of Sukuk in Islamic Finance International Conference on Sociality and Economics Development, IPEDR vol.10 (2011) © (2011) IACSIT Press, Singapore.

Zaidi, J. A. (2007) Sukuk A Global Trend, Chartered Financial Analyst. September 2007

Zakaria, N. B., Md Isa, M. A., & Abidin, R. A. Z. (2012). The construct of Sukuk, rating and default risk. Procedia-Social and Behavioral Sciences, 65, 662-667.

Zarqa, M. A. (1997). Istisna Financing of Infrastructure Projects. Islamic Economic Studies, 4(2), 69-70.

Zawya (2011). Sukuk Intelligence. Retrieved from http://www.zawya.com/story/USD_85_billion_Sukuk_issued_in_2011 -ZAWYA20120110175320/

Zaman, S. H. (1993). Indexation of Financial Assets: An Islamic Evaluation (Vol. 4). IIIT.

Zeghal, D., &Ahmed, S.A. (1990). Comparison of social responsibility information disclosure media used by Canadian firms. Accounting, Auditing and Accountability Journal, 3(1), 38-53.

Zeti Akhtar Aziz, Tan Sri Dato' Sri Dr., (2010) Governor of Central Bank of Malaysia, Quarterly Bulletin, First Quarter 2010,

Zikmund, W. (1997). Business research methods (8th ed.). Fort Worth: The Dryden Press - Harcourt Brace.

Zin, M. Z. M., Hashim, N., Khalid, N. K., Opir, H., & Sulaiman, R. (2011). The Implementation of Sukuk in Islamic Finance. International Proceedings of Economics Development & Research, 10.

Zin, M. Z. M., Sakat, A. A., Ahmad, N. A., Nor, M. R. M., Bhari, A., Ishak, S., & Jamain, M. S. (2011). The Effectiveness of Sukuk in Islamic Finance Market.Australian Journal of Basic & Applied Sciences, 5(12).

Zulkhibri, M. (2015). A synthesis of theoretical and empirical research on Sukuk. Borsa Istanbul Review, 15(4), 237-248.